The Explorations of
William H. Ashley
and
Jedediah Smith,
1822–1829

GW00497931

The Explorations of William H. Ashley and Jedediah Smith, 1822–1829

with the original journals edited by
HARRISON CLIFFORD DALE
(Revised Edition)

Introduction to the Bison Book Edition by James P. Ronda

University of Nebraska Press
Lincoln and London

Copyright 1941 by the Arthur H. Clark Company
Introduction © 1991 by the University of Nebraska Press
All rights reserved
Manufactured in the United States of America

First Bison Book printing: 1991
Most recent printing indicated by the last digit below:
10   9   8   7   6   5   4   3   2   1

Library of Congress Cataloging-in-Publication Data
Dale, Harrison Clifford, b. 1885.
[Ashley-Smith explorations and the discovery of a central route to the
Pacific, 1822–1829]
The explorations of William H. Ashley and Jedediah Smith, 1822–1829
/ with the original journals edited by Harrison Clifford Dale; introduc-
tion by James P. Ronda.—Rev. ed.
p.   cm.
"A Bison book."
Reprint. Originally published: The Ashley-Smith explorations and the
discovery of a central route to the Pacific, 1822–1829. Glendale, Calif.:
A.H. Clark, 1941.
Includes bibliographical references and index.
Partial Contents: The Ashley narrative—The Smith narrative—Journal
of Harrison G. Rogers—The second journal of Harrison G. Rogers.
ISBN 0-8032-6591-3
1. West (U.S.)—Description and travel—To 1848.   2. West (U.S.)—Dis-
covery and exploration.   3. United States—Exploring expeditions.   4.
Ashley, William Henry, 1778–1838—Diaries.   5. Smith, Jedediah
Strong, 1799–1831—Diaries.   6. Fur trade—West (U.S.)—History—
19th century.   7. Overland journeys to the Pacific.   I. Ashley, William
Henry, 1778–1838.   II. Smith, Jedediah Strong, 1799–1831.   III.
Rogers, Harrison G., d. 1828.   IV. Title.
F592.D13 1991   978—dc20   91-16834   CIP   ∞

Reprinted by arrangement with the Arthur H. Clark Company
Originally titled *The Ashley-Smith Explorations and the Discovery of a Central
Route to the Pacific, 1822–1829*

To
PAUL RUSSELL TEMPLE
In memory of days and nights among the mountains and
along the streams traversed
and revealed
by
William Henry Ashley
and
Jedediah Strong Smith

Contents

Illustrations

Introduction to the Bison Book Edition
By James P. Ronda

No two names are more intimately associated with the halcyon days of the Rocky Mountain fur trade than those of William H. Ashley and Jedediah Smith. In the popular imagination these two adventurers have come to symbolize all that was daring and romantic about the age of the mountain man. Ashley and Smith drift through popular fiction and films like *Jeremiah Johnson* as figures of epic proportion. As symbols of what sometimes seems a wilder, freer time, their exploits continue to spark the imaginations of many Americans.

But the lives of Ashley and Smith meant far more than western romance and frontier adventure. Each man was at the heart of a key process or crucial series of events in western history. We miss the larger meaning of the story if we neglect the wider context. For Ashley, that context was the coming of global capitalism to the West. Long before railroads and extractive industries like agriculture, ranching, and mining made the West part of the international marketplace, the fur business transformed the economic and human geography of the region. The many fur and hide trades of western North America involved peoples, goods, markets, and capital resources on a vast scale. With a business enterprise of such large size, there were bound to be important changes in strategy and organization over time. Early fur trade companies like the Hudson's Bay Company built fixed trading posts and invited Indians to bring pelts in exchange for iron and textile items. Other adventurers cut loose from the posts, and took goods directly to native trappers. Whatever the variation, Indians remained as the principal trappers and initial processors of the furs. Although this strategy did not always yield profits in equal measure to both partners, the system required at least some measure of trust and cooperation.

That strategy, and the cultural conditions upon which it was based, changed dramatically in the 1820s. Missouri River Indians, especially the Arikaras, were increasingly concerned about their own loss of economic power as the fur trade pushed past them and headed upriver. William H. Ashley attempted to send a large trading party up the Missouri from St. Louis. That expedition numbered among its company such future notables as James Clyman, William L. Sublette, Hugh Glass, and Jedediah Smith. Despite Ashley's best efforts, the party came to grief under the withering fire of Arikara warriors. It was the Arikara disaster and an effective Indian blockade of the river that forced Ashley to become a fur-trade innovator. Expediency demanded that the Ashley men become trappers, no longer relying on Indians to scour the streams and river banks for beaver and other fur-bearing animals. That same expediency compelled Ashley to abandon the Missouri and look west to the Rockies. To his credit, Ashley embraced necessity and built his Rocky Mountain trapping system on it. At the same time he developed a supply and rendezvous schedule, allowing his trappers to stay in the mountains over the winter.

But as Harrison Dale points out in his pioneering study, Ashley was more than an astute frontier entrepreneur who turned necessity to profit. He also had some genuine claim on the title of explorer. By the end of the eighteenth century exploration was an integral part of the fur business. The Canadian traders, especially those in the service of the North West Company, were busy pushing west in search of new beaver grounds. Fur traders quickly became agents of commerce and empire. Ashley knew that his own financial success depended on expanding the range of his trappers and further refining his system of operations. During the fall and winter of 1824–1825, Ashley led a party west from Fort Atkinson through present-day Nebraska and eastern

Wyoming, over the Medicine Bow Range and into the Green River country. Ashley and some of his company then made a hazardous descent of the Green River. Ashley's 1825 letter to General Henry Atkinson, one of the most important documents for that journey, is printed in the Dale volume.

Ashley had some claim on the explorer title, but few could match the accomplishments of Jedediah Smith. Like the Nor'wester David Thompson, Smith combined the skills of a frontier traveler, geographer, and beaver scout. He became an Ashley man in 1822, and soon rose to the top rank of that elite mountain man fraternity. Smith had a keen eye for the landscape and could portray its essentials in both written and cartographic form. One of Smith's most daring journeys was a reconnaissance into the Mexican province of California. Crossing the Mojave Desert in the fall of 1826, Smith became the first American explorer to reach California by an overland route. Once on the Pacific coast, he made several important exploratory probes—including a passage over the Sierra Nevada Mountains via Sonora Pass—before heading to the Oregon country in 1828. Smith's clerk was Harrison G. Rogers. His journal, covering parts of the period 1826–1828, is printed by Dale and provides a valuable record of the California venture.

In the years since Harrison Dale published his pathbreaking findings, several important books have appeared to enrich our understanding of Ashley, Smith, and the fur trade era. The early chapters of William H. Goetzmann's magisterial *Exploration and Empire: The Explorer and the Scientist in the Winning of the American West* (New York: Vintage Books, 1966) are important for their reassessment of the fur trader as explorer. Ashley's life is the subject of a fine biography by Richard M. Clokey entitled *William H. Ashley: Enterprise and Politics in the Trans-Mississippi West* (Norman: University of Oklahoma Press, 1980). Ashley's impact on the organization of the western fur business is traced in David J. Wishart, *The Fur Trade of the American West, 1807–*

1840: A Geographic Synthesis (Lincoln: University of Nebraska Press, 1979). Dale L. Morgan's masterful *Jedediah Smith and the Opening of the West* (Indianapolis: Bobbs-Merrill Co., 1953; reprint, University of Nebraska Press, 1964) set a biographical standard of western literature that has rarely been equaled. Fresh sources to illuminate Smith's time in California are printed in David J. Weber, ed., *The Californios versus Jedediah Smith, 1826–1827* (Spokane: Arthur H. Clark Co., 1990). Perhaps no book so fully captures the flavor of those times as well as Dale L. Morgan, ed., *The West of William H. Ashley, 1822–1838* (Denver: Old West Publishing Company, 1964). This collection of documents—government reports, contemporary newspaper accounts, and personal letters—offers the fur trade world in all its rich complexity.

Preface to the Revised Edition

The growing interest in the early development of the west, and particularly in the pioneer explorations and discoveries of Jedediah Smith, has focused attention not only on the original narratives describing these achievements but on the geographical and economic setting within which these explorations and discoveries were undertaken. Twenty years have elapsed since the first edition of this book was written. In the interval much new material has been brought to light, including the fragmentary Smith journals, some of it necessitating a correction or modification of my earlier interpretations, some of it, also, happily strengthening conclusions that had been hazarded in the first edition. I have found the only satisfactory way to use this new material effectively has been to recast many portions of the book. This edition, consequently, is something more than a revision, something less than a complete rewriting.

HARRISON C. DALE

University of Idaho
January 1941

Preface to the First Edition

Since the appearance of Brigadier-general Hiram M. Chittenden's *The American fur trade of the far west*,[1] there has been printed a considerable volume of source material covering the operations throughout the west of American and British fur-traders with their attendant discoveries. The publication of the Trudeau, Ross, and Ogden journals alone has necessitated the reconstruction of the history of geographic discovery in the trans-Missouri area. The reprinting in Reuben G. Thwaites's *Early western travels*[2] of a number of hitherto very rare narratives of exploration, together with the collection of a considerable quantity of scattered and hitherto unpublished historical data, and the more recent monograph literature on particular phases of western exploration have all thrown much new light on geographic history. For this reason it has seemed advisable to introduce this account of the Ashley-Smith explorations with a brief summary of the progress of discovery attending the operations of the fur-traders prior to 1822.

The expeditions of William Henry Ashley and Jedediah Strong Smith are but two divisions of one enterprise, the discovery and utilization of a central route to the Pacific by way of the Platte, the interior basin, and the Colorado river. Ashley and his men plotted the course as far as Green river and the Great Salt lake by way of the North Platte and the South Platte; Smith,

---

[1] Chittenden, H. M., *The American fur trade of the far west*, 3 vols.

[2] Thwaites, R. G. (editor), *Early western travels, 1748-1846*, 32 vols.

Ashley's successor in business, continued the latter's explorations, reaching California by way of the Colorado river and the Mojave desert, returning from central California, eastward, across the present state of Nevada to the Great Salt lake again. A second expedition carried Smith, the first white man to traverse it, the entire length of California and Oregon to the Columbia. The narratives of these explorations, comprising a recently discovered manuscript account by William H. Ashley describing his journey to and down Green river in 1824-1825, a letter of Jedediah Smith covering his first expedition to California, an unpublished letter, also by him, describing his second expedition through California to Fort Vancouver, and the unpublished fragmentary journals of Harrison G. Rogers, covering both the Smith expeditions, all preserved among the papers of the Missouri Historical society, are here for the first time brought together.

In the preparation of this volume I am deeply indebted to the Missouri Historical society and the Kansas Historical society for generously placing their collections at my disposal and to the Academy of Pacific Coast History for furnishing me copies of manuscripts in their possession. In particular I wish to express my thanks for the scholarly assistance rendered me by Miss Stella M. Drumm, librarian of the Missouri Historical society, whose intimate acquaintance with the bibliography of western history frequently expedited my work. I wish, further, to express my obligations to the Wisconsin Historical society, the Library of Congress, the Adjutant-general's and Chief of Engineers' offices of the War department, Washington, the Grosvenor library, Buffalo, and the American Antiquarian society, Worcester.

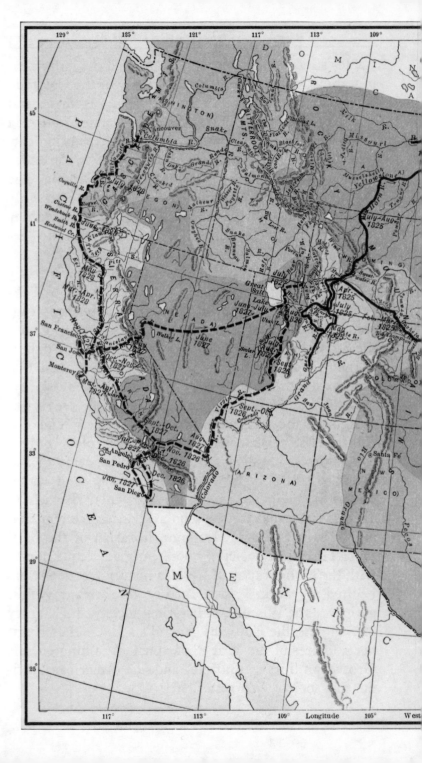

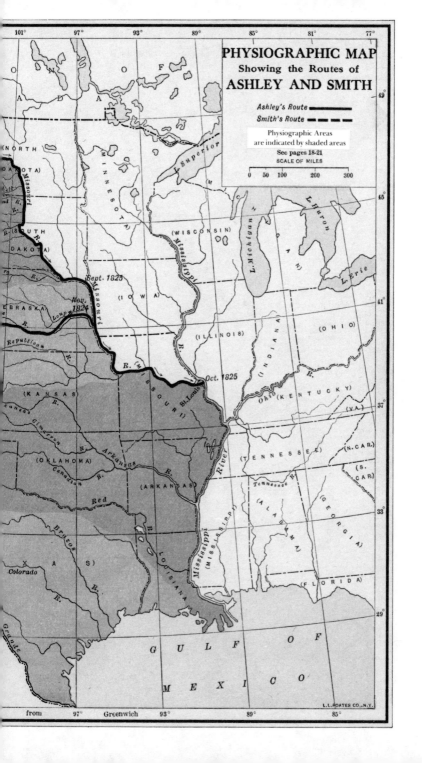

The Fur-trade and the Progress of Discovery to 1822

Not a few of the most significant geographical discoveries in all ages have been made by men who entirely lacked special scientific training. This is notably the case in western America. With the possible exception of Lewis and Clark and, in less degree, of a few others, the discoverers within the trans-Missouri area have not been professional geographers. Principally they have been missionaries, prospectors, trappers, Indian-traders, and the like, men who have entered a hitherto unknown region not with the object of adding to the stock of human knowledge about the face of the earth, but accidentally, in some cases, or for a distinct personal object, the attainment of which demanded their penetration of the unknown. The fur-traders and trappers form one of the most important classes in this group, furnishing such discoverers as Colter, Larocque, Crooks, Ross, Ogden, Bridger, and the Sublettes.

Though William Henry Ashley and Jedediah Strong Smith were men of this same stamp they nevertheless approach more nearly the scientific type than any of their fur-trading contemporaries. Recognizing fully the value of their work, they strove seriously to record the itineraries of their journeys, especially within uncharted regions, with such a measure of care and minuteness that the results of their operations, instead of being lost, might be utilized by professional geographers.

The American west, far from being a single geographic unit, comprises, as a matter of fact, six or seven distinctly defined drainage areas separated from each other in some places by rocky and lofty mountain barriers, in others by almost imperceptible divides. River courses have always been the natural approaches to the interior of a country, but they served this purpose in the highest degree in the trans-Missouri region, where fur-traders and hunters sought the most valuable peltries in and along the streams.

The first area[3] to be noted, beginning at the north, is the upper Missouri. This may be defined as including the valley of the main stream itself, from its three source rivers, the Jefferson, Madison, and Gallatin, eastward and southward to the mouth of the Niobrara, together with the great upper tributaries, Milk river, the Musselshell, Little Missouri, and the Yellowstone, with the main affluents of the last, the Big Horn (Wind river), Little Big Horn, Tongue, and Powder rivers. A number of minor streams enter the Missouri between the mouth of the Little Missouri and the Niobrara whose valleys may also be included. In the north the upper Missouri area extends into Canada. From about the intersection of the international boundary with the one hundred thirteenth meridian to a point near Lander, Wyoming, this area is bounded by the Flathead, Bitterroot, Absaroka, Grosventre, and Wind River ranges, a lofty barrier on whose western slopes gather the waters of the Columbia. From Lander the southern boundary runs almost due east to the Missouri. This is the largest of these geographic units.

A second division comprises the region drained by the great central affluents of the Missouri, the Platte

[3]See map on pages 14–15.

and the Kansas, with their tributaries. The valley of the
Sweetwater, the main tributary of the North Platte,
with that stream itself, lies just south of the upper Missouri area, roughly separated from it by the southern
spurs of the Big Horn mountains and, along the boundary of Wyoming and South Dakota, by the Black hills.
The valley of the South Platte, whose sources lie in the
mountains of central Colorado, is separated by only a
low divide from the Blue, Republican, Solomon, and
Smoky Hill forks of the Kansas, all to be included
within this geographic district. The western boundary
of the second division is, in the north, the low divide
separating the Atlantic waters from those of the Colorado, and, in the south, the lofty Colorado mountains
separating the same waters from the upper reaches of
the Rio Grande.

The cis-Rocky southwest comprises two drainage
areas which, however, because of the low divide separating them, may be considered as one. The first includes
the regions watered by the tributaries of the lower
Missouri and Mississippi, principally, of course, the
Arkansas; the other, the valleys of streams flowing into
the Gulf of Mexico, the chief and westernmost of which
is the Rio Grande with its great affluent, the Pecos. The
lower Mississippi area is separated from the central
Missouri area by an almost imperceptible divide in the
west but by the rugged Ozark plateau in the east.

Returning to the north, beyond the high range marking the western boundary of the upper Missouri area,
lies a fourth district, the Columbia basin, extending
southward to approximately the forty-second parallel
and including the Clark and Lewis forks of the Columbia with their numerous tributaries. The short
streams of Washington and Oregon flowing directly

into the Pacific may also, for convenience, be included in this area.

South of the forty-second parallel lies the interior basin, comprising most of Utah and Nevada with a portion of California, Oregon, and Wyoming. Only a low divide separates this area from the Columbia basin on the north and from the Colorado drainage area on the northeast, southeast, and south, while to the west, on the other hand, the lofty Sierras clearly define it. This series of low divides to the north, northeast, and southeast largely accounts for the fact that the interior basin remained so long unidentified and for the natural supposition that it was a part either of the Columbia or of the Colorado drainage areas. Had it been approached from California instead of from the east, its real nature would undoubtedly have been recognized early.

South of the interior basin and west of the Rio Grande the Colorado river drainage area extends as far as the Mexican boundary and the Gulf of California, comprising most of Arizona with parts of Utah, Nevada, and California. As stated above, only a low divide separates it at most points from the interior basin.

Last of all, beyond the Sierras, is the Pacific drainage area, divided into a northern and southern half by the Sacramento and San Joaquin rivers. To this belongs also the narrow littoral between the Coast range and the sea.

Each of these areas may be said to be dominated by a single stream, the upper Missouri by the Missouri, the central Missouri by the Platte, the lower Mississippi by the Arkansas, the gulf by the Rio Grande, the Columbia by that river, the interior basin by Bear river and the Humboldt, the Colorado by Green river and the Colorado itself, the Pacific by the San Joaquin-Sacramento.

The operations of the fur-traders were not extended equally into all these areas. Generally speaking their contributions to geographic discovery were confined to the upper Missouri, the central Missouri, the interior basin, and the Columbia drainage areas. The lower Mississippi, the gulf, Colorado river, and Pacific areas were not only less productive of furs but had been discovered and in large measure explored before the extensive development of the fur industry began. Fur-traders, to be sure, penetrated these regions from time to time in search of peltries, and in their wanderings contributed to geographic knowledge, but their results were less significant here than in the north. The geographic contributions of Ashley and Smith were made chiefly within the central Missouri area and the interior basin, though their operations extended into nearly all the other districts, while Smith made discoveries of first importance within the northern part of the Pacific drainage area.

St. Louis was the center of the fur-trade and consequently the starting-point of expeditions of discovery. Even before the coming of Laclede, French *coureurs de bois* and half-breed whites, following in the steps of La Harpe and Du Tisné, of De Bourgmont and Mallet, without probably ever having heard of these gentlemen, pushed up the Missouri and its central tributaries at least as far as Kansas City and perhaps to Omaha. After 1764 a greater number pressed farther and farther into the interior, continuing up the Missouri to the Great Bend and up the Platte and Kansas to the foothills of the Rockies. The farther they penetrated, however, and the more diverse the reports of what they had seen, the more confused became the actual geographic knowledge of the interior. This was notably the situation in 1793, when, at the instigation of the lieutenant-governor of the province, Zenon Trudeau, who wished "to enlighten the age in regard to that portion of the globe as yet so little known," [4] nine or ten fur-traders, out of some twenty odd who were invited, organized *La Compagnie de Comerce pour la Decouverte des Nations du haut du Missouri.*[5]

The patron of this undertaking, recognizing how important were the discoveries that the Missouri fur-traders were making each year, resolved to follow them up by careful exploration.

To effect this, he required in pursuing this trade, those engaged in it, would pay attention to unite to the employees they might send to the country, enlightened persons, who would use every exertion to penetrate to the sources of the Missouri, and beyond, if possible, to the Southern ocean – take observations and heights of localities and notices of the tribes who inhabit them, their habits and customs, the trade that might be established with them – note them as suitable marts for trade, or forts for the protection of commerce, in a word, to acquire a correct knowledge of a country until this period solely inhabited by Indian tribes, and almost entirely unknown.[6]

A schoolmaster, Jean Baptiste Trudeau, a relative of the lieutenant-governor, was accordingly selected, as an "enlightened person," to accompany the first expedition, sent out in the spring of 1794. Trudeau was unable to ascend the river far enough to learn much that was not already known, but he kept a journal of his trip, which was the first recorded description of a long

---

[4] Billon, F. L., *Annals of St. Louis*, 283.

[5] Douglas, W. B., "Manuel Lisa," in Missouri historical society *collections*, III, 238 ff; Billon, *op. cit.*, 283; Teggart, F. J., "Notes supplementary to any edition of Lewis and Clark," in American historical association *annual report, 1908*, 189. The company was organized october 15, 1793, and the first apportionment of trade under its regulations was made may 3, 1794. Douglas states that the company was formed may 12, 1794.

[6] Billon, *op. cit.*, 283 ff.

stretch of the river made by one who had actually ascended it.[7]

Following this first attempt at exploration, Juan or John Evans, accompanying James Mackay, a Spanish subject, ascended the river to a point near the present Omadi, Nebraska, spent part of the winter of 1795-1796 in camp there, and the following spring pushed on alone as far as the Mandan villages on a voyage of positive discovery.[8] Despite the admirable designs of the company and its genuine efforts to carry them out, it is probable that it offered more hindrance than incentive to the cause of discovery and exploration.[9] To be sure part of Trudeau's journal and Mackay's and Evans's maps subsequently fell into the hands of Thomas Jefferson and by him were transmitted to Lewis and Clark for their guidance. Jefferson valued them highly, perhaps more highly than did Lewis and Clark, who seem to have made but slight use of either the journal or maps.[10]

Not only did the *Compagnie du haut du Missouri*

[7] The "Trudeau journal," part iii (ii), Missouri historical society *collections*, IV, part i; *American historical review*, XIX.

[8] "Havia atravezado felizmente la nacion mandana."—Teggart, *op. cit.*, 192, footnote and *passim*.

[9] It is not improbable that the company's interest in geography was something of a cloak to cover a concerted effort to outstrip the British in their westward advance and to undermine the hold which they had secured on the savages. Mackay himself stated that through his hands "were distributed, principally, the presents of merchandise necessary to secure the friendship of the Indians, and to estrange them from the influence and traffic of the British, Northwest, and Hudson's Bay companies."—Teggart, *op. cit.*, 193. The company took pains to establish at least three forts, one opposite the mouth of the Platte, another, Fort Charles, about six miles below the present town of Omadi, Nebraska, and a third above the mouth of the Niobrara, on the left bank of the Missouri. See Perrin duLac, *Voyages dans les deux Louisianes*, map.

[10] The Mackay and Evans maps have not come to light. It is the opinion of Teggart that Mackay's map is substantially the same as that of Perrin duLac, accompanying his *Voyages dans les deux Louisianes*. Teggart, *op. cit.*, 188 ff.

fail to push its discoveries and explorations beyond the Mandans into the real *terra incognita,* but, by monopolizing the trade, it placed a rigid check on the efforts of other individuals in that direction. One of those to feel this most keenly was Manuel Lisa,[11] who had come to St. Louis in the last decade of the eighteenth century and who in 1799, with several others, memorialized the government complaining that "the trade in peltries, the sole and only resource which for a long time has supported the commerce of this country, being forbidden to the greater part of the citizens, must necessarily involve the ruin of the merchants" who undertook to venture into the Indian country. Lisa and his comrades went on to urge that the trade monopoly of the company be abolished and that "general freedom of commerce be restored." [12] Lisa's petition, however, was made in vain. The company continued to monopolize the trade of the upper river, while in the southwest, among the Osages, the Chouteau interests, which had been granted a monopoly for six years, effectually blocked all competition and consequently the prosecution of geographic discovery in that direction.

The United States government fell heir to the scientific designs of the *Compagnie du haut du Missouri,* if not to its commercial policy. The transfer of upper Louisiana was effected march 10, 1804, and on may 14 Lewis and Clark commenced their journey, arriving at St. Louis on their return september 23, 1806. While Lewis and Clark were in camp, their first winter out, a number of Canadian *voyageurs* and Indians visited their quarters, from whom the explorers endeavored to obtain every shred of information available about the

---

[11] For a sketch of Lisa see Douglas, W. B., "Manuel Lisa," in Missouri historical society *collections,* III.

[12] *Idem,* III, 239.

country lying between the Missouri river and the ocean. This data Lewis embodied in a map which was sent back to Washington on their departure the following spring.[13] A glance at this map, called the Lewis map of 1806, and a comparison of it with the one of 1810 "copied by Samuel Lewis from the original drawing of Wm. Clark" [14] shows to how great an extent Lewis and Clark were actual discoverers. In the first place, they learned that the continent was much wider than had been supposed and than they had represented it on their map of 1806. The Columbia, instead of being only a Pacific coast stream, was found to drain a vast interior territory or series of valleys between the Cordilleras and the Coast range. Instead of one mountain system lying between the headwaters of the Missouri and the Pacific, they found two, separated from each other by four hundred miles and more of intervening valleys. They discovered the whole interior drainage of the Columbia with its two main arteries and their network of tributaries fittingly named for the discoverers themselves. The Missouri they found to head in the northwest and not in the southwest. The upper waters, though not the source, and many of the higher tributaries with those of its affluent, the Yellowstone, they were the first white men to cross.[15] The network of ridges that characterizes the Rocky mountain system along the forty-fifth parallel they also sighted for the first time.

[13] The map is printed in *Science,* old ser., X, 222 and in Coues, *History of the expeditions under the command of Captains Lewis and Clark,* IV, pocket.

[14] The original drawings by Clark are reproduced in Thwaites, *Original journals of the Lewis and Clark expedition,* VIII (atlas).

[15] The lower course of the Yellowstone with its southern tributaries was explored by Larocque a month before Clark. Burpee, L. J. (editor), "Journal de Larocque," in *Publications des archives Canadiennes,* no. 3, 30 ff. They were also familiar to the French fur-traders from St. Louis and perhaps also to the Spaniards from New Mexico.

With the return of Lewis and Clark the government abandoned for a considerable time its support of western discovery and exploration, leaving both to private enterprise, which was quick to take advantage of the work of the pathfinders. Lewis and Clark had reached St. Louis on their return september 23, 1806. Only a little over six months later the enterprising Manuel Lisa, whose efforts in the fur-trade during the Spanish regime had been baffled by the *Compagnie du haut du Missouri,* dispatched an expedition up the river from St. Louis, the real forerunner of all subsequent fur-trading expeditions within the upper Missouri area. Lewis and Clark were the trail-makers, Lisa the trade-maker. The former laid the foundation of scientific geographic exploration of the far west, the latter, the foundation of a great industry in that same region, which, profiting by the information brought out by the first explorers, in turn contributed more than any other single agency to the prosecution of the work of discovery begun by them.

All Lisa's expeditions were attended by discoveries which one is tempted to surmise might have been accomplished nearly a decade earlier but for the policy pursued by the *Compagnie du haut du Missouri.* In the interval, however, Lisa had had opportunity to study carefully the trade and its possibilities and to observe that the failure of earlier ventures, including those of the monopolistic company itself, was attributable to the lack of stability and permanence of occupation which invariably characterized their undertakings. Small parties only, "vagrant hunters and traders" Major Thomas Biddle had called them, had undertaken to conduct operations from merely temporary trading-posts, always soon abandoned. Lisa determined to depart from this policy altogether and instead to erect at suitable points along the upper river substantial forts or factories to serve as places of protection and permanent headquarters for the men in his employ. As a result, Lisa's expeditions were enabled to penetrate the interior country to a much greater distance and, consequently, to make a number of important discoveries.

His first expedition, in 1807, ascending the Missouri and the Yellowstone, erected the first fort at the mouth of the Big Horn, where Lisa wintered with his men, returning to St. Louis in the summer of 1808.[16] Before his departure for the lower country steps had been taken to investigate the region lying above the mouth of the Big Horn. John Colter, who, with George Drouillard and one Dickson, was of the party of Lewis and Clark, had already joined Lisa.[17] Colter, who had assisted in the building of the fort, was dispatched either in the fall of 1807 or in the spring of 1808 to confer with the Crow Indians and probably with the tribes on the upper Missouri to induce them to bring in their furs to Lisa's posts.[18]

Alone, with a pack weighing thirty pounds, he first traveled southward into Absaraka, the land of the Crows, and thence northward with a band of these Indians until, together, they met a war party of Blackfeet with whom hostilities ensued. In the course of this engagement Colter was wounded in the leg, which pre-

[16] Brackenridge, H. M., *Views of Louisiana,* 91; Douglas, *op. cit.,* III, 255 ff; Vinton, *John Colter,* 45 ff.

[17] James, Thomas, *Three years among the Indians and Mexicans,* 23; Gass, Patrick, *Journal,* 252; Douglas, *op. cit.,* III, 251. See Thwaites, *Original journals of the Lewis and Clark expedition,* V, 341, footnote.

[18] Brackenridge, *op. cit.,* 91 ff. See also Chittenden, *American fur trade,* II, 714. The Americans knew little about the Crows, although François Larocque, of the Northwest company, had visited them in the summer of 1805 and had written an interesting description of them, "Quelques remarques sur les sauvages Rocky mountain avec lesquels j'ai passé l'été de 1805."—Burpee, L. J. (editor), *Journal de Larocque,* 59 ff.

vented him from standing. Meanwhile his companions
had apparently abandoned him. Nothing daunted, however, alone and unaided he made his way back to Lisa's
post on the Big Horn.[19] Brigadier-general Chittenden
places this engagement on the western side of the continental divide, in Pierre's Hole, and infers that it was
on his return from the battle that Colter entered the
Yellowstone national park, discovering the natural
wonders of that region.[20] Thomas James, however, specifically states that the battle took place on the Gallatin
river, and Clark's map bearing the legend, "Colter's
route in 1807," based on information derived from Colter himself in 1810, nowhere places him on waters tributary to the Columbia. If this account is correct, it is
unlikely that Colter penetrated to the country associated a few years later with the name of Andrew
Henry and the overland Astorians.[21] Colter was a man
of superior courage, and his reputation does not suffer
from the fact that, in addition to his many adventures,
he did not cross Jackson's Hole, negotiate the Teton
pass, enter Pierre's Hole (Teton basin), and then re-
cross the continental divide to the Yellowstone.[22] Others
who went from Lisa's fort in the spring and fall of 1808
traversed much of the country lying between the Yellowstone and the Missouri, determining the general

[19] Brackenridge, *op. cit.,* 92. James places the engagement in 1808 and
states that there were fifteen hundred Blackfeet against eight hundred Crows.
See James, *op. cit.,* 19.

[20] Chittenden, *American fur trade,* II, 715.

[21] James employed Colter to guide him in the spring of 1810 from Lisa's
fort to the Three Forks. On the way, they passed through ravines and mountains to the Gallatin river, which they crossed and descended passing the
battlefield of 1808. James adds that Colter "was thoroughly familiar with the
route, having twice escaped over it from capture and death at the hands of
the Indians."—James, *op. cit.,* 19.

[22] There may even be some question of his having entered the Yellowstone
park area at this time. "Colter's route in 1807" lies wholly west and north of
Lake Eustis (Yellowstone).

features of the region and the course of streams whose mouths alone Lewis and Clark had passed.

In Lisa's first venture he had met opposition from the Chouteau interests, against whom he had contended earlier and by whom he had been cleverly balked in the Osage trade.[23] Scarcely had he left St. Louis when Pierre Chouteau likewise embarked with a party of traders for the upper country. He got no farther than the Arikara villages however. There, owing perhaps to the machinations of Lisa himself, he was forced to abandon his journey, returning in high dudgeon to St. Louis.[24] On Lisa's return in august 1808, however, the rival interests were brought together.

During Lisa's sojourn in the city the small company of 1807, of which he had been the leader, was reorganized and enlarged by the admission of Pierre and Auguste Chouteau, Benjamin Wilkinson, of a family, like the Chouteaus, long hostile to Lisa, Reuben Lewis, brother of Meriwether, William Clark, Andrew Henry, subsequently an associate of Ashley, and several others. The reorganized company was called the St. Louis Missouri Fur company. Its founders sought by heavier capitalization and by the substitution of monopoly for competition to revolutionize the fur-trade.[25]

[23] Douglas (*op. cit.,* III, 243 ff) describes the amusing ruse by which Pierre Chouteau nullified Lisa's long-sought permit to trade with the Osages.

[24] The character of Manuel Lisa has been painted in consistently dark colors. See "Letter of Nathaniel Pryor to William Clark, october 16, 1807," in *Annals of Iowa,* third ser., I, 615 ff. Thomas James (*Three years among the Indians and Mexicans,* 3) declared that "rascality sat on every feature of his dark-complexioned Mexican face, gleamed from his black Spanish eyes, and seemed enthroned on a forehead villainously low." John Bradbury, the naturalist, charged him with a breach of good faith. See Thwaites, *Early western travels,* V, 25-26. Pike had a not very elevated opinion of him.

[25] Lisa's capital in 1807 is said to have been sixteen thousand dollars, Billon, F. L., *Annals of St. Louis in its territorial days,* 32; that of the Missouri Fur company in 1809 forty thousand dollars, Chittenden, *American fur trade,* I, 140.

The first expedition sent up the river by the new company, in the spring of 1809, consistently followed Lisa's policy, by establishing first a post at the Gros Ventre villages and, in april of the following year, pushing far up the river to the Three Forks and erecting another fort there in the very heart of the Blackfoot country.[26] The same year, one Howes, an enterprising Hudson's Bay man, established himself west of the Three Forks, on a small tributary of the Flathead river, beyond the continental divide.[27] From the Missouri Fur company's post trapping detachments began at once to operate in the region between the Great Falls and the Three Forks and up the valley of the Jefferson river, crossing and recrossing the route of Lewis and Clark. The vicinity of the Three Forks was dangerous country for any white man. The implacable Blackfeet were given to picking off detached hunters at the most unexpected moments. It became utterly out of the question for the men to venture from the post unless they went in groups so large that their efficiency as hunters and trappers was impaired. George Drouillard, a man of unusual astuteness in dealing with Indians, was instantly shot one morning on venturing out alone.[28] The effect of this danger on the employees became daily more noticeable. The swiftness and suddenness of the Blackfoot attack had such an air of mystery, was so incapable of being side-stepped by ordinary human precaution, that the employees, once they had felt the ter-

---

26 James, *op. cit.*, 10, 22. A detailed account of this expedition is given by James, who accompanied it.

27 Ross, Alexander, *Fur hunters of the far west*, II, 9; Elliott, T. C. (editor), "Journal of Alexander Ross, 1824," in the Oregon historical society *quarterly*, XIV, 371. See also Lewis and Phillips, *Journal of John Work*, 26 and note.

28 James, *op. cit.*, 32 ff. Compare, however, Menard to Chouteau in Chittenden, *American fur trade*, I, 143; III, 894.

ror of it, declined even to leave the protection of the fort.[29] Many of the Americans, including Thomas James, the chronicler of the expedition, resolved to return to the settlements. The fort was accordingly abandoned, and a prolonged check given to geographic investigation within the country lying between the Bitterroot and Flathead mountains.

With the abandonment of the post, however, Andrew Henry and a small party proceeded up the Madison fork of the Missouri, crossed the continental divide, the first Americans to do so since Lewis and Clark, and discovered the northern branch of Snake river which now bears his name, followed that stream south to a sheltered valley, where, in the vicinity of what is now St. Anthony, Idaho, he built the first American trading-post on the Pacific slope of the Cordilleras. Here he was in a country hitherto unvisited by whites. To him is to be credited the discovery of the headwaters of the Lewis fork of the Columbia and of the radiating valleys that encircle its upper reaches. Henry and his men spent the winter at his post with indifferent success and in the spring abandoned the fort, some striking out for the Spanish country, others turning east, while Henry himself, with a handful of men, returned to the lower country by way of the Missouri.[30]

Thus the first efforts to operate beyond the Rockies were abandoned. From now on, too, the Missouri Fur company, declining in importance, drops out of sight as an agent of discovery. The partners had abandoned their fort at the Three Forks in the summer of 1810, and, in the course of the same year, or the following, their

---

[29] Letter of Pierre Menard to Pierre Chouteau, april 21, 1810, in Chittenden, *American fur trade,* III, 893 ff. See James, *op. cit.,* 30 ff; Brackenridge, *op. cit.,* 92 ff.

[30] Brackenridge, *op. cit.,* 233.

post at the mouth of the Big Horn as well. Their store-houses, located probably on Cedar island near Chamberlain, South Dakota, were also unfortunately burned. Henry, moreover, had met with very indifferent success beyond the mountains, securing only forty packs of fur, so that altogether the outlook of the company was dark. Reorganizations were effected in 1812, 1814, 1817, and 1819, but for a time the trade was largely restricted to the country below the Mandans. By 1819 the situation had somewhat improved, and following the reorganization of that year, which admitted many new members to the company, including Joshua Pilcher, Andrew Drips, and Robert Jones, the company began to regain its hold on the upper country. The next year Lisa died, and his place was taken by Joshua Pilcher, who proceeded to develop Lisa's project by establishing another post at the mouth of the Big Horn and by undertaking to prosecute the trade even among the Blackfeet again. This last effort terminated in a crushing defeat in 1823, and the gradual shifting of the company's operations from the upper Missouri to the lower river again and eventually to the Great Salt lake region.

The Missouri Fur company had felt the pressure of competition on all sides but most keenly from the Pacific Fur company representing the Astor interests. This company's overland expedition of 1811 to the mouth of the Columbia, headed by Wilson P. Hunt, reentered the field just abandoned by Andrew Henry and contributed many details to the geographic knowledge of the southern Columbia basin.[31] Three of Henry's men, in fact, accompanied the expedition, John Hoback, Edward Robinson, and Jacob Rezner. They

---

31 The most recent and authoritative account of the overland Astorian expedition is in Rollins's *The discovery of the Oregon trail,* lxv ff, containing Robert Stuart's journals.

had joined it in the spring of 1811 on its way up the Missouri. On leaving the Arikara villages july 18, 1811, the company proceeded almost due west into the largely unexplored country between the Missouri and the Big Horn, crossing the Grand, Moreau, Big Cheyenne, and Belle Fourche rivers. Some of the earliest trappers had ventured up these tributaries of the Missouri a considerable distance, and nearly seventy years earlier La Verendrye had pushed westward into this same area.[32] From the Yellowstone, too, Lisa's traders had penetrated eastward into the great plains of southern Montana and northern Wyoming, visiting an isolated valley here and there. Edward Rose, the interpreter with the expedition, was also, no doubt, familiar with the Crow country through which they passed after rounding the Black hills and crossing the streams between Grand river and the Popo Agie. Continuing westward they reached the Big Horn, which they ascended to the Wind River mountains. Continuing up Wind river till they reached an Indian trail leading over the Wind River range, the Astorians were now traversing an entirely unvisited country, though Colter and others of Lisa's men had penetrated far to the south, perhaps into the Wind River valley itself and over the crest of the mountains at least as far as Jackson's Hole. The fifteenth and sixteenth of august were occupied with crossing the range, apparently in the neighborhood of Union pass, and the next day they encamped at evening on Green river well towards its source. This stream was known soon after, if not already, as Spanish river.[33]

[32] See maps, nos. 1-4, in Thwaites, *Original journals of the Lewis and Clark expedition,* VIII (atlas).

[33] Brackenridge, *op. cit.,* appendix, 298-300; Irving, Washington, *Astoria,* I, 280, II, 159. The following entry occurs in the books of the Missouri Fur company, printed in Missouri historical society *collections,* IV, 197, "1812,

From the summit of the pass Hoback, Robinson, and
Rezner had caught a glimpse of the Tetons, familiar
landmarks, reminiscent of the long winter at Henry's
post beyond. Crossing the low divide between Green
river and the south fork of the Snake, in the vicinity of
Bondurant, they followed down Hoback river to its
confluence with the Snake, where they arrived september 27. Leaving four men here, Hunt, on the advice of
the three men, pushed across Snake river and the Teton
pass to Henry's abandoned post, arriving there october
8, 1811. Four more trappers were detached here to
operate in this country.

From this point, having left their horses, the main
body proceeded down Snake river in canoes on a voyage of positive discovery until disaster overtook them
near Caldron Linn. Here a division was effected, a portion of the men under McKenzie striking north over the
desert, only to return to the river, to abandon it again,
and finally to cross the mountains to the Clearwater,
where they touched the route of Lewis and Clark. This
stream they followed to its confluence with the Snake,
down the Snake to the Columbia, and so to Astoria,
where they were joined a month later by the major
division of the party under Hunt, which had followed
the main stream of the Snake and then crossed the Blue
mountains to the Columbia. A third division, accompanied by Ramsay Crooks and John Day, did not arrive until may. Thus nearly the entire length of the
great Lewis fork of the Columbia had been coursed,
the upper stream by Henry in 1810-1811, and the central and much of the lower portions by the overland

Fbre 7. Pour serche les Chasseurs qui etet sur la Pre. des Espagnols et
Arapaos." W. B. Douglas, in a summary of the evidence covering the wanderings of Ezekiel Williams, is inclined to believe that this refers to Williams
and his companions, who started south from Lisa's fort on the Big Horn in
1810, 1811, or 1812.

Astorians the following year. Furthermore, a new cross-ing of the continental divide, though a difficult one, had been traced over the Union pass, across Jackson's Hole, and over the Tetons. So far as is known, the Astorians were likewise the first Americans to visit Green river, though "Colter's route, 1807," on the Lewis and Clark map, in crossing three upper tributaries of a stream named Rio del Norte, one of which is legended "Col-ter's R.," may indicate that he, too, had reached the up-per waters of this stream.[34]

---

[34] It is dangerous to attempt to establish a definite itinerary for Colter from the Lewis and Clark map, as the most that can be said about his route is that he never believed he reached streams flowing into the Columbia, that he passed to the west of a lake (Biddle)—rather appropriately called Lake Riddle on some of the later maps—which he believed to be the source of the Big Horn and therefore an Atlantic water, and that he passed to the west and north of another lake (Eustis), which he believed to be the source of the Yellowstone. Some of the companions of Ezekiel Williams, the hero of Coyner's *Lost trappers,* may have been on Green river in 1810 or even a year earlier. See "Letter of Ezekiel Williams," in Missouri historical society *collections,* IV, 203. The entire evidence for Williams's wanderings, which is very confusing, is printed in Missouri historical society *collections,* IV. Edward Rose, Hunt's guide, had been one of Williams's companions. Williams states that he went with a detachment of the Missouri Fur company to the mountains in 1810, where he hunted, apparently in their employ, for two years, that in august 1812 he started south through the Crow country with nearly twenty men, all operating independently, that after forty or fifty days they struck the Arkansas, where they wintered, and that the next june (1813), having assembled on the headwaters of the Platte, eight or ten of them crossed the Rocky mountains, while Williams, continuing south, spent another year among the Indians, reaching Arrow Rock on the Missouri river, after prolonged wanderings, in the spring of 1814. The statement is incorrect as to date, for according to David H. Coyner [*The lost trappers,* 90] Edward Rose, who was with the expedition, abandoned it on reaching the Crow country, preferring to remain with the savages. As he joined Hunt's party in the spring of 1811, it, of course, precludes the possibility of Williams's expedition having left Lisa's fort in august 1812. It is specifically stated, further-more, by George Sibley, a trustworthy gentleman, that Williams reached Arrow Rock on his return to civilization in the summer of 1813. Coyner, however, states that Williams went up the Missouri in 1807 with the expedition which conducted the Mandan chief, Shehaka, and implies that he started south the same year. See Coyner, *op. cit.,* 19, 86, 87. Coyner's dates are erroneous, for the expedition of 1807, commanded by Ensign Pryor, con-

The geographic discoveries of the Astorians did not end here. On june 29 or 30, 1812 a party, ostensibly under command of Robert Stuart, carrying with them letters and papers for Colonel Astor, set out from Astoria to return overland to the states. Stuart was accompanied by Ramsay Crooks, Robert McClellan, and four others. Following up the Columbia and the Snake, familiar country to them all, they encountered on the twentieth of august, below Caldron Linn, the party of four, Miller, Hoback, Robinson, and Rezner, which had been detached at Henry's fort the preceding october.[35] These men stated that they had traveled south about two hundred miles and had trapped on a river, which, according to their account, discharged into the ocean but

ducting Shehaka, never reached the Mandans, although Coyner describes with much circumstantial detail the reception accorded that long-absent savage. He does not definitely state the length of time that Williams was absent but implies that he reached Arrow Rock in the second winter after his departure, i.e. 1809-1810, which is manifestly incorrect. Williams postdates his adventures; Coyner antedates them. The most reasonable assumption is that Williams and Rose went up the river in 1809 with Lisa's party, although he is not mentioned by James, and that the following year, 1810, he turned south in company with Rose, who was left in the Crow country, to be picked up by Hunt the next spring, and that in june 1811 a portion of his company set out for the Spanish country. If they reached Green river, as seems likely, they would in this case have antedated the Astorians by three months or so. The two divisions of Henry's men, who separated from him in the early spring of 1811 and of whom nothing further is known, may also have reached Green river. One of the divisions, it is certain, started for the Spanish country. "Sometime after this (1809-1810) a party of hunters south of the Yellowstone were taken prisoners by the Spaniards and carried into Santa Fé." *American state papers, Indian affairs,* II, 451.

[35] The other four men left at the mouth of Hoback, october 1, 1811, had trapped in that country and had perhaps ventured some distance down the Snake. In the spring they had turned north and west through Jackson's Hole and over the Teton pass, following Henry's route to the headwaters of the Missouri. On their way they had been attacked by the Crows and one of their number slain. The remainder then made their way to the lower Snake country, where they were picked up by Reed in the summer of 1812. Irving, *Astoria,* II, 196; Ross, Alexander, *Oregon settlers,* in Thwaites, *Early western travels,* VII, 215; Chittenden, *American fur trade,* I, 206. They made no discoveries of consequence.

at a point south of the Columbia. Washington Irving understood by this description Bear river and the Great Salt lake. Their account of their wanderings, however, was most incoherent. After hunting on this river they had proceded due east, they said, for two hundred miles, when they had encountered sixty lodges of Arapahos, who had robbed them. They then wandered fifty miles further and halted for the winter. In the spring they again wandered on foot "several hundred miles," traversing barren wastes until they were discovered by Stuart and his party.[36] Vague as is their narrative, it seems not unlikely that they were the first to penetrate the interior basin from the north.

They then joined Stuart and his party but, a few days later, all but Miller abandoned them again. Miller undertook to guide Stuart's party but his services did not prove valuable. Under his direction they followed the Snake some distance until they reached a country of great sandy plains. On september 7 they abandoned the Snake and, still under Miller's guidance, wandered in a vague fashion up the Portneuf and its tributaries until, crossing a low divide, they reached Bear river, to which they gave Miller's name.[37] This stream they ascended until september 12. They then turned east over a range of hills,[38] and then north up a large branch of Miller's river which came in from the north.[39] Along this they traveled, the first day twenty-five miles, and the next twenty-one miles, encamping on the margin of a stream flowing north.[40] Two days more brought them to an-

[36] Irving, *Astoria,* II, 128 ff; Rollins, *Discovery of the Oregon trail,* 86.

[37] Irving, *Astoria,* II, 134; Rollins, *op. cit.,* 129.

[38] Preuss range (?).

[39] Smith's fork or Thomas fork according to Coues (*New light on the great northwest,* II, 884 footnote). Thomas fork, Rollins, *op. cit.,* 131 and note 56.

[40] Salt river. Chittenden, *American fur trade,* I, 209; Irving, *Astoria,* II, 138; Rollins, *op. cit.,* 132.

other stream "running due north, which they concluded
to be one of the upper branches of Snake river." [41] This
stream they descended to its confluence with the south
fork of the Snake, which they followed to the vicinity
of Pierre's Hole.[42]

They then abandoned the river and struck northeast
across the Teton range, fording several streams, including the south fork of the Snake, ascending the Hoback
and, bending their course constantly to the east and
southeast, finally on october 11 found themselves "encamped on a small stream near the foot of the Spanish
River mountain." [43] They crossed the mountain on the
twelfth to Green river. On the seventeenth, they passed
two large tributaries of this stream rising in the Wind
River mountains.[44] On the nineteenth and twentieth
they continued their course, striking a large Indian
trail running southeast.[45]

Continuing in a generally southeasterly direction
they followed this trail the remainder of the nineteenth
and part of the twentieth, but, when they found it turning northeast, abandoned it, continuing their own way
southeast. Next day, the twenty-first, however, they
turned east, striking the trail again. That day they made
fifteen miles; on the twenty-second they made twenty,
but they crossed the divide. The twenty-third they
reached a stream running south-southeast, which they
concluded could not, however, be a tributary of the
Missouri. They then turned due east all that day and
on the twenty-fourth and twenty-fifth. The next day an

[41] Irving, *Astoria*, II, 137. Grey's river according to Rollins, *op. cit.*, 132
and note 67.

[42] Rollins, *op. cit.*, 150 ff.

[43] Irving, *Astoria*, II, 153. The southern spur of the Grosventre range near
the sources of Green river.

[44] Boulder creek and East fork. Rollins, *op. cit.*, 178, notes 106 and 107.

[45] *Ibid.*, 162.

easterly and northeasterly course brought them to Muddy creek and on the twenty-eighth they reached the Sweetwater.[46] Thus they were the first to cross the continental divide by the famous South pass.[47]

The next expedition to cross the continental divide by or near this pass was one of Ashley's detachments a dozen years later.

The beginning of British expansion in the northwest is associated with the name of David Thompson. A skilled astronomer and mathematician, educated in London, he had journeyed in the summer of 1795 from Hudson bay to Lake Athabasca in the service of the Hudson's Bay company. Eager to undertake further exploration, he pressed the company's agent at Fort York for another commission, but in vain. Finding himself out of employment, he hastened to present himself at the summer rendezvous of the Northwest traders at Grand Portage. Having made known his qualifications, he was immediately appointed astronomer and surveyor

---

[46] *Ibid.,* 166 ff and 181-186, notes 147, 151, 193.

[47] Elliott Coues in his edition of the Henry-Thompson journals concluded that "the pass they made can be no other than the famous South pass of the Rocky mountains." (Coues, *New light on the great northwest,* II, 884 footnote.) In his review of a new edition of Irving's *Astoria,* 1897, however, he concluded that they followed a course "very near South pass—perhaps within twelve or fifteen miles of it, where they wandered off the Indian trail which would have taken them through this pass, and kept about south-east till they had headed the Sweetwater entirely. Then they struck east, south of that river, and finally fell on it lower down." This change of view he was induced to make after a discussion of the problem with Brigadier-general Chittenden (Coues, *Forty years a fur trader,* 29 footnote). This interpretation is confirmed by the entries in Stuart's journal. See Rollins, *op. cit.,* chapt. VII and notes. After all the South pass is no "narrow mountain corridor" but some twenty miles in width, extending over undulating plateaus and ridges. Ramsay Crooks's claim, in a letter of 1856 published in the *Detroit free press* in july of that year, is consequently correct. For this letter and a discussion of the problem see Dale, "Did the returning Astorians use the South pass," Oregon historical society *quarterly,* XVII. See also the map facing page 145 in Gilbert, *Exploration of western America.*

to the company, and, in that capacity, journeyed to
Lake Winnipeg, up the Saskatchewan to Lake Winni-
pegoosis, north to Swan river, and subsequently to the
Assiniboin with a side trip to the Mandan Indians on
the Missouri.

After the union of the Northwest company with the
so-called X. Y. company in 1805, it became necessary
to extend careful surveys into the great unknown beyond the Rocky mountains. Thompson, accordingly,
was selected to go up the Saskatchewan, explore the
Columbia river, and examine the vast sea of mountains
bordering on the Pacific. He crossed the Rockies in
1807, discovering the upper reaches of the Columbia,
where the next year he erected a post called Kootenai
House. Here he wintered, 1807-1808, and again 1808-
1809. In 1809, determining to extend his operations
down the Columbia river, he pushed a short distance
across the present international boundary and established Kullyspell House near Hope, Idaho. The winter
of 1809-1810 he spent at the newly-erected post near
Thompson's falls on Clark fork in Montana.

Two years later, he descended the Columbia, being
the first white man to follow that stream as far as the
confluence of Lewis's fork with Clark's fork, from
which point Lewis and Clark had, of course, preceded
him to the sea. Continuing down the Columbia he
reached Astoria, where he found the Americans installed. Thus were discovered the upper courses of the
Columbia and the adjacent country in eastern Washington, Idaho, and Montana. What Andrew Henry and
the overland Astorians accomplished in the way of discovery along Lewis's fork, Thompson accomplished
along Clark's fork. The course and main valleys of the
two great arteries were thus determined. East of the

Rockies Lewis and Clark and the Missouri Fur company carried discovery nearly to the forty-ninth parallel; and now, west of the mountains, the British, operating southward, penetrated to the Columbia. Only the intervening mountain region, the home of the Blackfeet, still baffled the whites.

Following the cession of Astoria and the erection of posts at Oakanagan, Spokane House, and among the Nez Perces and the Flatheads, the British company not only filled in the details of discovery but, through its so-called Snake country expeditions, widely extended geographic knowledge in that region which had been first sighted by the Astorians. For five years, to be sure, the Northwest company made no systematic effort to operate in the valley of Snake river or in the country of the Snake Indians to the south. But in 1816 it was proposed to extend operations "on the south and west toward California and the mountains, embracing a new and unexplored tract of country." [48]

A new method of conducting the business, however, very similar to that adopted later by Ashley, had first to be devised in order safely to operate in so remote a region. "To obviate the necessity of establishing trading posts, or permanent dwellings, among so many warlike and refractory nations, formidable trapping parties were, under chosen leaders, to range the country for furs; and the resources thus to be collected were annually to be conveyed to the mouth of the Columbia, there to be shipped for the Canton market." [49] In other words, these Snake country expeditions, as they were subsequently called, were to be self-supporting during the period of their absence, which would frequently ex-

[48] Ross, *Fur hunters of the far west*, I, 73.
[49] *Idem.*

tend from six to nine months. They were to have no permanent base with which they might constantly keep in touch. To command such expeditions men of rare ability were needed. They were found in Donald McKenzie, Alexander Ross, John Work, and Peter Skene Ogden.

The first of these expeditions under Donald McKenzie, who had accompanied the overland Astorians, operated only as far as the cascades of the Columbia and, accordingly, contributed nothing to geographic knowledge. In 1818, however, a post was erected near the confluence of Clark's and Lewis's forks, called Fort Nez Perce (Walla-Walla) from which the first Snake expedition, accurately so called, set out in september. Part of this expedition, under the command of McKenzie himself, journeyed up the Snake river twenty-five days, until they found themselves in a rich beaver country lying between Snake river and the "Spanish waters," where the Indians were inclined to be hostile.[50] Leaving his people in this region, McKenzie took a circuitous route along the foot of the mountains, through an extremely dreary country, until he reached the headwaters of the great south branch (Snake river), regretting every step that he had been so long denied such a resourceful country. From the headwaters of the Snake he followed a course down that stream, sighting many points with which his expedition of 1811 as an Astorian had familiarized him.

In 1819 he accompanied a second Snake country expedition. Leaving a part of the men to winter near the river and to operate on its tributaries, McKenzie determined, "should the natives prove peaceably inclined

---

[50] Ross, *Fur hunters,* I, 200 ff. The expedition, therefore, ventured into the country traversed by the detached Astorians of 1812, probably in the valley of Bear river along its course through southern Idaho.

and the trapping get on smoothly among them, to spend part of the winter in examining the country further south. He was likewise anxious to have an interview with the principal chiefs of the Snake nation, not having hitherto seen them." [51] Keeping his resolve, he set out to the south on a journey of positive discovery and had gone only five days when he fell in with the main body of the Snake nation accompanied by two of their chiefs.[52] Just where he encountered them is uncertain, but in the course of his journey he had occasion to write to Alexander Ross, dating his letter "Black Bears lake, sept. 10, 1819," [53] which presumably indicates that he traveled up Bear river at least as far as Bear lake, a journey farther south in this section of the interior basin than any white man had taken heretofore.[54]

In describing the country he had traversed, he wrote, "South of Lewis river, at the Black Feet lake, this article [salt] is very abundant, and some of it is six inches thick, with a strong crust on the surface. Near the same lake, our people found a small rivulet of sulphurous water bubbling out from the base of a perpendicular rock more than three hundred feet in height. It was dark blue and tasted like gun-powder." "Black Feet

---

[51] Ross, *Fur hunters,* I, 227.

[52] *Idem,* I, 248.

[53] *Idem,* I, 227.

[54] The returning Astorians abandoned Bear river probably twenty miles north of Bear lake, crossing the mountains between Georgetown and Montpelier, Idaho, and may, accordingly, have never seen Bear lake. The Bear lake country was familiar five years later to the Snake country men, although no other of their expeditions in the interior is known to have penetrated so far south. In 1824 the Snake party of that year had reached a point on Salmon river, Idaho, where it was necessary to adopt one of two routes. "I then told them that the country to our left, or southwest, would lead us along the foot of the Rocky mountains to Henry's fork, and crossing there Lewis's river, or the main south branch, we might proceed by the Blackfeet river to the Buffalo Snakes, the Sherrydikas, and Bear's lake, *where the country was already known."*—Ross, *Fur hunters,* II, 63.

lake" probably refers to one of the small lakes, the sources of Blackfoot river, Caribou county, Idaho, where sulphur springs and salt deposits abound.[55]

The Snake country expeditions of 1820-1821 under McKenzie, and that of 1823 under Finan McDonald, his successor, were confined to areas already familiar.[56] In february 1824, however, Alexander Ross, the new commander, left Flathead House on a more extended tour. Proceeding south and a little east the party headed straight for the Missouri valley into the dangerous and, as yet, little-known Blackfoot country till they struck the trail of Lewis and Clark in the valley of the Bitterroot. Ross followed their course as far as the Lemhi river in Idaho, though to him the country was unfamiliar.[57] From this point he and his men proceeded to Salmon river, and then southwest into a "country that was in many places unknown to the whites." [58] They trapped along the upper tributaries of Salmon river until the sixteenth of june, when a detachment was sent eastward to the Three buttes,[59] the appointed rendezvous, to meet a party of Iroquois hunters that had been dispatched earlier in the season to trap the country lying east. They encountered instead a gang of Blackfeet and returned without the trappers.[60] On the fourteenth of october, however, the Iroquois themselves came into camp pillaged and destitute. With them "arrived seven American trappers from the Big Horn river, but whom," says

---

[55] It is strange that the name Blackfeet should be applied south of Snake river.

[56] Ross, *Fur hunters*, I, 276-280; II, 2-3.

[57] *Idem*, II, 13; Ross, "Journal of the Snake river expedition, 1824" in Oregon historical society *quarterly*, XIV, 369 ff.

[58] Ross, *Fur hunters*, II, 63 ff.

[59] Misnamed by Ross the Trois Tetons. *Idem*, II, 124. See also Oregon historical society *quarterly*, XIV, 382, footnote.

[60] Ross, *Fur hunters*, II, 127.

Ross, "I rather take to be spies than trappers. There is a leading person with them." [61] This leading person was Jedediah Smith.[62] As the season was advanced, Alexander Ross with his own party and the Americans now returned to Flathead House where he met Peter Skene Ogden, his successor. The next five Snake country expeditions were under Ogden's command. Much interest centers about the first of these as the one on which Ogden reached Great Salt lake. Leaving Flathead Post december 20, 1824, he reached the Snake river probably by way of Big Lost river on april 2. From the Snake he crossed to the Bear which he described "and found it discharged into a large lake of one hundred miles in length." [63] It is not unlikely that Great Salt lake had already been visited that spring or even the preceding fall by a party of Ashley's men who were wintering in Cache valley.[64]

The Snake country expeditions of 1825-1826 carried Ogden from Fort Nez Perce westward along the Columbia to the Deschutes (Ogden's River of the falls) and up this stream, through an untraversed country, to the headwaters of its eastern fork in Crook county, Oregon. From this point he and his men crossed to the sources of John Day's river, also hitherto unvisited.

On the expedition of 1826-1827 Ogden visited regions even more remote. Departing from Fort Vancouver september 12, 1826, he proceeded as before to Deschutes river, thence to Crooked river and the head-

[61] Ross, "Journal of the Snake river expedition, 1824," in Oregon historical society *quarterly*, XIV, 385.

[62] See page 96.

[63] Merk, "Snake country expedition" in *Mississippi valley historical review*, XXI, 55. No journal has come to light for Ogden's first expedition but Doctor Merk has discovered a letter of Ogden's, dated july 10, 1825, describing his route in some detail.

[64] See page 100 f.

waters of John Day's. A detachment was sent to Syl-
vaille's river and the Malheur and Harney lake country of southern Oregon. Thither Ogden with the main
party journeyed and then proceeded westward in the
direction of the "Clammiitte" (*sic*) country.[65] Crossing the headwaters of the Deschutes they found themselves in a familiar region,[66] and then turned south to
the headwaters of the Klamath, probably reaching
Williamson river somewhere east of Crater lake.

Ogden's unfamiliarity with this portion of the country is evidenced by the following entry, "The waters of
the Clammittee do not discharge in the Columbia and
must discharge in some river to the ocean. It is from this
river I have hopes of beaver." [67] Continuing south they
reached Klamath River lake, passing "the camps from
where Mr. McDonald turned back last year and are
consequently strangers to the country in advance." [68]
But they did not proceed far, for beaver were scarce.
Wintering among the Shasta Indians they resumed
their southerly course in the spring, reaching a stream
having "no connection with the Clammitte river," but
flowing "south then west to a large river." [69] The In-

---

[65] Klamath. See Ogden, "Journal, 1826-1827," entry of november 5, 1826,
in Oregon historical society *quarterly*, XI, 209.

[66] Ogden enters in his journal, november 18, 1826, "Reached the River of
the falls, so desired by us all. Thank God. The road to the Clammitte we all
know."—*Idem*, XI, 210. Finan McDonald had trapped in the Klamath country the previous year in company with Thomas McKay, though only on the
headwaters of the stream above Klamath lake. See *idem*, XI, 211. "From Mc-
Donald," says Elliott, "must have come the first report of a name of the
Indians of that quarter, either a French-canadian rendition of the native
name or a French name assigned by the trappers because of local conditions."
—*Idem*, XI, 202. Elliott suggests Klamath ("Tlamath," Rogers and Fremont)
from the French *Clair-metis*, light mist or cloud.

[67] Ogden, "Journal, 1826-1827," entry of november 27, 1826, in *Idem*, XI,
210.

[68] Entry of december 5, 1826, in *Idem*, XI, 211.

[69] Pitt river (?), but Ogden states that he strikes it by going *west*. Entry
of february 10, 1827 in *Idem*, XI, 213.

dians knew nothing of the ocean beyond, but, from an advance party sent ahead Ogden learned that the Klamath, itself, took a westerly course and that below the forks it was a river of considerable volume.[70] One detachment actually reached a point only four days' journey from the sea.[71] Thomas McKay was dispatched beyond the Klamath to trap its southern and eastern tributaries,[72] while Ogden turned northwest to the northern branches of Rogue river. Here his guide "went to visit the Indians and returned with the information that Umpqua chief with the trappers from Williamettee [*sic*] has visited this region and taken all the beaver." Soon after McKay's return from the Klamath, it was designed to send him "to explore the sources of the Williamettee, which to this day have not been discovered," [73] but this plan was changed. The whole party then turned east into the difficult and, for the most part, untrodden country comprising the southern tier of Oregon counties, until they reached Snake river and so down to Fort Vancouver.[74]

The expedition of 1827-1828 left Fort Vancouver in august and confined itself to a region already frequently trapped, the valley of the Snake river itself.[75] In the course of the winter, which was spent near the Portneuf, the camp was visited by a party of Americans in the employ of Smith, Jackson, and Sublette. By the middle of july Ogden was back at Fort Vancouver, where pre-

[70] Entry of february 12, 1827, in *Idem*, XI, 213.

[71] Entry of february 21, 1827, in *Idem*, XI, 215.

[72] Entry of march 1, 1827. He did not proceed far, however. See *Idem*, XI, 217.

[73] Entry of may 13, 1827, in *Idem*, XI, 218.

[74] Ogden's journal of the expedition is printed in Oregon historical society *quarterly*, XI, 204-222.

[75] Ogden's journal of this expedition is printed in Oregon historical society *quarterly*, XI, 361-379.

sumably he was still sojourning when Jedediah Smith arrived the following month.[76] The expedition of 1828-1829 took Ogden into an unvisited country lying north and west of the Great Salt lake and the valley of the Humboldt.[77] The latter part of the journey carried him into California again as far as the country of the Modocs. Here he saw rifles, ammunition, and arms which he believed to be part of the plunder of Jedediah Smith's party of the previous year. Ogden then returned in the early summer to Fort Nez Perce.

The net result of the operations of the Northwest and Hudson's Bay companies in the Columbia and interior basin areas was, first, a detailed exploration of the country lying between the route of Lewis and Clark and that of the overland Astorians; second, the penetration and criss-crossing of that vast triangle formed by the two forks of the Columbia with the Cordilleras. South and west of Snake river McKenzie and Ross had pushed into the interior basin, to be followed a few years later by Ogden. To the west and southwest McDonald, McKay, and Ogden penetrated from the Great Salt lake across the deserts of southern Oregon and northern Nevada into the Sierras of the north Pacific, crossing to the headwaters of the Sacramento, the Klamath, and Rogue rivers, streams within the Pacific drainage area. For the most part, however, they operated north of the forty-second parallel, leaving the task of discovery and exploration south of that line to American trappers and traders, chief among whom were William H. Ashley and Jedediah S. Smith. American enterprise and discovery touched British enterprise in the upper valley of Green river, in the Bear lake region, about the

[76] See page 278.

[77] The journal of this expedition is printed in Oregon historical society *quarterly,* XI, 381-396.

Great Salt lake, across Nevada, and in northern California and southern Oregon.

One of the most noteworthy features of all the discovery and exploration crowded into this first third of the century is the simultaneity of it. Wherever an Englishman penetrated, there an American was sure to be a few months before or a few months after him. This, of course, was more true of the region north of the forty-second parallel than south of it. In the interior basin the American trappers had free rein, though their rewards were less.

By the year of Ashley's first venture in the fur-trade, 1822, the known area of the west comprised, in the first place, the main valley of the Missouri and its great tributary, the Yellowstone. The intervening country had been criss-crossed by Americans and to some extent by British trappers. South of the Yellowstone occasional travelers, such as Colter and the overland Astorians, had pushed as far as Wind river and across the lofty range at its source. The general route of the Oregon trail eastward from the point where it follows the Sandy had been traced by the returning Astorians. Having struck that trail, however, by crossing from the upper reaches of Hoback, they had consequently avoided that portion lying within the interior basin. This area, however, had been skirted by the detachment of Astorians sent out from Henry's fort, then by the overland Astorians in their weird circumvolutions under John Miller's guidance, and again by McKenzie in 1819. The British, too, had probably reached the low divide separating the interior basin from Green river and had trapped in the upper tributaries of that stream.[78]

The Columbia basin had been crossed and recrossed

[78] See page 42.

in every direction. Lewis and Clark and David Thompson were the first to journey nearly its entire length. Andrew Henry had skirted it in 1810, and the Englishman, Howes, the same year. The overland Astorians had followed its main artery, Snake river. After them the Northwest and Hudson's Bay companies had completed the examination of the intervening area between the Lewis and Clark forks. The Snake country expeditions had not confined themselves to the Columbia drainage area, but had crossed, as noted above, to the Bear river valley of the interior basin and, subsequently, in the year following Ashley's first venture, to the area west of the Great Salt lake, including southern Oregon and northern Nevada. Similarly, they had overstepped the Columbia area to discover the sources of the Pacific streams of northern California and southern Oregon.

Meanwhile exploration to the southwest had not been neglected. The limited fur-trading possibilities of this region delayed exploration or rather forced it to become the by-product of different enterprise. The United States government, itself, dispatching Pike and Long, undertook to spy out the general features of the country between the Arkansas and Missouri and the Rockies. The earliest visitors to Santa Fe learned to trace their way across the arid plains that intervene between the two areas of white settlements. West of the Rocky mountains, which, in the state of Colorado, push much farther east than in Montana or Idaho, the country was, as late as 1822, entirely unknown to Americans, while even the Spaniards had but an indifferent acquaintance with its general features.[79] Beyond the

79 Much remains to be done in studying the history of early Spanish exploration from Santa Fe. One of the best representations of Spanish geo-

Rockies, within the drainage areas of the Colorado and the interior basin, no American had penetrated. Two adventurous Spaniards, a half century before, had reached the shore of Utah lake after traversing western Colorado and part of eastern Utah. Other exploring expeditions had been dispatched by the Spaniards from Santa Fe from time to time, but the constant state of war prevailing between the Spaniards and the Comanches, Utes, and other Indian tribes during the first half of the eighteenth century effectually checked any real advance into these untraversed regions.[80] After 1761 Tomas Velez Cachupin, the governor, sent exploring expeditions as far as the Gunnison country in search of gold and silver. After the beginning of the nineteenth century, however, the interests of the inhabitants of New Mexico centered about their internal political affairs and the development of the mines of Chihuahua.

A great strip, widening as it went westward from the Missouri to the Spanish missions of the Pacific could be laid down on the map of 1822 and inscribed *terra incognita*. To the north and west, the valley of the Missouri and its tributaries was known; to the south and west, the route to Santa Fe. Between lay a vast unexplored area. The central tributaries of the Missouri, to be sure, had been followed along part of their course toward the mountains by isolated fur-traders at inter-

graphic knowledge at this period is Alexander von Humboldt's map, portions of which are printed in his *Political essay on the kingdom of New Spain*, III, facing page 493. The main features of this map are embodied in a more intelligible form in the "Map of Spanish North America, published as the act directs, aug't. 20, 1818, by Longman, Hunt, Rees, Orme, and Brown, Paternoster row, London." This map is based largely on the explorations (and map?) of Dominguez and Escalante. Compare the Plano geografico de la tiera descubierta y demarcada por Dn. Bernardo de Miera, etc., MS map, undated (1777?), unsigned, in United States library of congress, Woodbury Lowery collection, no. 593.

[80] Twitchell, R. E., *Leading facts of New Mexican history*, I, 443.

vals ever since the close of the eighteenth century; but indefinite indeed was the knowledge of the upper stretches of these streams and of the tributary country north and south. Few white men had crossed it.[81] Some of Andrew Henry's men, it is true, may have made their way from Snake river to the Spanish settlements; and not far from the same time, apparently, Ezekiel Williams and his companions journeyed from the Crow country to the Arkansas. Stephen H. Long, furthermore, in 1820 met a French half-breed who had been to the source of the North Platte in North Park. These isolated journeys, however, had added nothing to the general stock of geographic knowledge. The great task of exploration, if not of prime discovery, between the Missouri and the mountains had yet to be accomplished. Beyond the Rockies the interior basin was still virtually a blank.

The withdrawal of Manuel Lisa from the upper country in 1811 marked a general decline of the American fur-trade. For a decade, the ambitious activity that had characterized the Missouri Fur company and its predecessors, and that had led to the first penetration and survey of so large a stretch of inland country, had been noticeably subsiding. Instead of pushing forward from the established outposts into unvisited valleys and mountain defiles, the traders had abandoned these very posts, the bases of all further advance.

One of the first causes of this decline was the failure of the great Astor enterprise. Starting with exalted ambitions and brilliant prospects and under the manage-

---

81 Larocque found a Snake Indian of the Big Horn whose tribe had had dealings with the Spanish to the south. "Il est arrivé ici un sauvage Snake qui avait été absent depuis le printemps et avait une partie de sa tribu qui avait fait des échanges avec les Espagnols." Burpee, L. J. (editor), "Journal de Larocque," in *Publications des archives Canadiennes*, no. 3, 45.

ment of some of the ablest men on the continent, British and American, the company had been forced to abandon entirely its Pacific project. This was partly due to the failure on the part of the maritime end of the enterprise to cooperate with the overland division and also to the war with Great Britain, which rendered the position at Astoria untenable. Competition had also, to no small degree, weakened the fur-trade. The Lisa-Chouteau interests had found the only road to success in replacing competition by combination. No sooner had the Missouri Fur company been formed, however, than other concerns, most of them with inferior capital, also undertook to operate in the upper Missouri area. The Astor enterprise was the most formidable rival, but the presence of other smaller concerns, all of them willing to resort to unscrupulous methods in dealing with the Indians tended to reduce the profits of them all.[82]

The incessant hostility of the Blackfeet placed a serious check on the extension of trapping operations beyond Three Forks and thereby restricted all the upper Missouri companies to an area already worked for half a decade. The Blackfeet, furthermore, controlled directly or indirectly for a considerable time the only two known passes over the mountains; and accordingly every band of trappers and traders which crossed the Cordilleras risked attack from these implacable enemies of the whites. The whole history of the Missouri Fur company had been one of conflict with this tribe, culminating finally in the great disaster of 1823. After the War of 1812, moreover, there was little capital in

[82] Chittenden gives a list of some of the companies of 1819 competing with the Missouri Fur company. They included Cerre and Chouteau, capital, $4000; Chouteau and company, capital, $6000; Robidoux and Papin in company with Chouteau and Berthold, capital, $12,000; Pratte and Vasquez, capital, $7000. See Chittenden, *American fur trade*, I, 150, footnote 15.

the west available for enterprises so uncertain and hazardous as the fur business.

The Indian policy of the United States government also proved unfortunate. The factory system of trade with the Indians, adopted in 1796, was intended to provide the savages with tools, blankets, seeds, and the like, as inducements to abandon nomadic for settled agricultural life, manifestly an object entirely at variance with the natural aboriginal life which made the fur-trade possible. Having established the factory system of trade, the government thereupon negatived its object from the start by licensing private traders who desired to enter the Indian country. The government and private enterprise thereby became competitors in the same field. The consequences were, perhaps, more disastrous to the government system than to the private concerns, though the latter also suffered. Of greater moment was the government's failure to furnish adequate protection to those traders whom it licensed. The policy of fostering care of the Indians was naturally incompatible with the use of force against them even for the protection of American citizens, who were pretty generally regarded as being in the wrong whenever clashes with the Indians occurred. The citizens of St. Louis had petitioned congress in the winter of 1815 for the establishment of military posts at the Falls of St. Anthony and at the Mandan villages,[83] but for three years received no response. When the government, awakening finally to the need for protection, dispatched the famous Yellowstone expedition in 1819 with the very sensible object of building forts at Council Bluffs, the Mandan villages, and the mouth of the Yellowstone,[84] it only further demon-

83 *Niles register,* august 14, 1819.

84 O'Fallon to Sibley, St. Louis, may 3, 1818, Sibley MSS, III, in Missouri historical society. It was expressly stated that the purpose of these military

strated its feebleness. A nautical monstrosity, the steam-ship "Western Engineer," a single post near Council Bluffs, soon abandoned, and an abortive exploring expedition was all that the government had to show for the money expended.[85] It was not until 1822 that the factory system was abolished.

It was now ten years since the fur-trade entered on its decline. In the interval changed conditions had arisen. Competition had reduced all concerns to a dead level of mediocre returns, the upper country had restocked itself, more capital was available, and the British companies had been definitely excluded from operations in the territory of the United States. The government had promised its citizens protection in the Indian country and, as an earnest of its good intentions, had abolished the factory system. Taking advantage of these altered conditions several new trading companies were formed with headquarters at St. Louis. One of these was the American Fur company representing the Astor interests, which, since the fall of Astoria, had been confined to the region of the Great lakes. The political influence of this powerful company had been largely instrumental in securing the abolition of the factory system. An office was now opened in St. Louis.[86] Another concern entering the field at this time was the

establishments was to control the operations of the Northwest and Hudson's Bay companies in their dealings with Indians resident within the United States and to protect American traders. See *Niles register,* may 9, 1818.

[85] It should be admitted, however, that the undertaking brought the power of the United States army to Omaha, furnishing a certain assurance to the fur-traders that in their operations as far up the Missouri river as this point, at least, they were reasonably sure of protection. The exploratory division of the expedition, under Major Long, found a route up the South Platte to the mountains, which, a few years later, Ashley was to utilize and extend.

[86] Chittenden, *American fur trade,* I, 319. See also Thomas Allen in De Bow, *Industrial resources,* III, 517. Allen, however, gives the date erroneously as 1819.

Columbia Fur company, founded only the year before.[87] Other companies now engaging in the business for the first time or with increased capital were Stone, Bostwick and company, Bernard Pratte and company, and Ashley and Henry. All planned to operate in the upper Missouri and Yellowstone country, the dangerous neighborhood of the Three Forks, and the transmontane area so long abandoned.

[87] Chittenden, *American fur trade*, I, 325.

William Henry Ashley

William Henry Ashley, born in 1778, was a native of Powhatan county, Virginia.[88] He came, accordingly, from that portion of the United States which produced many of the earliest trans-Mississippi pioneers. From Virginia and its offspring, Kentucky, haled most of the leaders in western discovery and exploration. Lewis and Clark were Virginians. The nine civilians who accompanied them were all Kentuckians.[89] So also were John Hoback, Jacob Rezner, and Edward Robinson, of Astorian fame, and the Sublettes, Milton, William, Pinckney, Andrew, and Solomon. John Day, another Astorian, and James Bridger, prominent a little later, were Virginians. The list might easily be extended. Ashley received a good education in the country schools, and there is ample evidence in his letters and speeches to indicate that he was better equipped intellectually than most of his contemporaries. Although he removed to St. Louis in 1808,[90] he retained an interest in Virginian affairs and as late as 1829 had business dealings

[88] Switzler, W. F., "General William Henry Ashley," in *American monthly magazine*, XXXII, 318. Ashley was not a common Virginian name. The Hanover county records contain a deed of 1791 to a William Ashley of Spotsylvania, William and Mary college *quarterly*, XXI, 160. Switzler conjectures that he was the son of the William Ashley, who in 1750 was given permission to construct a gallery in St. Paul's church, Norfolk. Compare Meade, *Old churches, ministers, and families of Virginia*, I, 276.

[89] Thwaites, *Original journals of the Lewis and Clark expedition*, I, xxxi and lv, footnote.

[90] *Missouri republican*, april 3, 1832; Switzler, *op. cit., loc. cit.* Not in 1802, as stated by Chittenden, *American fur trade*, I, 247.

in his native state that demanded his personal attention.[91]

The year of Ashley's arrival in St. Louis was the year of Manuel Lisa's return from his first successful venture to the upper Missouri country, an event of conspicuous importance in the fur-trade. For a time, however, other enterprises attracted Ashley's attention. A knowledge of surveying and a slight familiarity with geology furnished him opportunities for visiting the remoter portions of Missouri.[92] It was on one of his expeditions of this sort that he discovered "Ashley's cave" in a lonely valley on Cave creek, Texas county, about eighty miles southwest of Potosi.

This cave is situated in a high wall of lime-stone rock. The entrance to it is by a winding foot-path from the banks of the creek, and leads to the mouth of the cave at an elevation of about fifty feet above the level of the water. Its mouth is about ninety feet wide and thirty in height, a size, which, without great variation, it holds for two hundred yards. Here it suddenly opens into a room which is an irregular circle, with a height of eighty or ninety feet and a diameter of three hundred, having several passages diverging from it in various directions. The two largest passages lead southwest and south, and after winding along a considerable distance, in the course of which they are successively widened and narrowed, unite and lead in a south course about five hundred yards, where the passage is choked up by large masses of stalactite, formed by the water which has filtered through the superincumbent rock at that place. The largest passage from the circular amphitheatre of the cave diverging north opens by another mouth in the rock, facing the valley of Cave creek, at no great distance below the principal mouth. Several smaller passages diverge from each of the main ones, but cannot be followed to any

91 "I had determined to attend personally to some business in Virginia and on my way to visit Washington City,"—Ashley to Benton, january 20, 1829, in U.S. Senate, *Executive documents*, 20 cong., 2 sess., I, no. 67.

92 Ashley was one of the first to examine the Ozark mountains, which he pronounced metalliferous. Schoolcraft, *Scenes and adventures in the semi-Alpine region of the Ozark mountains*, 47.

great extent, or are shut up by fragments of the fallen rock. Near the centre of the largest opening, a handsome spring of clear water issues.[93]

Within the mouth of the cave Ashley erected a complete plant for the extraction of commercial saltpetre from the potassium nitrate with which the cave abounded.[94] The prepared saltpetre he hauled to a gunpowder factory, which he built at Potosi, the only one in that part of the country.[95] Here Ashley resided for a time, conducting his business in partnership with one Brown.[96] The total production of their factory in the eighteen months from december 31, 1816 to june 1818 amounted to sixty thousand pounds, valued at thirty thousand dollàrs.[97] It was probably during his residence at Potosi that Ashley made the acquaintance of Andrew Henry.

Although Andrew Henry had not gone to the mountains since 1811, he had retained his financial interest in the Missouri Fur company, being present at meetings of the directors in St. Louis in 1812 and 1813, and by proxy in 1814.[98] By this last year, however, he had removed from St. Louis to Potosi, where he was engaged in the lead-mining industry.

[93] Schoolcraft, *Journal of a tour into the interior of Missouri and Arkansas*, ii ff.

[94] The year in which Ashley began this undertaking is uncertain, but Schoolcraft, who visited the cave in november 1818, found no one in charge of the works, which appeared "to have lain idle for some time." Schoolcraft, *op. cit.*, 13; also *Scenes and adventures*, etc., 228. Ashley was in St. Louis as late as 1814. Compare Chittenden, *American fur trade*, I, 248.

[95] Schoolcraft, *View of the lead mines of Missouri*, 43; also *Tour into the interior*, etc., 10.

[96] Schoolcraft, *View of the lead mines*, etc., 47. Schoolcraft alludes to him as "Colonel Ashley of Mine à Burton" (Potosi) in *Tour into the interior*, etc., 10.

[97] Schoolcraft, *View of the lead mines*, etc., 47.

[98] Records of the St. Louis Missouri fur company, MSS. in the Kansas historical society (Topeka).

The beginnings of modern lead mining in Missouri date from the year 1798 when Moses Austin, of Connecticut and Virginia and subsequently of Texan fame, erected the first scientific smelter at Mine à Burton. His process of extracting the ore was so far in advance of the primitive methods employed by the Spaniards that a direct impetus was given to an industry which had hitherto attracted but little attention. The demand for shot, created by the War of 1812, together with the discovery of new and richer deposits of ore in the vicinity of Mine à Burton, made lead mining one of the principal industries of the territory.

Instead of investing in one of the existing mines, Henry, apparently, had sufficient capital to undertake independent operations. His shaft, known as "Henry's Diggings," was worked profitably for some years, although by 1818, in common with a number of other mines in this neighborhood, it was no longer operated.[99]

Potosi was a small town, having only about five hundred inhabitants in 1818, and consequently its prominent citizens were few in number. First in importance was Moses Austin, the pioneer of the mines, still living near Mine à Burton. Among the few other men of mark in this small community were Andrew Henry, who, apparently almost on his arrival, had been selected foreman of the first grand jury of Washington county,[100] and William Henry Ashley, who, with Moses Austin, was a member of the board of trustees of Potosi academy, an educational institution incorporated in 1817.[101] It was natural that Ashley and Henry should be much thrown together and that, with the decline of the min-

---

99 Schoolcraft, *View of the lead mines,* etc., 127. Ashley had for a time an interest in Mine Shibboleth, also at this date abandoned.

100 *History of Franklin, Jefferson, Washington, Crawford and Gasconade counties,* 494.

101 *Idem,* 516, 525.

ing business, they should look about for fresh opportunities for investment. Henry's experience in the fur-trade had not only acquainted him with the remote areas of the upper Missouri but had familiarized him with the details of that important industry. Observing the trend of the business, he had wisely withdrawn from the Missouri Fur company when, toward the close of the War of 1812, the trade was rapidly declining. By 1819, however, the outlook was beginning to appear brighter, and two years later Henry, in company with Ashley, abandoned the mining industry, turning to this more romantic, risky, and, in their case, lucrative enterprise.[102]

Ashley, meantime, had attained greater prominence and higher distinction than could attach to membership on the board of trustees of Potosi academy. Interested in the development of the territorial militia and active in politics, he had advanced in the former from the rank of captain in 1813, through that of colonel in 1819, to a generalship in 1822, while his ventures in politics won him in 1821, by a close margin, the lieutenant-governorship of the newly-formed state of Missouri. Three years later, after his successful engagement in the fur-trade, he ran for governor but was defeated.[103] None of Ashley's financial enterprises down to 1822, however, had been attended by marked success. After fourteen years residence in Missouri he not only had not made

[102] That is, in 1821. Although the first Ashley-Henry expedition was sent out in 1822, Henry had already resumed his interest in the business, having a group of men trapping from the post at the mouth of the Yellowstone. After reaching this post on october 1, 1822, "and receiving the furs of the LAST hunt Genl. Ashley started for St. Louis with a large Pirogue," Sullivan, *Travels of Jedediah S. Smith*, 8.

[103] Edwards, R. and M. Hopewell, *Edwards's great west*, 337; Davis, W. R. and D. S. Durrie, *Illustrated history of Missouri*, 72, 86. Compare Wetmore, *Gazetteer of Missouri*, 379; Switzler, *op. cit., American monthly magazine*, XXXII, 323.

a fortune, but was estimated to be nearly one hundred thousand dollars in debt.[104] The renewed activity in the fur-trade, however, was by 1822 attracting repeated notice. One observer wrote:

> Those formerly engaged in the trade have increased their capital and extended their enterprise, many new firms have engaged in it and others are preparing to do so. It is computed that a thousand men chiefly from this place [St. Louis] are now employed on the waters of the Missouri and half that number on the upper Mississippi.[105]

Ashley and Henry were among the former.

Henry's experience stood him in excellent stead. He was familiar with the details of the business and with the resources of the country beyond the mountains, a region neglected by Americans after the collapse of the Astor enterprise, but which Henry and Ashley seem to have chosen from the start as one of their principal fields of operation. The remoteness of this area, however, necessitated a new method of conducting the business. Hitherto it had been customary to erect trading-posts or forts at convenient points in the mountains, whither the Indians might repair with their peltries for trade or from which as a base the hired trappers might operate. This system, which had been developed largely by Manuel Lisa, had broken down because of the uncertain factors on which its success depended,

---

[104] Letter of Thomas Forsyth to Lewis Cass, october 24, 1831, in U.S. Senate, *Executive documents,* 22 cong., 1 sess., II, no. 90. Compare Letter of N. J. Wyeth to Messrs. Hall, Tucker, and Williams, Cambridge, Mass., november 8, 1833, in Young, *Sources of the history of Oregon,* I, 73. Wyeth says that Ashley was "bankrupt but a person of credit."

[105] *Missouri intelligencer,* september 17, 1822. That these new ventures were already justified is evidenced by the fact that, in the fall of 1822, Captain Perkins of the Missouri Fur company came down the river with a packet of furs valued at the unprecedented sum of fourteen thousand dollars, which was followed shortly by another worth ten thousand dollars. Both had come from the Yellowstone country. See *Missouri intelligencer,* october 29, 1822.

first, the quantity of goods at the post which needed to be constantly replenished, second, the ability of the men to hold the forts against hostile attack, and third, the willingness of the Indians to bring furs to trade.

Instead of depending on the savages to furnish their furs, Henry and Ashley determined to employ white men in the actual task of trapping, and for the regularly established post to substitute, in large measure, the annual rendezvous. The trapper was to supplant the trader. To be sure he might procure a considerable portion of his furs from the Indians or by shrewd bargaining from the employees of other companies, but it was his duty to secure all that he could by whatever means; and he was paid in proportion to the number and quality of the furs he brought to rendezvous. The rendezvouses were conducted at appointed points to which the annual supply of goods could be conveyed from the states and from which the year's accumulation of peltries could be transported down country. Later other companies adopted the Ashley-Henry business methods until, within the region not directly tributary to the Missouri, they became recognized and customary. Ashley has been credited with the invention of this system,[106] and it is true the first use of the term rendezvous, in its technical sense, occurs in Ashley's narrative of 1825;[107] but, as a matter of fact, such methods with certain modifications were already used by the Hudson's Bay company in the conduct of their Snake country expeditions, while even among the American companies who were in the field in 1821 and 1822, if not earlier, they were not unknown.[108]

---

[106] Chittenden, *American fur trade,* I, 273.

[107] See page 152.

[108] Benton, T. H., "Speech in the senate," reprinted in *Proceedings of the senate of the United States on the bill for the protection of the fur trade,* 29.

Such methods required a large force of young men capable of withstanding the rigors of life in the wilderness. A sufficient number for the first expedition sent out by Ashley and Henry was secured through an advertisement inserted in the *Missouri Republican* of march 20, 1822. A call was made for "one hundred young men to ascend the Missouri to its source, there to be employed for one, two, or three years.[109] Three weeks later Ashley and Henry secured licenses to enter the Indian country, and on may 8 the fully equipped party set out by boat from St. Louis under command of Andrew Henry.[110] En route the boat was overturned and foundered with a total loss including cargo and equipment estimated at ten thousand dollars. Nothing daunted, General Ashley on receiving word of this disaster completely outfitted another boat which he accompanied himself. Joining the first contingent which had camped near the scene of the disaster, he assumed command of the combined parties. Passing Fort Atkinson where Lieutenant-colonel Leavenworth was stationed, they entered the heart of the Sioux country, where every effort was made to conciliate the tribes and assure a peaceful progress. On september 8 they reached the Arikara villages. At this point Ashley, having bought horses for the party, set out at once by land for the

N. J. Wyeth, in a letter to Messrs. Hall, Tucker, and Williams, dated Cambridge, november 8, 1833, says, "In the course of this business [Ashley] perceived that there was plenty of beaver in the country to which he had resorted for trade but great difficulty to induce the Indians to catch it. After many trials of trading voyages, he converted his trading parties into trapping parties."—Young, *Sources of the history of Oregon*, I, 74.

109 *Niles register*, june 8, 1822. See also Chittenden, *American fur trade*, I, 262.

110 "Licenses to trade with the Indians, 1822" in U.S. Senate, *Executive documents*, 18 cong., 1 sess., no. 1. Joshua Pilcher stated that forty or fifty of the company proceeded by land, the remainder by water. See *American state papers, Indian affairs*, II, 455; Sullivan, *Travels of Jedediah S. Smith*, 1 f.

mouth of the Yellowstone while the boat continued its slower course up the Missouri. Jedediah Smith was a member of the land party, which proceeded with great caution for Ashley had become suspicious of the Arikaras. However no untoward incidents occurred and after a day at the Mandan villages the party pushed on, arriving at the Yellowstone on october 1. A fort had already been erected at this point, which from now on served rather as a base of operations for the men than a trading-post.[111] As the season was well advanced Ashley immediately reembarked for St. Louis with the accumulation of furs which his hunters, probably former employees of the Missouri Fur company, had procured during the previous season.

No unusual difficulty or danger seems to have been encountered until the ensuing summer, when a general wave of hostility swept over the Indian tribes of the upper Missouri, due perhaps to the sudden influx of whites following the revival of the trade. On Pryor's fork of the Yellowstone Jones and Immel of the Missouri Fur company suffered a crushing defeat in may at the hands of the Blackfeet. Both leaders with many of their men were killed. The same tribe of Indians, either just before or just after this massacre, fell on a party of eleven of Henry's men near the mouth of Smith's river, killing four.[112] A band of Assiniboines had already attacked Henry on the Missouri, stealing fifty of his horses.[113] The culmination of these disasters was the defeat of Ashley himself by the Arikaras.

[111] Joshua Pilcher, "Report, 1831," in U.S. Senate, *Executive documents,* 22 cong., 1 sess., II, no. 90.

[112] "Casualty list furnished by Smith, Jackson, and Sublette," Superintendent of Indian affairs, Letter book, Kansas historical society MSS. Compare also Letter of Benjamin O'Fallon to General Atkinson, july 3, 1823, in U.S. Senate, *Executive documents,* 18 cong., 1 sess., I, no. 1.

[113] Benton, *Proceedings of the senate,* etc., 29.

After his return to St. Louis in the fall of 1822 Ashley had set about organizing a second expedition, which he planned to conduct to the mountains the following spring.[114] Resorting again to advertising, he procured another hundred recruits with whom he left St. Louis, march 10, 1823, in two keel-boats, the "Rocky mountains" and "Yellowstone packet," arriving without incident at a point just below the Arikara villages on the thirtieth of may.[115]

The personnel of this party is of more than passing interest. Among others the expedition included James Clyman,[116] David E. Jackson, William L. Sublette,[117] and, after they reached the Indian country, Jedediah S. Smith who had been a member of the expedition of 1822.

The last three, now presumably brought together for the first time as employees of Ashley, were within a few years to succeed him in business and to carry into more remote regions and with greater enterprise the industry which he had built up. Their worthiness as mountain

114 A fresh license was issued Ashley and Henry, march 12, 1823, for a period of five years to trade with the "Ricaras, Score, Mandans, Milanawa, Blackfoot, and Crow tribes, within and west of the Rocky mountains."—U.S. House, *Executive documents,* 18 cong., 1 sess., 1, no. 7.

115 *Missouri intelligencer,* march 25, april 1, july 8, 1823.

116 James Clyman, a Virginian, born february 1, 1792. As a young man he moved into the Ohio country, fought in the War of 1812, learned surveying in Indiana, and joined Ashley's expedition of 1823 as a hunter. While in Ashley's employ he was one of the party which circumnavigated Great Salt lake in the late fall of 1825 or spring of 1826, but retired from the mountains in 1827, settling in Illinois where he participated in the Black Hawk war, a member of the same company as Abraham Lincoln. After pioneering in Wisconsin he joined one of the Oregon companies of 1844. Settling finally in California he died at Napa in 1881. Camp, *James Clyman,* 11, 45-53, 243, and *passim.*

117 William L. Sublette, one of five brothers, all of whom were interested in the fur-trade, was born in Kentucky in 1799, moved to St. Charles, Missouri in 1818, and thence to St. Louis. He died in 1845. A considerable mass of his correspondence and accounts are preserved in the Sublette MSS., Missouri historical society (St. Louis).

men was presently demonstrated in the awkward situation which arose at the Arikara villages. On his way up Ashley had been informed by agents of the Missouri Fur company that there had been a recent encounter with this traditionally hostile tribe in which two of the Indians had been killed. According to their representations, the Arikaras, who were on the war path against the Sioux, had fallen in with a party of the Missouri Fur company's men traveling in company with two or three of the latter. These the Arikaras had demanded should be surrendered. The traders had naturally refused.[118] Hostilities then ensued with the unfortunate consequences mentioned. The Arikaras then and there, it was stated, swore vengeance against the whites and were now only lying in wait for a good opportunity of taking it. As a matter of fact, the enmity of the Arikaras was as old as the trade itself, but in this particular instance, no doubt, could be regarded as part and parcel of the prevailing Indian hostility of this year.

Forewarned, Ashley on reaching the villages prepared to act with caution. Wisely anchoring his boats in the middle of the stream, below the villages, he went ashore accompanied by two men. A group of Arikara warriors, including the chiefs, instantly greeted him with protestations of friendship and very amiably suggested that he land a portion of his goods and begin to trade with them at once. This was precisely what Ashley was anxious to do, for he had just received word from Major Henry, probably conveyed by Jedediah Smith, desiring him to purchase all the horses he could procure to replace those recently stolen by the Assiniboines. Ashley was prepared to purchase a sufficient number of mounts to convey forty of his men overland

---

118 For a slightly different account of this incident see the Clyman narrative in Camp, *op. cit.,* 15.

to join Henry while the remainder proceeded by the boats. Still cautious, however, Ashley insisted that the trading be conducted not in the villages but on the open sand beach by the river. The Indians, after some consultation among themselves, agreed. Ashley thereupon made them a small gift of powder and muskets, seizing the occasion to let them understand that he was perfectly aware of their previous conduct toward the whites and warning them for the future. They professed to regret the late affair, assuring Ashley that they no longer harbored any ill feeling but regarded the Americans as their very true friends and intended henceforth to treat them as such.

Matters now seemed satisfactorily arranged, and the following morning, the first of june, Ashley began his purchases. As soon as he had secured the requisite number of horses, which did not take long, he made ready to proceed the next day. Late in the afternoon, however, a courier came from the Bear, one of the chiefs, requesting Ashley to pay him a visit. Ashley complied with the invitation, was cordially received, and returned shortly to his boats for the night. About half past three on the morning of june second he was suddenly awakened by one of his men, who informed him that Aaron Stephens, an employee, had just been killed by the Indians and that an attack on the boats was momentarily expected.[119] The night before Ashley had divided his force, leaving forty of his party on shore in charge of the horses, while the remainder, totaling about fifty, he had lodged on the ships. The shore party was camped on the beach at a point approximately midway between the two boats, which were anchored about ninety feet off shore.

---

[119] According to Clyman a group of men including Edward Rose, the interpreter, had gone without permission to spend the night in the village. Camp, *op. cit.*, 15.

With sunrise the Indians began a general attack directing their fire from a line extending along the pickets of their villages and from the shelter of the broken ground adjoining.[120] The men on shore, being in direct line of fire, suffered severe losses immediately. As the only retreat lay toward the river, Ashley undertook to have the horses swum across to a sand bar near the middle of the stream, where the water was only three feet deep. This move, however, was rendered impossible by the increased and concentrated fire of the savages, who were using Ashley's gift of powder and muskets to advantage. The only other course was to reinforce the land party. Ashley, accordingly, ordered anchors weighed and the boats put to shore. Most of the oarsmen were so panic struck, however, that, says Ashley, "notwithstanding every exertion on my part to enforce the execution of the order, I could not effect it." The men refused to expose themselves to the slightest danger. The situation was becoming desperate, with half his men enduring a terrific fire and the other half in virtual mutiny. The land party, however, displayed splendid courage. Two skiffs, sufficient to convey between twenty and thirty men were, at length, rowed to shore for their embarkation. Most of them, however, refused to avail themselves of this means of escape, preferring rather to avenge then and there the loss of their comrades than yield an inch of ground until forced to it.

Only four or five men, two of them wounded, climbed into the larger skiff and started for the vessels; at the same time two others, one of them mortally wounded,

120 For the official documents covering this episode and the punitive expedition of Colonel Leavenworth which followed, see Doane Robinson, "Official correspondence of the Leavenworth expedition into South Dakota in 1823," in South Dakota historical society *collections*, I.

set out in the other boat for the opposite bank. As soon as the wounded had been removed, the larger boat was ordered back to the shore again, but scarcely had it left the ship, when one of the oarsmen was shot down, and the craft began to drift helplessly down stream. Two of the men on the sand bar, Reed Gibson and James Clyman, swam out toward her. Scarcely had they got under way when Gibson was shot and mortally wounded. Clyman put him ashore and, at the latter's suggestion, fled for his life across the open country, hotly pursued by three Indians whom he fortunately managed to elude. Doubling back to the river he luckily reached the shore just in time to be taken aboard the boats on their way down the stream. Gibson had also been rescued but soon died of his wounds. By this time most of the horses were killed and about half the men were dead or wounded. Renewed efforts to get the boats to shore were in vain, although the land party was now so greatly reduced that it could no longer hope to keep up the fight. Cut off entirely from the vessels, with the skiffs gone, the only loop-hole of escape lay in swimming the ninety feet separating them from their comrades. Most of them made it. Some of the wounded, however, went under before they could reach the boats or, failing to make due allowance for the force of the current, were carried too far down stream. Some were shot down on the shore even before they could plunge into the water. In fifteen minutes it was all over and the last of the swimmers was scrambling into the boats. One ship weighed anchor, the other cut itself loose, and both drifted down stream.

The losses amounted to thirteen killed and ten or eleven wounded.[121] "To describe my feelings," says

---

[121] There are two casualty lists, one in a letter of Ashley's, dated june 4, 1823, printed in U.S. Senate, *Executive documents*, 18 cong., 1 sess., I, no. 1,

Ashley, "at seeing these men destroyed is out of my power. I feel confident that if my orders had been obeyed, I should not have lost five men." [122] This failure to obey orders, bewailed by the commander, does not clear him of a large share of the blame for the disaster. In the first place, to leave forty of his men on shore with the horses in a manifestly unprotected position, knowing full well the treachery of the Arikaras, was a grave mistake. The assurance of friendliness made on Ashley's arrival and, subsequently, in the lodge of the Bear seems quite to have lulled his natural suspicions and to have led him into this error, though he is said to have been warned by one of the Arikara chiefs, the craven Little Soldier.[123]

The only safe thing to have done after concluding his bargain would have been to move both the land party with the horses and also the boats down stream to a

and reprinted (inaccurately) in *Edwards's great west,* 333 ff; the other, in a letter of Ashley's, dated june 7 and printed in the *Missouri intelligencer* of july 8, 1823. Presumably the second is the more accurate. The first is as follows: "Killed, John Matthews, John Collins, Aaron Stevens (killed at night in the fort), James McDaniel, Westley Piper, George Filage, Benjamin F. Sneed, James Penn, jr., John Miller, John S. Gardner, Ellis Ogle, David Howard. Wounded, Reed Gibson (since dead), Joseph Mouse, John Larrison [brother perhaps of Daniel Larrison, one of Lisa's men, Missouri historical society *collections,* IV, 204], Abraham Ricketts, Robert Tucker, Joseph Thompson, Jacob Miller, David McClain, Hugh Glass, Auguste Dufier, Willis (black man)." The second is as follows: "Killed, John Matthews, John Collins, Benjamin F. Sneed, Thully Piper, James M. Daniel, Joseph S. Gardner, George Flager, David Howard, Aaron Stephens, James Penn, jr., John Miller, Ellis Ogle. Wounded, John Larrison, Joseph Manso, Reed Gibson (since dead), Joseph Thompson, Robert Tucker, James Davis, Aaron Ricketts, Jacob Miller, August Dufren, Hugh Glass, Daniel M'Clain, Thilless (black man)." The Indian losses were slight. These lists were evidently compiled and dispatched immediately since John Larrison, reported in both lists as among the killed, showed up stark naked three or four days after the battle with a bullet wound in his buttocks. Clyman narrative, Camp, *op. cit.,* 19.

[122] *Missouri intelligencer,* july 8, 1823.
[123] *American state papers, Indian affairs,* II, 452.

point sufficiently removed from the villages to have
made an attack, at least from behind the Indians' own
stockade pickets, impossible even of attempt. To make
bad matters worse, Ashley's error in judgment seems to
have been followed up next day by a distressing pusil-
lanimity. The boatmen refused to expose themselves at
Ashley's order; they declined to put to shore in the
skiffs; in a word, they mutinied. Ashley's statement that
he used every effort to enforce his commands is absurd.
Every commander has at his disposal, if he is bold and
determined enough to use it, an argument well suited to
the type of cowardice exhibited by these men, namely
the threat, made with the manifest intention of abiding
by it, to shoot the first man who disobeyed. A moment of
real resolve on Ashley's part might have prevented the
loss, as he himself estimated, of no more than five men.
His personal courage of the day before, which lead him
to go virtually unattended to the lodge of the Bear,
seems not to have been followed up by that other kind
of courage, so frequently required of a commander, the
courage that may demand the purposeful sacrifice of
one human life in order that others may be saved.

That his men sized him up correctly was evident at
once. The boats having fallen back to the first timber,[124]
a landing was made, and the general situation surveyed.
It was Ashley's desire to proceed at once with his boats
past the Arikara villages, but his men informed him
with decision that they would not undertake such a
move without adequate reinforcements. Next morning
Ashley approached them again on the subject only to

---

[124] In the vicinity of Ashley island. Compare Missouri river commission,
Map of the Missouri river, plate XLV. Here the party remained till reinforcements arrived, living much of the time on very scant rations. Camp, *op. cit.*,
19.

find the men, after a night's consideration, more determined than ever.

I had them paraded and made known to them the manner in which
I proposed fixing the boats and passing the Indian village. After saying all that I conceived necessary to satisfy them, and, having good
reason to believe that I should be, with but very few exceptions,
deserted in a short time by all my men, as some of them had already
formed a resolution to desert, I called on those disposed to remain
with me under any circumstances, until I should here [*sic*] from
Major Henry, to whom I would send an express immediately and
request that he would descend with all the aid he could spare from
his fort at the mouth of the Yellowstone. Thirty only volunteered,
among whom are but few boatmen; consequently I am compelled to
send one boat back, having secured her cargo here.[125]

Ashley, accordingly, dispatched the "Yellowstone packet" down stream with five of the wounded men to Fort
Atkinson, erected two years before near Council Bluffs,
some four hundred fifty miles below his camp. Smith,
who seems to have been the patroon or commander of
this contingent, was to continue the entire distance to St.
Louis,[126] but on the way was to advise Colonel Leavenworth at Fort Atkinson of the nature and magnitude of
the disaster, requesting military reinforcements with
which to force a passage through the Arikara villages.[127]

On the departure of the "Yellowstone packet," Ashley hastened to acquaint Henry with the disaster by
which he had been delayed and to urge him forthwith to
dispatch such aid as could be spared from the upper

---

[125] *Missouri intelligencer,* july 8, 1823. The above narrative of Ashley's
encounter with the Arikaras is based on his letters of june 7 and of june 4,
the latter to Colonel Leavenworth, printed in U.S. Senate, *Executive documents,* 18 cong., 1 sess., 1, no. 1 and on the Clyman narrative.

[126] Compare *Missouri intelligencer,* july 1, 1823.

[127] U.S. Senate, *Executive documents,* 18 cong., 1 sess., 1, no. 1.

country. Informed of the situation, Henry acted promptly. Leaving behind only twenty men, he proceeded down the Missouri with the rest of his force. Making excellent progress with the current, they soon approached the Arikara villages. The Indians, coming down to the shore, invited them to land and trade. Henry, however, acting with prudence and decision, sailed straight down the channel, declining to have any intercourse with them.[128] Soon after he joined Ashley in his camp at the mouth of the Cheyenne river.[129]

Meanwhile the "Yellowstone packet" had reached Fort Atkinson, june 18, with the wounded men and messages for Colonel Leavenworth. Only a few hours after its arrival an express came in announcing the massacre of Immel and Jones of the Missouri Fur company with most of their men on the Yellowstone. Two reports of this nature in such rapid succession determined Colonel Leavenworth to move promptly with the whole force at his command to protect Ashley in his further ascent of the river and to punish the Indians for so daring an outrage. Six companies of the Sixth regiment, amounting in all to about two hundred fifty men, together with two six-pound cannon were embarked june twenty-second. Three keel-boats, one of them the "Yellowstone packet," were used for conveying

---

[128] Letter of Brigadier-general Henry Atkinson to Major-general Gaines, St. Louis, august 15, 1823, in U.S. Senate, *op. cit.*

[129] The date of Henry's arrival cannot be determined exactly. Ashley expected him within twelve or fifteen days after Smith's departure, Ashley to Leavenworth, june 4, 1823. Chittenden states that he arrived "about the second of july," Chittenden, *American fur trade*, I, 269. It was certainly earlier, possibly within the fortnight set by Ashley, for shortly before the eighth of july two of Henry's men, who continued down stream with their furs, passed Fort Atkinson, over four hundred miles below Ashley's camp, en route to St. Louis, U.S. Senate, *op. cit.* It is probable that he joined Ashley about june 23, as it would take about a fortnight to proceed from Ashley's camp to Fort Atkinson.

the stores and part of the force.[130] The rest proceeded by land. On the twenty-seventh they were overtaken by Joshua Pilcher of the Missouri Fur company with sixty men, who placed his two boats and his force at Leavenworth's disposal. He had taken on board at Fort Atkinson a five and one-half inch howitzer with its equipment. His assistance proved very material a week later, when one of the government boats was sunk.

On the nineteenth of july, having "arrived at a trading establishment called by the Indian traders Fort Recovery and sometimes, Cedar Fort," [131] they were joined by a small band of Yankton Sioux who were anxious to have a share in fighting their old enemies, the Arikaras. Some days later, about two hundred Saone and Hunkpapa Sioux also appeared, while rumors came in that others were on the way. Pilcher, having explained the object of the expedition, easily induced them to join. Soon after, they reached Ashley's new camp near the mouth of the Teton river, whither he had removed on Henry's arrival.[132] He was not there when Leavenworth arrived, having hastily departed for his upper camp one hundred twenty miles above, where preparations were made to put the camp and his eighty men into military shape against the arrival of the troops.[133]

On reaching the camp, about the first of august, Colonel Leavenworth accepted the tender of Ashley's services. His men were divided into two companies of about forty each, officered as follows: Jedediah Smith [134] and

[130] The narrative of this expedition is in Colonel Leavenworth's official report, dated october 20, *Missouri intelligencer,* december 2, 1823.

[131] A mile below the present city of Chambersburg, South Dakota.

[132] Ashley to Colonel O'Fallon, dated Fort Brasseaux, july 19, 1823, in U.S. Senate, *op. cit.* The location of Fort Brasseaux is uncertain. See Chittenden, *American fur trade,* III, 953.

[133] Letter of Ashley to O'Fallon in U.S. Senate, *op. cit.*

[134] Some doubt has been raised as to Smith's participation in this engage-

Hiram Scott, captains; Hiram Allen and George C. Jackson, lieutenants; Charles Cunningham and Edward Rose, ensigns; Fleming, surgeon; Thomas Fitzpatrick, quartermaster; William Sublette, sergeant-major. The contingent furnished by Major Pilcher, comprising one company, was added to the Indian forces and the whole placed under the command of Pilcher. He named his officers as follows: Henry Vanderburgh, captain of the whites, Angus McDonald, captain of the Indians, Moses B. (?) Carson, first lieutenant, and William (?) Gordon, second lieutenant. After some delay occasioned by the Saone and Hunkpapa Sioux, who "wished them to come to a feast for they had killed a heap of dogs" but who were finally induced to postpone feasting till after fighting, on the eighth of august they reached a point fifteen or sixteen miles below the Arikara villages, where they encamped. Next day the Sioux cavalry, pushing ahead to skirmish, met a party of Arikaras and engaged them in a hotly contested encounter near their villages. The main force, coming up behind the Sioux, met parties of the latter returning to the rear with a number of horses which they had captured. Major Pilcher, finding the enemy in considerable force,

ment. After the battle of june second he had descended the river to St. Louis. A letter from General Atkinson, commanding the western department, dated St. Louis, august 15, 1823, contained the following, "I have received some unofficial information from the expedition under Colonel Leavenworth as late as the 19th ultimo [july 19] . . . A Mr. Smith, who came down with the proceeds of the trappers and hunters of General Ashley from the mouth of the Yellowstone, gives also some verbal news to the following effect, viz: He left the Yellowstone with Mr. Henry, with all the party under him, except twenty men left in the fort at the mouth of the Yellowstone, proceeded to join General Ashley at the mouth of the Shyan [Cheyenne] river. . . Mr. Smith informs me that Colonel Leavenworth was progressing on very well and expects to accomplish the object of his movement."—U.S. Senate, *op. cit.* Robinson suggests that the appointment was "nominal" or honorary. Robinson, "Official correspondence, etc.," South Dakota historical society *collections*, I, 254.

though fifteen of them had already been slain,[135] asked for instant reinforcements.[136] This induced Colonel Leavenworth to reform his entire line, which was now massed at one point.

In the new formation, General Ashley with his two companies was placed on the extreme right, resting on the river, while to the left were stationed five companies of the Sixth regiment, and on the extreme left a company of riflemen. This alignment was quickly made, and the order at once given to advance. A charge on the villages was impossible because the Sioux auxiliaries, still ahead of the whites, were keeping up their fire. When the Arikaras saw the main body of troops advancing to support the Sioux, they broke from their hiding places, which were nothing but rudely constructed and partially covered trenches, and fled, the Sioux firing on them as they ran toward the shelter of their villages. Colonel Leavenworth then advanced his men to within three or four hundred yards of the villages, where he halted to await the arrival of the boat conveying the artillery, taking the precaution, however, to send Captain Riley ahead with his company to engage the Arikaras in their villages. Meanwhile the Sioux amused themselves by cutting up the slain Arikaras and attaching cords to the detached arms, legs, hands, and feet, which they dragged over the ground.[137] Just before sunset the artillery arrived and it was decided to camp for the night, postponing an organized attack till the next day.

---

[135] *Missouri intelligencer,* september 9, 1823. Chittenden (*American fur trade,* II, 592), says thirteen. Colonel Leavenworth in his "Report" (*Missouri intelligencer,* december 2, 1823), says ten. The casualty list furnished by Smith, Jackson, and Sublette gives fourteen. See Superintendent of Indian affairs, Letter book, 299, Kansas historical society MSS.

[136] Report of Colonel Leavenworth, october 20, 1823, in the *Missouri intelligencer,* december 2, 1823.

[137] Clyman gives a graphic account of the engagement, Camp, *op. cit.,* 20.

On the morning of the tenth the attack was opened
by artillery fire under direction of Lieutenant Morris,
who was inadequately supported by Sergeant Perkins
with one of the six-pounders from a position within one
hundred yards of the Arikara barricades but at too high
an elevation to be effective. At the same time the infantry advanced to within three hundred yards and fired
one volley "to discharge their guns which had been
loaded for some time." Inasmuch as this combined infantry and artillery attack had accomplished nothing,
Colonel Leavenworth undertook to investigate the
strength of the Indian positions with the hope of being
able to carry them by storm. Meanwhile, to create a
diversion, Ashley was ordered to attack the lower and
smaller village. Taking a position in a ravine, within
twenty paces of the village, he opened a brisk fire.
Leavenworth, however, believed a charge would be unsuccessful unless supported by the Sioux auxiliaries.
The latter, declining to abandon their devastation and
robbery of the Arikara cornfields, refused to cooperate,
and the charge was accordingly abandoned. The Sioux
were then notified that it had been decided to withdraw
from the upper village. They were also advised to retire
from the cornfields in order "to save their stragglers
from the tomahawks of the Arikaras." [138] As it was now
well on in the afternoon, orders were given for the men
to retire to eat.

Not long after, Colonel Leavenworth left his cabin,
where he had gone for lunch, to consult with Ashley
and Pilcher. In the midst of their conversation an opportunity seemed to offer for opening negotiations with
the enemy. A Sioux, observed in parley with an Arikara, was instructed to inform him that, if his people

[138] *Missouri intelligencer,* september 9, 1823.

wished to discuss terms of peace, they should at once send out their chiefs. Soon ten or twelve Indians were observed approaching, and a preliminary interview was opened. Colonel Leavenworth informed the Indians at the start that an essential of peace would be the restoration of Ashley's property, the giving of hostages, and assurances of good behavior for the future. Some bickering ensued in which the Arikaras asserted that, as most of the horses had been slain, they could only restore other property. Colonel Leavenworth dwelt at some length on the power of the United States, of which, however, up to now the Indians had seen no striking evidence. The pipe of peace was produced, and passed the rounds till it came to Joshua Pilcher, who at first declined it, but, urged by Leavenworth, at last consented to smoke. His reluctance produced a noticeable effect on the Arikaras, who had been informed that Pilcher was the most prominent of the whites. On the conclusion of the interview, when Leavenworth undertook to select his hostages, a disturbance ensued, shots were exchanged, and the Indians retired to their villages.

Perhaps the most deplorable result of the campaign up to this point was the effect produced on the Sioux. They had joined the expedition with the expectation of procuring a quantity of plunder and with the firm conviction that so determined an expedition, sanctioned by the Great Father, himself, would promptly and effectually efface their enemies. They had borne the brunt of the attack on the ninth and tenth, but, at the moment of victory, were warned "to save their stragglers from the tomahawks of the Arikaras." They had had enough. During the night of the tenth to eleventh, having stolen six government mules and seven of Ashley's horses, which they loaded with corn gathered in the fields of the Arikaras, they "made a preciptate movement no one knows whither." [139]

Next day negotiations were resumed on the appearance of Chief Little Soldier, a traitorous savage, who had warned Ashley of his danger in june. He explained that the Indians had been alarmed at the action of Pilcher the previous evening, whereupon Leavenworth assured him that in the matter of making peace Pilcher had no choice but to abide by the terms agreed upon. This seemed to satisfy the Indians, who soon after dispatched several other chiefs to negotiate a treaty. Colonel Leavenworth, anxious now apparently to shift the responsibility, appealed to Pilcher as sub-Indian agent to assist or at least to prepare a draft of the treaty. He declined however. Leavenworth then appealed to Andrew Henry, a special sub-agent, but "he politely replied that it was a matter in which he felt himself wholly incompetent to act as his powers were for a special purpose." [140] There was nothing left for Leavenworth to do but draw up the treaty himself. The final instrument was simple, embodying merely the three essentials insisted upon the previous day, viz: (1) the restoration by the Arikaras of "the arms taken from Ashley's party and such other articles of property as might remain in their hands, which were obtained from General Ashley in exchange for horses;" (2) promises by the Indians that the navigation of the Missouri should be free and unobstructed and that all Americans duly authorized to enter their country should be treated by them with civility; (3) an exchange of mutual expres-

---

[139] The *Missouri intelligencer,* september 9, 1823, says "all the horses belonging to the United States troops and ten of those belonging to General Ashley's company." Compare Chittenden, *American fur trade,* II, 597.

[140] Colonel Leavenworth, "Report," in *Missouri intelligencer,* december 9, 1823.

sions of friendship and goodwill.[141] The treaty was
signed by eleven Indians, five army officers, and Ashley.

As the campaign was now ended, Colonel Leavenworth four days later ordered the withdrawal of his
force. The total number engaged on the ninth had been
about one thousand one hundred whites, with auxiliaries, against six to eight hundred Arikara warriors
with some three to four thousand men, women, and children.[142] After the withdrawal of the Sioux, on the night
of the tenth, the American force must have been reduced by half. Aside from the casualties of the first day,
inflicted by the Sioux, the Arikaras suffered altogether
the loss of only about thirty, including women and children. The American losses were even more insignificant, consisting of but two whites slightly wounded.
The cost of the expedition was about two thousand dollars.

The expedition had had two objects in view, the first
immediate, and the other ultimate. The immediate object had been to clear the way for General Ashley and to
secure the restoration of his property. In this the expedition had succeeded. The ultimate object had been
to impress on the Indians respect for the strength of the
American arms and, in a measure, to seek revenge for
the severe losses suffered by the trappers and Indian
traders. Here the expedition failed utterly. The Sioux
had abandoned the undertaking in disgust. The Arikaras, not having been defeated and having observed the
extent to which the whites relied on their Sioux auxiliaries, had no reason to respect the power of the Ameri-

---

[141] The treaty in full is printed in the *Missouri intelligencer*, november
18, 1823.

[142] This is Chittenden's estimate based on a study of the sources, Chittenden, *American fur trade*, II, 591.

can military. Despite the peace treaty they did not hesitate to massacre several parties of trappers near the Mandan villages that very summer and the following winter to commit other outrages in the Platte country.

Perhaps Joshua Pilcher did not put it too strongly when he wrote to Colonel Leavenworth (who had charged him with the burning of the Arikara villages, an unfortunate event that occurred the day of the withdrawal of troops, but for which Pilcher seems not in the least to have been to blame)

> You came to restore peace and tranquillity to the country and to leave an impression which would insure its continuance. Your operations have been such as to produce the contrary effect and to impress the different Indian tribes with the greatest possible contempt for the American character. You came (to use your own language) to "open and make good this great road," instead of which you have by the imbecility of your conduct and operations created and left impassable barriers.[143]

As the summer was well advanced Ashley and Henry decided to push operations into the upper country as rapidly as possible in order to take full advantage of the fall hunt. Ashley returned to St. Louis, as he had done the year before, while a division of the remaining men was effected, Andrew Henry with thirteen men and a few horses proceeding as rapidly as possible to the Yellowstone post, while the remainder under command of Jedediah Smith, who by this time had certainly rejoined the party, pushed directly west.[144]

The names of some of those who accompanied the expedition are recoverable. Altogether they formed one

[143] Pilcher to Leavenworth, quoted by Chittenden, *American fur trade,* II, 606. In reviewing the campaign, Chittenden, while scoring Leavenworth for his failure to achieve the ultimate object of the expedition, fails to credit him with having accomplished its immediate aim.

[144] Cooke, P. St. George, *Scenes and adventures in the army,* 137.

of the most remarkable groups of mountain men ever brought together. Some were experienced traders of the older generation, including Andrew Henry and Edward Rose, the latter having been a companion of Ezekiel Williams during the first stretch of his remarkable wanderings in the interior, and subsequently one of the overland Astoria party as far as the continental divide. Rose had also dwelt for a time among the Arikaras.[145] Louis Vasquez of a family long associated with the trade, and probably a member of the expedition of the previous year, was also with the party. Another man of 1822 was James Bridger, afterwards Vasquez's partner and one of the ablest mountain men of the period. William L. Sublette was a member and possibly one or more of his brothers.[146] Fresh from the states and about to receive their first taste of mountain life were James Clyman, Hugh Glass,[147] Thomas Fitzpatrick, David E.

---

[145] Leavenworth, "Report," *Missouri intelligencer,* december 9, 1823.

[146] *St. Louis reveille,* march 1, 1847.

[147] A native of Pennsylvania, Glass had drifted to St. Louis, where he joined Ashley's second expedition. He was slightly wounded in the first engagement with the Arikaras. After the Leavenworth campaign he continued toward the mountains with Henry. On the evening of the fifth day of their journey Glass was attacked by a grizzly bear and horribly mangled. It was necessary for Henry to hurry on, and, accordingly, two men, Fitzgerald and a youth of some seventeen or eighteen years, were left to care for Glass until he should die or recover sufficiently to move, neither of which he showed any inclination of doing. His attendants, however, confident that in the end he must succumb, cravenly decided to abandon him, taking with them his rifle and all his other belongings. On discovering his plight, Glass made a new resolve to recover if only to have vengeance on his cowardly companions. Living for some time on berries and spring-water, he finally pulled himself together sufficiently to crawl on his hands and knees. He set out and, gradually recovering enough strength to walk, struck across country toward Fort Kiowa on the Missouri, about one hundred miles distant. Reaching this post after untold hardships, he soon joined a party of trappers, probably of the Missouri Fur company, bound for the Yellowstone. Undertaking to make a short cut alone by crossing overland to Tilton's fork, instead of following the bends of the river, he again barely saved his life, while the rest of the party were slain by the Arikaras. Unaware of danger, Glass, on approaching

Jackson, and Seth Grant. The wanderings of this group during the next ten or fifteen years cover the entire west from the Missouri to the Pacific and from Canada to Chihauhua. It was the most significant group of continental explorers ever brought together.

Misfortune still attended the luckless Henry. He had scarcely left the Mandans when he was attacked by the Arikaras once more, suffering on this occasion the loss of two men.[148] A little farther on Hugh Glass was nearly torn to pieces by a grizzly bear and two men had to be detached to remain with him, while the remainder hastened on toward the Yellowstone. There they were

Fort Tilton, saw a group of Indians, whom he recognized as having been among his late enemies at the villages. Unable to flee from them, he was in grave danger of capture when two Mandans galloped up. One of them shouted to Glass to mount behind him, and away they dashed to the fort. Determined still on vengeance, Glass left Fort Tilton and set out alone up the Yellowstone toward the mouth of the Big Horn, where he knew Henry's men would be stationed for the winter. After thirty-eight days' wandering he discovered them, but only to find that his sworn enemy, the elder of the two men who had deserted him, had gone down the river. The younger he forgave out of pity for his youth. Still seeking revenge he left winter quarters to convey dispatches to Fort Atkinson. After another series of marvelous adventures he reached his destination in january 1824, only to find that the faithless Fitzgerald had enlisted in the army. Glass perforce decided to forgive him. Nothing further is known of Fitzgerald. Tradition has it that the younger of Glass's companions was James Bridger. Glass's career after this date is uncertain. He was at Fort Union about 1830 but was finally slain by his old enemies, the Arikaras, in the winter of 1832-1833. There is a naive and charming account of Glass's adventures with Henry's party in the *Missouri intelligencer,* june 18, 1825. More elaborate accounts are contained in Cooke's *Scenes and adventures,* 137-150. A brief narrative is in Sage's *Rocky mountain life,* 159 ff. Sage erroneously states, however, that Glass was living in Taos in 1843. See also Maximilian (Prince of Wied), *Travels in North America,* in Thwaites, *Early western travels,* XXII, 294; XXIV, 102 ff. For a critical account see Chittenden, *American fur trade,* II, 698 ff. The story of Glass's adventures has been done into verse by John G. Neihardt, *The song of Hugh Glass.* See also "Chronicles of George C. Yount" in California historical society *quarterly,* II, 24 f.

148 J. Anderson and A. Neil, "Casualty list," furnished by Smith, Jackson, and Sublette, Superintendent of Indian affairs, Letter book, 300, Kansas historical society MSS.

again attacked by Indians, whom they took to be Gros Ventres, losing four more men.[149] On arriving at the post Henry discovered that twenty-two of his horses had been stolen by the Blackfeet and Assiniboines. Not long after he lost seven more. Convinced of the futility of remaining in a region so hostile, he decided to push up the Yellowstone toward the mouth of the Big Horn. On the way he fell in with a party of Crows, who much to his relief sold him forty-seven horses. He continued to the forks, and prepared to winter, probably near the abandoned posts of Lisa and the Missouri Fur company.

Meantime the party of eleven commanded by Jedediah Smith and including William Sublette and Thomas Fitzpatrick left Fort Kiowa late in september, pushing westward across the present state of South Dakota under the guidance of Edward Rose of Astoria fame. Striking the White river they worked up this stream for a day and a half and then leaving the river course behind them moved out into the treeless and waterless country to the west. Before reaching water again two of their men gave out completely and were buried in the sand with only their heads protruding, in order to conserve body moisture and prevent the tortures that come with excessive dehydration. Eventually a small water-hole was discovered and it was Smith who is alleged to have scooped up some of the precious liquid and to have ridden back to the relief of his exhausted companions.[150] Next morning they hurried on, overtaking Rose four or five miles distant on the banks of a clear running stream.[151] Stopping near a Bois Brule

---

[149] "Decharle, Trumble (two others, names not recollected)," "Casualty list,"—*Idem.* Compare Benton, *Speech in the senate,* 29.

[150] Smith figured in a similar episode four years later on his return from California across the Nevada and Utah deserts. See page 225.

[151] Teton or Bad river?

Sioux encampment they purchased sufficient horses to provide two for each man and a few to spare. Their route then led across the south fork of the Cheyenne through the Bad Lands west of this stream and into the Black hills. Crossing the first divide Rose, the half-breed interpreter, was sent ahead to get assistance from the Crows while the main party continued on through an extremely rugged country. Five days later, so the story goes, as they were proceeding in single file they suddenly came upon a huge grizzly bear.

Although the narratives of the period are replete with bear stories, Clyman's naive account of this encounter deserves repeating. Attacking Smith, who was heading the single file, the bear, according to Clyman, seized his head and sent him sprawling to the earth, cutting him badly and breaking several ribs. Though badly mauled, Smith showed sufficient presence of mind to give instructions for the treatment of his wounds, a task which James Clyman undertook to perform. "I asked the captain what was best," says Clyman, "he said one or two [go] for water and if you have a needle and thread git it out and sew up my wounds around my head which was bleeding freely. I got a pair of scissors and cut off his hair and then began my first job of dressing wounds. Upon examination I [found] the bear had taken nearly all his head in his capacious mouth close to his left eye on one side and close to his right ear on the other and laid the skull bare to near the crown of the head leaving a white streak where his teeth passed. One of his ears was torn from his head out to the outer rim. After stitching on the other wounds in the best way I was capable and according to the captain's directions, the ear being the last, I told him I could do nothing for his ear. 'Oh you must try to stitch it up some way or other,' said he. Then I put in my needle stitching it through and through and over and over laying the lacerated parts together as nice as I could with my hands." [152]

If we may believe Clyman's account, Smith, following this painful ordeal, was nevertheless able to mount his horse and ride to camp. After resting several days the party followed the old Cheyenne trail northwest into Powder River valley, where they were rejoined by Rose and a party of Crow Indians, from whom they procured a few additional horses. They continued to Tongue river, where they struck the old Crow trail. This they followed south and, crossing the low divide that marks the southern extension of the Big Horns, came on Wind river, which, as Clyman says, "is merely another name for the Big Horn above the Big Horn mountains." [153] Continuing up Wind river they established winter quarters at the foot of the Wind River range. During the winter they made a futile attempt to cross these mountains. In february 1824 they decided to attempt a more southerly crossing and so moved up the Popo Agie to the vicinity of the present town of Lander, whence they went south to the valley of the Sweetwater just above the so-called "Three crossings." With the breaking up of winter the expedition cached part of

[152] Clyman, op. cit., 25-26.

[153] Clyman, op. cit., 26-27. This route is not the same as that indicated by Camp in his edition of Clyman's journal (map facing page 38). Camp assumes that the party kept south to a point near the headwater of Powder river, that they moved northwest along the eastern flanks of the Big Horn mountains, rounded the northern end of the range and then followed the Big Horn (Wind river) south. Clyman's description does not seem to me to justify such a conjectural route for the following reasons: (1) They struck the Crow Indian trail on Tongue river. This goes southwest and northeast. Had they followed the trail in the latter direction they would not have reached either the Big Horn or the Wind river. (2) Clyman states that from the Crow trail they crossed a ridge of mountains and came on Wind river. (3) On the more roundabout route indicated by Camp they would have encountered great difficulties in travel.

their powder and lead, and in the last days of february 1824 started westward through a barren land where their only water was secured from melting snow. They discovered shortly that they had crossed the main divide [154] when they reached the banks of the Sandy. On the twentieth of february [155] they were on Green river.[156]

This is the first recorded use of the South pass from east to west.[157] The returning Astorians had apparently been unaware of its existence until they actually came through it in the opposite direction nearly twelve years before.[158] Smith thus becomes not the discoverer of the South pass but the first to cross it from east to west. To Etienne Provot, however, has been given this distinction and, equally erroneously, that of prime dis-

154 South pass.

155 Perhaps march, since Clyman crowds most of the winter's events into the month of february which, despite the fact that 1824 was a leap year, remains the shortest of the twelve.

156 "In the spring of that year [1824] the gentleman in charge of the expedition, crossed the mountains, and fell into the waters of the Colorado (then supposed to be the Rio del Norte) which, together with a large section of the country to the west of them, were found to be very rich in furs." Pilcher, Joshua, "Report," in U.S. Senate, op. cit. Cf. also Chittenden, American fur trade, I, 271.

157 Clyman's narrative on which the above is based indicates that Smith rather than Fitzpatrick, as has been frequently alleged, commanded the party on its first penetration of the pass. Fitzpatrick, however, might well claim to be a co-discoverer. "Solitaire" (pseudonym of John S. Robb), "Major Fitzpatrick as the discoverer of the South pass," in St. Louis reveille, march 1, 1847.

158 Stuart, who commanded the eastbound Astorian party, having reached Green river october 12, 1812, turned south and east across the Wind River range not, at least at first, because he knew of the pass but because his party was so famished that they had to keep to open buffalo range in search of meat. The Snake (Shoshone) Indians whom they encountered six days later, october 18, very likely told them about the pass, for they were familiar with the Indians on the other side, and Stuart's party twice crossed the well-worn trail that led them through this convenient gap in the continental divide. Three days later Stuart's party had crossed the pass. Stuart narrative in Rollins, Discovery of the Oregon trail, 160, 161, 163, 164. For a discussion of this discovery of the South pass see also ibid., ciii ff.

covery.[159] Tradition has it that Provot, in the fall of 1823, preceded Smith and Fitzpatrick through the South pass to the "Pacific waters." Proof is lacking either way but some doubt may be cast on the tradition. In the first place it is certain that Provot and LeClerc, his partner,[160] operated during the year 1823 in the vicinity of the Mandan villages, though it is possible that he spent only the spring in that neighborhood. More to the point is the fact that Henry and his party, by whom Provot was probably outfitted, did not leave the Arikara villages till the middle of august 1823, and did not reach their headquarters at the mouth of the Big Horn till some time in september. To have crossed from the mouth of the Big Horn to Green river at so late a season of the year would have been, to say the least, a hazardous undertaking and not likely to be attempted. There is also the possibility that Provot was himself a member of Smith's party in the winter of 1823-1824.

Almost every prominent figure in the west has been credited at one time or another either by himself or by his biographer as the discoverer of the South pass – Smith, Fitzpatrick, Provot, Bridger, even Fremont. The actual credit for discovery belongs to none of these but to the returning Astorians. Only Smith, who died too young to build up a case for himself or to answer the claims of his more long-lived contemporaries, may claim the distinction, not of actual discovery but of being the first to utilize the pass from east to west.

During the winter at Henry's fort men were sent out in various directions to operate in this newly re-opened

159 Chittenden, *American fur trade,* I, 271; Dodge, G. M., *Biographical sketch of James Bridger,* 6 ff. Dodge states that Bridger accompanied him.

160 "Casualty list," Superintendent of Indian affairs, Letter book, 1830-1832, Kansas historical society MSS. Perhaps the same LeClerc or LeClair employed by Ezekiel Williams in 1812. See Missouri historical society *collections,* IV, 206.

territory. Some of them trapped in the vicinity of the
Yellowstone and Big Horn, an area directly tributary to
their post and, though worked for a number of years,
still rich in beaver. Other parties went northwest toward the land of the Blackfeet, where peltries were
plentiful and danger imminent.[161] A small detachment
had been sent down to Fort Atkinson in february and in
the summer Henry also descended the river to convey
his accumulation of furs and to procure fresh supplies
for the men left in the mountains. However after disposing of his furs, he concluded his business relations
with Ashley, definitely and permanently withdrawing
from the fur-trade. He had intended to return with supplies but, says Pilcher, it was "his partner [Ashley,
who] set out with a party of men and the outfit required, [and] crossed the mountains in the spring following." [162] Lack of financial success probably explains
Henry's withdrawal at this point. He had met with one
series of misfortunes after another ever since he entered the mountains and, although the prospect must
have seemed brighter after the discovery of the richly-
stocked transmontane streams, nevertheless the net situation from the financial standpoint was far from en-
couraging.[163] His place in the fur-trade seems to have

161 "Several causes, however, combined to confine the operations to the
Missouri below the Great falls and to the waters of the Yellowstone until
the spring of 1824,"—Pilcher, "Report," St. Louis, december 1, 1831, in U.S.
Senate, *Executive documents,* 22 cong., 1 sess., II, no. 90.

162 Compare Ross, "Journal of the Snake river expedition, 1824," in Oregon
historical society *quarterly,* XIV, 385. Chittenden (*American fur trade,* I, 272)
in stating that Henry left St. Louis october 21, 1823 with a new expedition
for the mountains is mistaken.

163 Chittenden (*American fur trade,* I, 272) states that "the expedition of
1823 was on the whole successful," but this can scarcely be substantiated.
N. J. Wyeth, in a letter written ten years later, stated that the Ashley-
Henry ventures to this point (1824) had not been successful and that Ashley's
credit had been seriously impaired. Young, *Sources of Oregon history,* I, 74.

been taken in large measure by Jedediah Smith.[164]
Meanwhile Smith's party on Green river had divided
for the spring hunt, Smith with a group of seven men
moving southward to trap the tributaries of Green
river while other divisions, probably under Fitzpatrick
and Sublette, worked up stream. Clyman went with one
of the latter. Having agreed to meet on the Sweetwater
by june 10, Clyman's party cached part of their outfit
and, recrossing the South pass, reached the appointed
rendezvous by june 15. With Smith's arrival it was
agreed that the latter should remain in the mountains
to conduct the summer and fall hunt while Fitzpatrick
should convey their accumulated furs down stream by
boat. All went well until Fitzpatrick's party reached
the mouth of the Sweetwater. Here they found themselves caught by the rapid current and swirled along
into the dangerous canyon between the mouth of the
Sweetwater and Goat island. At the very spot where,
eighteen years later in company with Fremont, Fitzpatrick was caught by the rapids and upset with the loss
of journals and instruments, a similar misfortune now
befell him.[165] The rude boats were instantly capsized
and the precious cargo flung into the raging stream. By
great exertions, however, the men recovered a sufficient
quantity of Fitzpatrick's furs to square his account with
Ashley, who had outfitted him. Caching the rescued
furs and leaving most of his men, Fitzpatrick hastened

Joshua Pilcher also stated that their business to the spring of 1824 had been
unprofitable. See U.S. Senate, *op. cit.*

[164] Compare Thwaites, *Early western travels,* XIX, 237, footnote.

[165] "Eighteen years previous to this time, as I have subsequently learned
from himself, Mr. Fitzpatrick, somewhere above on this river had embarked
with a valuable cargo of beaver. Unacquainted with the stream, which he
believed would conduct him safely to the Missouri, he came unexpectedly
into this canon, where he was wrecked with the total loss of his furs."—
Fremont, J. C., *Report of the exploring expedition to the Rocky mountains,* 73.

on down the valley of the Platte to Fort Atkinson, where, on his arrival, he despatched a report to Ashley recounting the successful spring hunt, the discovery of the South pass, the descent of the Sweetwater to the North Platte, and the late disaster.[166] Having obtained horses at Fort Atkinson and accompanied by Robert Campbell and "Jim" Beckwourth, he turned back in september to recover his furs and bring in the men he had left behind.[167] By the first of december he was back at Fort Atkinson.

During the summer and fall of 1824 Ashley's men were divided into two groups, both operating in the recently opened country beyond the mountains. Jedediah Smith commanded the smaller division, comprising only six men, and William L. Sublette probably headed the other, which was somewhat larger. With the latter went also James Bridger, one Williams, one Marshall, and a score of others. Following once more the great primitive highway soon to be known the country over as the Oregon trail, they emerged from the South pass, striking the waters of the two Sandys, tributaries of Green river. Here they separated. Smith with his men crossed from the headwaters of Green river to the Lewis fork of the Columbia (Snake river), which he followed down for a hundred miles or so, and then struck across country to Clark's fork of the Columbia.[168] Their route in part was probably the reverse of that of the returning Astorians.[169] In the course of their wan-

---

166 St. Louis reveille, march 1, 1847. This, presumably, was the first word that Ashley had received from the mountains, as it is unlikely that Henry, by his more circuitous route, had as yet reached the settlements.

167 James Kennerly, "Journal," Kennerly MSS, Missouri historical society.

168 Compare page 153. Ross, "Journal of the Snake river expedition, 1824," in Oregon historical society quarterly, XIV, 385; Ross, Fur hunters, II, 127.

169 The details of their course are given in Washington Hood's Original draft of a report of a practicable route for wheeled vehicles across the mountains, written at Independence, august 12, 1839. He says, "After striking

derings they secured a large quantity of beaver on the streams tributary to Green and Snake rivers, which they packed along with them.

Late in september or early in october, they fell in with a party of Iroquois under command of one Pierre, who had been detached june 16 from the main Snake river expedition of the Hudson's Bay company, conducted this year by Alexander Ross.[170] These half-breeds were in a pitiful condition. In the course of their wanderings they had penetrated far to the south of Snake river, probably as far as the interior basin, where they had believed themselves secure. A war party of Snakes, however, discovering them shortly before the Americans appeared, had robbed them not only of a considerable portion of their furs but had stolen their traps and guns as well. Learning of their misfortune, Smith struck a shrewd bargain, by which he agreed to relieve them of their remaining furs, and, in return, to convey them, so the Iroquois themselves afterwards asserted, to the vicinity of the Three Tetons (Pierre's Hole) where they would meet Alexander Ross with the main body.[171]

the Colorado, or Green river, make up the stream toward its headwaters, as far as Horse creek, one of its tributaries, follow out this last mentioned stream to its source by a westerly course, across the main ridge in order to attain Jackson's Little Hole, at the headwaters of Jackson's fork [Hoback river?]. Follow down Jackson's fork to its mouth and decline to the northward along Lewis's fork, passing through Jackson's Big Hole to about twelve miles beyond the Yellowstone pass [sic], crossing on the route a nameless beaver stream. Here the route passes due west over another prong of the ridge, a fraction worse than the former, followed until it has attained the headwaters of Pierre's Hole, crossing the Big Teton, the battleground of the Blacksmith's fork; ford Pierre's fork eastward of the butte at its mouth and Lewis fork also, thence pass to the mouth of Lewis fork."—Missouri historical society, Hood MSS.

[170] Ross, *Fur hunters*, II, 124. Ross ("Journal of the Snake river expedition, 1824" in Oregon historical society *quarterly*, XIV, 382) states that the Iroquois were dispatched june 7.

[171] Ross, *Fur hunters*, II, 128.

On their arrival, Ross objected, probably with justification, that, inasmuch as this was the first time Smith
had ever entered this country, his services as a guide
were scarcely worth the heavy price paid. He was convinced, in fact, that Smith had procured the beaver by
promising the Iroquois fancy prices for them at Ashley's headquarters.[172]

Whatever may have been the actual terms of the
transaction, Smith, having now secured the peltries
amounting in all to nine hundred skins, which were deposited in two caches, proceeded with the combined
party in the direction of Pierre's Hole. On their way
they fell in with a search party sent out by Ross to discover the whereabouts of the Iroquois, which now
guided the Americans and the Indians to Ross's headquarters near the confluence of the Salmon and Pahsi-
mari rivers, Custer county, Idaho, where they arrived
the fourteenth of october.[173] Here Smith interviewed
Alexander Ross, who was impressed by the former's
intelligence and natural leadership. Smith told his story
of meeting the trappers, but, as Pierre had already
given his version, Ross was left to form his own conclusions. The disagreement in their narratives confirmed
him in his suspicion that a secret understanding had
been entered into between his men and Smith.[174]

Fearing that a fate similar to that of the Iroquois
might befall them, Smith and his six men determined
not to risk turning back to their headquarters at this late
season of the year but, instead, to accompany Ross and
his party northward to the Hudson's Bay company's

[172] *Idem,* II, 129; Ross, "Journal of the Snake river expedition, 1824," in
Oregon historical society *quarterly,* XIV, 385.

[173] *Idem,* XIV, 380, 385; Ross, *Fur hunters,* II, 127.

[174] *Idem,* II, 129 ff; Ross, "Journal of the Snake river expedition, 1824,"
in Oregon historical society *quarterly,* XIV, 385.

post, Flathead House, in the vicinity of Thompson
Falls, Montana. This would give him an opportunity to
view a region which no Americans since the Astorians
had penetrated, and also perhaps to pick up much useful information concerning the extent and success of the
British operations.[175] This part of his mission he performed with eminent success, learning from Alexander
Ross and subsequently from Peter Skene Ogden, whom
he met at Flathead House, that the British had some
sixty men employed as trappers in the Snake country
and that, in the previous four years, they had taken no
fewer than eighty thousand beaver, weighing in all
about one hundred sixty thousand pounds.[176]

Before reaching Flathead House, Smith and his English companions felt the dangerous presence of the
Blackfeet. As they proceeded rumors had come in from
a party of Nez Perce Indians that Blackfeet were lurk-
ing in the vicinity of their line of march. Precautions
were taken to prevent a sudden attack. As their road lay
through a narrow defile, Ross sent about two score of
his men ahead to explore the way, "taking care," as he
said, "to have two of the Americans and the most
troublesome of my own men among the party," presumably with the idea that these could best be spared if any
sacrifice must be made. Passing this point in safety, they
soon after discovered a party of Indians, whom they
suspected were Blackfeet but who insisted that they

---

[175] Ross recorded Smith's arrival at rendezvous thus, "With these vaga-
bonds [the Iroquois] arrived seven American trappers from the Big Horn
river but whom I rather take to be spies than trappers," Oregon historical
society *quarterly*, XIV, 385.

[176] See page 153. Compare, also, Letter of W. H. Ashley to T. H. Benton
St. Louis, november 12, 1827 (U.S. Senate, *Executive documents*, 20 cong.,
2 sess., I, no. 67), in which Ashley gives the figures somewhat differently,
stating that Ogden "boasted" that the English had taken from the Snake
country "85,000 beaver equal to £150,000."

were Crows and who fled precipitately on the approach
of the whites. Unable to engage them in parley, Ross
and his men left them, thankful at having recovered on
the same day a considerable number of horses which
had been stolen from their camp. The culprits had been
caught red-handed but allowed to go without punishment, "for," said Ross, "depriving them of life would
have done us no good, neither would it have checked
horse stealing in these barbarous places." [177] All along
their march to Flathead House they were accompanied
by the band of Nez Perces, who pointed out the sites of
many a battle with the Blackfeet.[178]

On the first of november they crossed the Bitterroot
mountains and entered the Valley of Troubles (Ross's
Hole), visited by Lewis and Clark nineteen years before and where Ross had been blockaded by snow the
previous spring.[179] Hastening on, lest they be similarly
delayed, they reached Flathead House by the end of the
month.[180] Here Smith spent some weeks before he set
out again for the south in company with Peter Skene
Ogden and the outgoing Snake expedition of 1824-
1825.

The importance of this first expedition of Smith's lies
in the fact that he was the first American since Lewis
and Clark, of whom there is definite information, to
cross the continental divide within the area lying north
and west of the Three Forks of the Missouri. He was
the first since Andrew Henry, in 1810, to explore the
Columbia drainage area south and west of the Three

---

177 Ross, *Fur hunters,* II, 137.

178 *Idem,* II, 133 ff.

179 Thwaites, *Original journals of the Lewis and Clark expedition,* III, 52;
Ross, *op. cit.,* II, 20, 21, 139; Ross, "Journal of the Snake river expedition,
1824" in Oregon historical society *quarterly,* XIV, 374, 385.

180 Ross, "Journal, Flathead post, 1825," in Oregon historical society *quarterly,* XIV, 386; Ross, *Fur hunters,* II, 140.

Forks, the country, that is to say, of Pierre's Hole and upper Snake river. He linked up and summarized the work that had been done by isolated groups of Americans before him and extended American exploration of the Cordilleras from the South pass to the North pass of Lewis and Clark.

Meanwhile the route of the other division of Ashley's men, having abandoned Smith at Green river, is uncertain but they probably followed that stream southward, trapping as they went, believing themselves, perhaps, on the upper reaches of the Rio Grande del Norte. As they proceeded they probably sent out detachments westward to view the country lying beyond the low sprawling barren hills that constantly paralleled their course.

If they investigated the country very far they must have been puzzled by its peculiar configuration, for there are few portions of the continent more confusing topographically. Not far to the east of Green river and south of the Wind River mountains lies the South pass, separating the Sweetwater branch of the Platte from the Sandy, a tributary of the Green. It bridges the almost imperceptible watershed dividing the waters of the Missouri-Mississippi system from those of the Gulf of California. To the west of upper Green river only a low divide separates that stream from Big Gray's and Salt river, tributaries of the Snake and hence members of the Columbia drainage system. Only a little to the south of Big Gray's river, and flowing in precisely the same direction, is Bear river, an affluent of the Great Salt lake and hence within the interior basin, and, like Big Gray's river, separated from the Green by an easy, though barren, divide. The headwaters of Bear river, moreover, issuing from the angle formed by the Wa-

satch and Uintah ranges, are intimately entangled with
the tributaries of Weber river, a direct affluent of the
Great Salt lake, and of Henry's fork, a western tributary of Green river. In other words, within a compara-
tively small area, not at all clearly defined by mountain
barriers, rise streams which flow into the Atlantic by
way of the Missouri, the Pacific by way of the Columbia, the Pacific by way of the Colorado and the Gulf of
California, and into the interior basin, directly by way
of Weber river and circuitously by Bear river.[181]

This complicated area would have been puzzling
enough had its discoverers been burdened with no pre-
conceived notions of geography, but their erroneous
ideas made confusion worse confounded. The first Ashley contingent seems to have mistaken Green river for
the upper waters of the Rio Grande, consequently believing themselves to be east of the continental divide
and on streams emptying into the Gulf of Mexico. The
men who followed in the fall of 1824 presumably la-
bored under the same misapprehension, although Ashley, who came out next year, rightly suspected Green
river to be the Rio Colorado of the West.[182] That Ashley's men might reach streams flowing into the Pacific,
they would have to cross the divide west of Green river.
They would then reach, so they supposed, the Multnomah, or the Buenaventura, or the Rio S. Felipe, that
hypothetical stream which for years was represented on
maps of the west as flowing from the interior to the Pacific. The stream was called by a variety of names. To
Ashley it was the Buenaventura, a direct tributary of
the Multnomah, which, in turn, was supposed to flow

181 For physiographic maps of this area, see Fenneman, N. M., "Physiographic boundaries within the United States," in the Association of American
geographers *annals*, IV, 134.
182 Chittenden (*American fur trade*, I, 274) to the contrary notwithstanding.

into the Columbia.[183] Searching for this river, his men explored the country west of Green river and, somewhere along their way, actually crossed the divide, perhaps in the vicinity of Ham's fork,[184] striking Bear river or one of its tributaries (Smith's fork or Tullock's fork). Bear river they followed down, thinking, no doubt, that they were on the Multnomah; then they turned sharply west and south in southern Idaho until they found themselves in Cache or Willow valley, where they prepared to spend the winter.[185] On their

---

[183] The knowledge of the country west of the mountains, which Ashley and the intelligent men associated with him, such as Henry, Smith, and Fitzpatrick, possessed, was derived from the half-breeds and Indians whom they encountered and from the maps and atlases of the period. A reference to the latter will probably indicate the minimum of their information but it will serve to furnish the nomenclature and fundamental geographical conceptions to which they would naturally adjust the information they derived from other sources. A number of American atlases were in circulation in Ashley's day, from which I have selected three, with any one or all of which he may have been familiar: (1) Carey, M., *General atlas* (Philadelphia, 1814); (2) Melish, John, *Map of the United States with the contiguous British and Spanish possessions* (Philadelphia, 1816); (3) Darby, William, *Map of the United States* (New York, *circa* 1818). (1) Represents the Rio Grande heading in the continental divide; just to the west, across the divide, heads the Colorado; west of the divide there are no lakes but, heading in the mountains a little north and west of the Colorado and the Rio Grande, is the Multnomah river flowing into the Columbia near the latter's mouth. (2) Shows the headwaters of the Rio Grande just east of the continental divide, designating the uppermost branch, "Coltier's river." Just west of Coltier's river and across the divide heads the Rio Buenaventura flowing westward into an unnamed lake, emerging from which, to the west, flows a hypothetical river (unnamed) into the bay of San Francisco. North of this lake is still another (also unnamed) corresponding to the Lake Timpanogos of other maps, from which flows a river in a northwesterly direction, labelled the Multonmah, which joins the Columbia. (3) Shows the Rio Grande much as in (2), just to the west of which, across the divide, heads the Rio Buenaventura, flowing into Lake Timpanogos.

[184] Possibly by "Sublette's cut-off." Sublette was a member of this group. Ham's fork was known to Ashley's men the following year. "Casualty list," Superintendent of Indian affairs, Letter book, 1830-1832, 298, Kansas historical society MSS.

[185] Letter of Robert Campbell, St. Louis, april 4, 1857, in Warren, "Memoir," in *Report of explorations and surveys for a Pacific railroad*, XI, 35.

way one of the men was killed by the hand of a comrade
on Bear river, and during the winter another of the
party, Marshall by name, was lost in Cache valley.[186]

Etienne Provot, instead of accompanying the main
body of Ashley's men and entering the interior basin by
way of Bear river and Cache valley, probably followed
Green river until he came to one of its large eastward
flowing tributaries, perhaps Black's fork. Following
this he would find an easy pass to the upper reaches of
Bear river. By continuing west he probably struck one
of the tributaries of Weber river. In general his route
seems to have been that followed by the Union Pacific
railroad down Weber river, which, like Ashley the next
spring, he probably assumed to be the Buenaventura.[187]
At the mouth of the Weber he reached Great Salt lake,
where seven of his men were killed by the Snake Indians and where he wintered.[188]

If it be true that Provot reached Great Salt lake before winter set in, he must be credited with its discovery. That distinction, however, was given by Robert
Campbell to James Bridger. While the main body of
Ashley's men were camped in Cache valley, a dispute
not unnaturally arose as to the outlet of Bear river. A
wager was laid and Bridger, so the story goes, was selected to follow its course. Louis Vasquez, who was
afterwards his partner and intimate friend, is erroneously said to have accompanied him.[189] He descended

---

[186] "Casualty list," Superintendent of Indian affairs, Letter book, 1830-
1832, 298 ff., Kansas historical society MSS.

[187] See page 148. Provot was certainly familiar with Weber river when
Ashley met him in the spring of 1825, having lost a man on that stream the
same year.—*Idem.*

[188] *Idem.*

[189] *Daily national intelligencer* (Washington, D.C., february 25, 1860),
citing the Sacramento *Standard*. This is disproved, however, by a letter of
Louis Vasquez, St. Louis, december, 1824, in Missouri historical society,
Vasquez MSS.

the stream to the point where it passes through a canyon from Cache valley into Bear river valley, near the present Cache junction. On emerging from the canyon, he is supposed to have discovered the Great Salt lake.[190] Still following Bear river, it is said, he reached the borders of the lake, tasted the water, and, returning, reported his discovery to his companions. His statement that the water of the lake was salt induced the belief that he had found an arm of the Pacific ocean.[191]

Early in the spring Jedediah Smith arrived at the camp in Cache valley, having, as noted above, accompanied the Snake river expedition of 1824-1825 from Flathead post under command of Peter Skene Ogden.[192] The party, having left the post five days before Christmas, followed in general the route of Alexander Ross the previous year, up the Missoula river to the confluence of the Bitterroot, thence probably eastward over the Gibbon pass to the source of the Missouri,[193] and

[190] Great Salt lake is easily visible from the hills just above the canyon of Bear river.

[191] Warren, *op. cit.*, XI, 35. It should be borne in mind, however, that in 1826 Provot broke with the Ashley interests, to which Campbell, Sublette, Smith, and Jackson succeeded, and that, accordingly, Campbell might incline to overlook his claims. His insistence that it was James Bridger who discovered the Great Salt lake perhaps points in this direction. For a discussion of Ogden's claims as discoverer of Great Salt lake, see page 45.

[192] Ogden had first entered the western country in october 1823, when he met Ross in central Idaho. That winter he had probably remained at Spokane House. In the spring of 1824, with John Work, he journeyed down the Columbia to Fort George (Astoria), where he arrived may 13, returning in the course of the summer to Spokane House. Here he received his appointment as commander of the next Snake river expedition and, accordingly, journeyed to Flathead House, where he arrived november 26, 1824. Elliott, "Peter Skene Ogden," in Oregon historical society *quarterly*, XI, 244 ff. "1824, november, friday, 26, from Prairie de Chevaux, myself and party arrived at this place [Flathead House] in the afternoon, where terminated our voyage of ten months to the Snake. Mr. Ogden and Mr. Dears, with people and outfit from Spokane reached this river expedition, 1824"—Oregon historical society *quarterly*, XIV, 386.

[193] See Merk, "Snake country expedition," *Mississippi valley historical re-*

thence over the Bitterroot mountains, probably by Lemhi pass, to Salmon river, which they reached in march.[194] Encountering great difficulties because of the deep snows, it was not till the second of april that Smith and Ogden reached Snake river. Proceeding thence up the Blackfoot river the various contingents of the party reached Bear river on the fifth of may. Here Smith and his six men left Ogden and began working up Bear river. Later he seems to have turned west again, perhaps following Ogden's party, for before joining Ashley's men in Cache valley, he "fell on the waters of the grand lake or "Beaunaventura" (*sic*), (Great Salt lake).[195]

The group which had wintered on Bear river opened the spring hunt by trapping the waters of sheltered Cache valley. Into this valley from the east flow Blacksmith fork, Logan river, Smithfield fork, Strawberry creek, and numerous smaller streams, all rich in beaver. To the west, beyond the Mendon ridge, the trappers struck the lower reaches of Bear river and its final tributary, the Malade.[196] Southward they operated along the western slopes of the Wasatch mountains in the present Boxelder and Weber counties, Utah, and as far as the Salt lake valley, already familiar to Provot and LeClerc. Following James Bridger's examination of Great Salt lake near the mouth of Bear river no further effort seems to have been made this year to explore it. Bridger's visit must have convinced them all that the lake and its shores offered no very promising field for

view, XXI, 55. Although there is no specific evidence on this point, Ogden wrote a letter to Simpson dated, "Sources of the Missouri," january 25.

194 Elliott, "Peter Skene Ogden," in Oregon historical society *quarterly*, XI, 248.

195 See page 154.

196 Ogden ("Journal, 1828-1829," in Oregon historical society *quarterly*, XI, 391), while on this stream, wrote, "It is strange that there should be beaver here as the Americans have been in this country for four years."

the prosecution of their business. South of Great Salt lake they probably pushed as far as Utah lake, which territory was certainly familiar to Ashley's men this year.[197]

By may the united parties comprising Smith's, Sublette's, and Provot's divisions were in the vicinity of Great Salt lake. On the twenty-third of that month Johnson Gardner, one of Ashley's men, accompanied by a considerable party fell in with the Ogden expedition. In camp nearby Gardner hoisted the American flag and next morning persuaded twenty-three of Ogden's men to desert.[198] They not only deserted but took all their furs with them, disposing of them to Ashley's men just as Ross's Iroquois had sold out to Smith the previous fall. Again the inducement was the offer of a higher price for the peltries.[199] Johnson Gardner, who consummated the transaction, was probably at this time one of Ashley's free trappers.[200] He appears later in this role, and it is certain that Ashley had a number of such men associated with him at this period.[201]

The ethics of the transaction are questionable, although this sort of thing was being done constantly, a

---

[197] See page 183.

[198] Journal of John Work, quoted by T. C. Elliott in "Peter Skene Ogden," in Oregon historical society *quarterly,* XI, 248. Ashley places the number of deserters at twenty-nine, see page 152. Merk, "Snake country expedition," *Mississippi valley historical review,* XXI, 65 f.

[199] The story that they were seduced by the distribution of liquor is unsubstantiated. See letter of N. J. Wyeth in Young, *op. cit.,* I, 73.

[200] Johnson Gardner was the avenger of Hugh Glass. See Maximilian (Prince of Wied), *Travels in North America,* in Thwaites, *Early western travels,* XXIII, 197; XXIV, 101 ff. In 1832 he was a free trapper doing business with Smith, Jackson, and Sublette, successors to William H. Ashley, and with the American Fur company at Fort Union. Extracts from his accounts are given in Chittenden, *American fur trade,* III, 942 ff. See Sublette MSS., carton 10, Missouri historical society.

[201] Compare Pilcher, "Report, 1831," in U.S. Senate, *Executive documents,* 22 cong., I sess., II, no. 90.

party of Hudson's Bay company men having deserted in 1822, selling their furs to the Americans on the Yellowstone.[202] It has even been said that Smith was a party to the transaction and consequently was implicated in a decidedly shady deal.[203] In describing the affair two months later in his report, Ogden goes to considerable length to describe the transaction in detail and, in particular, Gardner's tactics in persuading Ogden's men to desert. Nothing is said about Smith's participating, though as a "natural" as well as official leader, Smith might have been expected to take the initiative in any considerable transaction affecting Ashley's interests. Ashley himself, at any rate, is exculpated, for he had not yet arrived in the country, although when he reached rendezvous in july he was glad enough to accept the British furs.[204] Gardner's conduct was condemned two years later by Samuel Tullock, one of Ashley's men, although his willingness to do so may have

---

202 "Regarding our deserters of 1822, accounts do not agree. It is evident part of them reached the American post on the Yellowstone and Big Horn with much fur."—Ross, "Journal of the Snake river expedition, 1824," in Oregon historical society *quarterly*, XIV, 385.

203 Merk, "Snake country expedition," 67 note. Professor Merk bases his charges against Smith on Ogden's statement at a later point in his report that it "was these fellows [Smith and his party] that *guided and accompanied* [italics not in original] them [Gardner and his party] to our camp." Four years later Governor Simpson in a report to the governor and committee of the Hudson's Bay company dissociated Smith from the affair. See Sullivan, *Jedediah Smith*, 143.

204 Ashley himself afterward testified to the quality of Ogden's character. "Mr. Tullock further states that some time after separating from Mr. Ogden and party, but while within about fifteen miles of his encampment, he, Mr. T. and party, were attacked by a large party of Black-feet Indians (1828); the result was the loss of three of his party, killed, about four thousand dollars' worth of beaver fur, forty horses, and a considerable amount of merchandise. Notwithstanding I do not believe from the idea I have of the character of Mr. Ogden, that he could dictate such conduct to the Indians."—MS. letter of Ashley to an unknown correspondent (Benton?), december 26, 1828, Ashley MSS., Missouri historical society.

been induced by his anxiety to secure certain favors from Ogden at that time.[205]

Within a month after Gardner's profitable encounter with the Hudson's Bay company men, Ashley arrived in the mountains to conduct the first great rendezvous ever held by Americans beyond the continental divide.

These Ashley expeditions of 1824-1825 mark a new chapter in the history of the western fur-trade. Instead of operating in the region east of the mountains, accessible by the Missouri and Yellowstone rivers, they had abandoned that entire area in the spring of 1824 and, by the summer of that year, the whole company had been transferred to the waters of the three drainage areas beyond the mountains. For the first time since the ill-starred days of Astoria, American traders and trappers were making a concerted effort to extend their field of operations into the vast area drained by the "River of the West," which the British had monopolized since the naming of Fort George. Such a step had not been taken earlier largely because the South pass, on the great midland route, had remained unused and unknown since Robert Stuart led through it, or near it, his dejected band of returning Astorians in 1812.

The only known way to the Columbia was by the northern passes, discovered and used by Lewis and Clark, and after them by the Missouri Fur company in its palmier days. But the northern passes were scarcely ways, they were rather obstacles. Lofty and difficult in

---

[205] "Monday, 24 december [1827], The American party of six joined us, their leader a man named Tullock, a decent fellow. He informed me his company would readily enter into agreement regarding deserters. He informed me the conduct of Gardner's at our meeting four years since has not been approved... I should certainly be shocked if any man of principle approved of such conduct as Gardner's." Ogden, "Journal, 1827-1828," in Oregon historical society *quarterly*, XI, 367.

themselves, they presented a further danger to all whites who undertook to cross because they lay in the area continually harassed by the implacable Blackfeet. The disasters that had befallen Lisa's men at the Three Forks and, more recently, the Missouri Fur company and Andrew Henry, rendered all efforts to conduct the trade beyond the mountains by this route too hazardous for profit. The utilization of the South pass changed all this by opening up a road in a lower latitude and of gentler grades. The Crows and Snakes, moreover, who dwelt along the approaches to the South pass, while occasionally unfriendly, maintained no such policy of uncompromising and unyielding hostility to the whites as had characterized the Blackfeet ever since the days of Lewis and Clark. The Crows were not infrequently the positive friends of the whites through common hatred of the Blackfeet; the Snakes were a cowardly lot easily routed by a show of numbers.

Other reasons combined to induce Ashley to abandon the Missouri-Yellowstone area. Besides the danger from the Blackfeet, the hostility of other Indian tribes was making the work of the fur-trader increasingly dangerous in that region. The ineffective chastisement inflicted on the Arikaras in the Leavenworth campaign had only served to embolden these dangerous savages and their neighbors. The Assiniboines, who ranged between the mouth of the Yellowstone and the Mandan villages, had become notorious horse thieves. Altogether the Ashley-Henry expeditions had suffered in the years 1822 to 1824 a loss of about twenty-five men killed and nearly as many more wounded, and property to the value of many thousands of dollars. In the newly opened area beyond the mountains all the Indians were less dangerous, save of course the Blackfeet, while several tribes such as the inoffensive and fairly intelligent Flatheads and Pend d'Oreilles were really friendly.[206]

A further reason for abandoning the old territory was the increasing competition which the Ashley-Henry interests were having to face. The Missouri Fur company had made a vigorous effort to control this area before 1823, and only their crushing disaster of that year, at the hands of the Blackfeet, had thwarted them. They had begun, however, to recover in large measure from their losses. Their heavy capitalization greatly strengthened them in their efforts to secure the lion's share of the trade on the upper Missouri. Other smaller but constantly growing companies had also entered the race and were closely pressing the older enterprises. Among these were the Columbia Fur company and Stone, Bostwick, and company.[207]

Finally, the new method of conducting the business adopted by Ashley greatly facilitated this change of field. So long as the fur companies had been engaged merely in trade with the Indians, they had been obliged to maintain posts at various commercially strategic points, to which the savages might repair with their peltries. The more remote the region penetrated, the more difficult became the task of maintaining such posts, while the number of abandoned establishments, which dotted the upper Missouri country even as early as this period, pointed to the futility of ever attempting to follow such methods beyond the mountains. For the trading-post Ashley had substituted the rendezvous. The

---

[206] Ross, *Fur hunters,* I, II, *passim.* Ashley afterwards boasted, though without warrant, that in the year 1824-1825, in the area west of the mountains between the thirty-eighth and forty-fourth parallels, he had suffered the loss of but one man killed.

[207] Chittenden, *American fur trade,* I, 322 ff; "Licenses to trade with the Indians," in U.S. House, *Executive documents,* 18 cong., I sess., I, no. 7.

trappers, proceeding in small self-supporting groups, penetrated the most remote valleys and streams, assembling only in winter for the encampment in some sheltered valley and in summer for the rendezvous, both of which could be changed from year to year as circumstances demanded. The rendezvous, being movable and temporary, required no permanent residence. In fact, the only requisite was that it be conducted at a point accessible to the supply trains which came into the mountains with the annual stock of ammunition, Indian goods, traps, etc., and took out the year's accumulation of furs. An experimental rendezvous had been conducted by Thomas Fitzpatrick on the Sweetwater in 1824, but the first general meeting of this sort and the real prototype of all that followed was conducted by Ashley in Green River valley in the summer of 1825.[208]

The abandonment of the older territory and the penetration of the transmontane country under changed business conditions led naturally to a new line of approach and, consequently, to a new method of transportation. The traditional means of reaching the fur country had been by boat up the Missouri river. Those who had followed Lewis and Clark had used the keelboat, a craft sixty to seventy-five feet long, with a beam of fifteen to eighteen feet and a draft of three to four feet.

Rising from the deck some four or five feet was the cargo box, cut off at each end about twelve feet shorter than the boat. This part of

[208] The credit of having decided on this new field has been accorded Ashley. See Victor, *River of the west,* 33; Chittenden, *American fur trade,* I, 273. It would, however, seem more reasonable, *a priori,* to assume that it was Andrew Henry's idea. He alone knew the transmontane country from his winter on Henry's fork in 1810-1811. It had been his intention, furthermore, to cross to that region to trade with the Indians "within and west of the Rocky mountains." See "Licenses to trade with the Indians," in U.S. House, *Executive documents,* 18 cong., I sess., I, 33.

THE SUMMER RENDEZVOUS

Ashley was the first to establish the summer rendezvous on a large scale as a method of conducting the fur-trade.

the boat, as the name implies, was generally used for freight, but was occasionally fitted up with state-rooms when used for passengers only. The boat was built on thorough principles of ship craft and was a strong, substantial vessel.[209]

The boat was propelled by the cordelle, by poles, by oars, or even by sails. This remained the principal craft for upstream navigation from the earliest utilization of the river to the advent of the steamboat, but it was slow and expensive, requiring a crew of from twenty to forty men under ordinary circumstances. The normal rate of speed was only from twelve to fifteen miles a day.[210] For downstream navigation the mackinaw, a flat-bottomed boat pointed at both ends, was extensively used. It required only a half dozen men to handle and was capable of making seventy-five or even one hundred miles a day.

Occasionally the bull-boat, made of buffalo skins sewn together and stretched over a frame of willow or cottonwood poles, was employed. It had the least draught of any river craft and was therefore best adapted to such shallow streams as the Platte.[211] Even the canoe was used at times. All these craft, it is needless to say, were confined to the Missouri and its navigable tributaries. As the field of fur-trading operations was extended farther inland, away from the main streams, the more inaccessible by water became the men engaged in the business and more expensive the work of transporting supplies to them and of bringing down their annual accumulations of furs.

The only other method of transportation was with

[209] Chittenden, *American fur trade*, I, 33.

[210] *Idem*, I, 34; Chittenden, *History of early steamboat navigation on the Missouri river*, I, 103.

[211] This was the craft used by Ashley in descending Green river and the Big Horn. Compare page 137.

horses or mules, which Ashley and Henry had used in
a measure during the years 1822 and 1823. But this
method had serious drawbacks. Henry's loss of horses
in the spring and again in the fall of 1823, together with
the destruction of a considerable number of Ashley's
mules by the Arikaras, had seriously handicapped
them. So long as they followed the old route to the
mountains up the Missouri through the lands of hostile
Indians, they were certain to suffer such severe losses
regularly. The farther inland they penetrated, moreover, the more indispensable became the maintenance of
an adequate supply of mounts.[212]

Once the use of horses had been definitely decided on,
however, the reasons for following the customary routes
naturally vanished. A less dangerous and above all a
more direct approach to the mountains was available.
By the year 1824 Ashley's men were operating on the
upper reaches of Green river. Now if a point be selected on this stream in the vicinity of the subsequent
Fort Bonneville, for example, it will be found that from
Fort Atkinson, near the mouth of the Platte, to this
point by way of the Missouri, Yellowstone, and Big
Horn, and over the mountains is a distance of not less
than thirteen hundred fifty miles, while by way of the
North Platte and through the South pass, the distance
is only about eight hundred fifty miles, through a country of gentle grades, easy passes, and comparative im-
munity from Indian attack.

The fact that this approach to the mountains and to

212 Ashley's dependence on horses and his difficulty in retaining them is
illustrated by the narrative of the expedition of 1824-1825 and by the mission of "Jim" Beckwourth (who seems to have been employed by Ashley in
the role of wrangler as well as body-servant) to the Pawnees in 1823 and
1824 to purchase mounts. See Bonner, *Life and adventures of James P. Beckwourth*, 23, 24, 37.

the interior basin and the Pacific remained so long un-
utilized is explained, of course, by the impossibility of
navigating the Platte, which has been fitly described as
"a thousand miles long and six inches deep." Had it
been possible to use boats all the way on this stream, the
area which it drained and the region beyond would
have been penetrated much earlier. This situation was
clearly pointed out in that curious book, *Memoir of a
captivity among the Indians of North America,* by
John Hunter, published in London the year of Ashley's
successful utilization of this route (1824). Hunter
states:

> The river La Platte rises in the Rocky mountains, runs nearly east,
> is about one thousand six hundred miles in length, broad, shoal, and
> not navigable. The route of the Missouri is widely circuitous, the
> river of difficult ascent, and the mountains next to impassable for
> loaded teams, even though human art and means be exhausted in the
> construction of roads. That of the La Platte from the seat of govern-
> ment, is perhaps the most direct communication; but there, as before
> remarked, this river is not navigable, nor can it be made so for any
> expense at present justifiable by the object in view.[213]

Only the substitution of horses for boats could render
the valley of the Platte available for communication
with the interior.

In general this was the route which Ashley determined to follow in the year 1824. Thomas Fitzpatrick
had returned by the North Platte in the summer and
had reported the way feasible.[214] Still, Ashley's undertaking was a bold experiment, for it was not till the

---

[213] Hunter, John. *Memoir of a captivity among the Indians,* 157 ff.

[214] "General Ashley was at this period in St. Louis, where he received a
letter from Fitzpatrick, relating to him the discovery of the South pass, their
success in trapping on the newly found streams, and their disasters. In that
letter, the major stated that the new route would easily admit of the passage
of wagons."—*St. Louis reveille,* march 1, 1847.

third of november that he left Fort Atkinson, at a season when there was little prospect of obtaining adequate feed for his horses. He followed Fitzpatrick's course only a portion of the distance. At the forks of the Platte he selected the south branch instead of the north, in the hope of finding a greater supply of grass in a lower latitude. He was the first white man to travel this route in the dead of winter and the first to use that variation of the South pass, called by the name of one of his own employees, James Bridger. He was the first American to investigate the mountains of northern Colorado, the first to enter the Great Divide basin, to cross almost the entire length of southern Wyoming, and the first to navigate the dangerous canyons of Green river.

In 1824-1825, Ashley plotted the first section of the central overland route to the Pacific. The following year Jedediah S. Smith, marking out first a southern and then a central route, plotted the remainder of the distance to the coast. Lewis and Clark, in reaching the Pacific, discovered and utilized the northern passes; Ashley and Smith, in reaching Great Salt lake, utilized the southern passes. From this point, Smith, in tracing a new course to the Pacific, was the first American to reach the coast by a route other than that in general followed by Lewis and Clark. The latter crossed but one divide between the Atlantic and the Pacific drainage areas. Lewis and Clark were able to follow the course of large rivers almost the entire distance from St. Louis to the mouth of the Columbia; Ashley and Smith, crossing from one complicated drainage area to another, were obliged to traverse a series of lofty mountain barriers as well as vast stretches of difficult and trying desert.

Ashley's own narrative of his discovery and exploration of the first portion of the midland route, as far as the interior basin, is as follows:

SAINT LOUIS, dec. 1, 1825.

DEAR SIR, Yours of the 23 november is at hand, and in compliance with the request therein contained, I herewith enclose you a sketch of the country over which I passed on my late tour across the Rocky mountains.[215] The following remarks relating to my journey have been cursorily put together, but as they afford some better information as to the practicability and means of traversing that region, at the season of the year presenting the greatest privations, they may not be uninteresting to you.

I left Fort Atkinson on the 3rd november, 1824.[216]

---

[215] This letter was written to General Henry Atkinson. On the date mentioned (november 23, 1825) General Atkinson wrote from the adjutant-general's office of the western department, Louisville, Kentucky, to Major-general Brown at Washington, "I learn from General Ashley that there is an easy passage across the Rocky mountains, by approaching them due west, from the head waters of the river Platte; indeed so gentle in ascent, as to admit of wagons taken over. . . The general is now preparing for me a topographical sketch of this section of the country, which shall be forwarded to you as soon as received."—U.S. House, *Executive documents,* 19 cong., 1 sess., VI, no. 117. All efforts to locate this sketch and the map accompanying it in the files of the war department, Washington, have proved fruitless.

The letter, which fills thirty-six pages of letter paper, 26 cm. by 20 cm., and is in two different hands, neither of them Ashley's, is in the Ashley MSS., Missouri historical society.

[216] Ashley had reached Fort Atkinson nearly a fortnight before. "Oct. 21, Gen'l Ashley arrived to-day with party of trappers and hunters destined for the Spanish country."—Kennerly MSS., Missouri historical society. According to Beckwourth (Bonner, *Life and adventures of James P. Beckwourth,* 33 ff) a false start had been made in the spring, which they were obliged to abandon because the Indians stole most of their horses. Ashley had then returned to St. Louis. During the summer of 1824 Thomas Fitzpatrick had come in from the mountains, having descended the North Platte with a party of men and a supply of furs accumulated beyond the mountains. On his arrival Ashley had dispatched him to rejoin the men he had left behind and to bring in the remainder of the furs. This party, which included among others Robert Campbell and "Jim" Beckwourth, set out in september, *idem,* 35. Beckwourth

On the afternoon of the fifth, I overtook my party of
mountaineers (twenty-five in number), who had in
charge fifty pack horses, a wagon and teams, etc.[217] On
the 6th we had advanced within —— miles of the villages of the Grand Pawney's, when it commenced snowing, and continued with but little intermission until the
morning of the 8th. During this time my men and
horses were suffering for the want of food, which, combined with the severity of the weather, presented rather
a gloomy prospect.[218] I had left Fort Atkinson under
a belief that I could procure a sufficient supply of provisions at the Pawney villages to subsist my men until
we could reach a point affording a sufficiency of game;
but in this I was disappointed, as I learned by sending
to the villages, that they were entirely deserted, the
Indians having, according to their annual custom, departed some two or three weeks previous for their
wintering ground. As the vicinity of those villages af-

probably antedates their departure for he states that "after several days
travel" they found them; but it is certain that Fitzpatrick and his party
were back at Council Bluffs by october 26. "October 26, Fitzpatrick and party
have come in and brot beaver." During Ashley's sojourn at Fort Atkinson
he spent much of his time at the neighboring camps of Andrew Drips and
Lucius Fontenelle, famous mountaineers.

217 This is the party to which Fitzpatrick had been dispatched, and whose
furs he had brought in. Beckwourth, who gives their number as twenty-six,
describes their attitude of mind on Fitzpatrick's arrival among them. See
Bonner, *Beckwourth*, 37.

218 Beckwourth says there were thirty-four men all told. Ashley's figures,
however, are confirmed further in the narrative when he dispatched two
parties of six men each, one of seven, and himself with six descended Green
river. Beckwourth confirms Ashley's statement regarding their short rations
and the gloomy attitude prevailing among the men. "Our allowance," he
says, "was half a pint of flour a day per man, which we made into a kind of
gruel; if we happened to kill a duck or a goose, it was shared as fairly as
possible. . . We numbered thirty-four men, all told, and a duller encampment,
I suppose, never was witnessed. No jokes, no fire-side stories, no fun; each
man rose in the morning with the gloom of the preceding night filling his
mind; we built our fire and partook of our scanty repast without saying a
word,"—Bonner, *Beckwourth*, 37 ff.

forded little or no game, my only alternative was to subsist my men on horse meat, and my horses on cotton-wood bark, the ground being at this time covered with snow about two feet deep. In this situation we continued for about the space of two weeks, during which time we made frequent attempts to advance and reach a point of relief, but, owing to the intense cold and violence of the winds, blowing the snow in every direction, we had only succeeded in advancing some ten or twelve miles, and on the 22nd of the same month we found ourselves encamped on the Loup fork of the river Platt within three miles of the Pawney towns.[219] Cold and hunger had by this time killed several of my horses, and many others were much reduced from the same cause. On the day last named we crossed the country southwardly about fifteen miles to the main fork of the Platt, where we were so fortunate as to find rushes and game in abundance, whence we set out on the 24th and advanced up the Platt as expeditiously as the nature of things under such circumstances would admit.[220] After ascending the river about one hundred miles, we reached Plumb point on the 3d december, where we found the encampment of the Grand Pawney Indians, who had

[219] Ashley had been following the Indian trace extending from the Missouri river to the Pawnee villages, the same which Benjamin O'Fallon and his detachment of Long's expedition had followed in the spring of 1820, and the main body of that expedition the ensuing june. The trace, in the vicinity of the Pawnee villages "consisted of more than twenty parallel paths of similar size and appearance." At this season it was, of course, as Ashley states, deeply covered with snow. O'Fallon and his men had halted near the site of Ashley's camp april 24, 1820, James, Edwin, *Account of an expedition from Pittsburgh to the Rocky mountains* (Stephen H. Long's expedition) in Thwaites, *Early western travels*, xv, 143 ff. The first Indian village encountered was probably in the vicinity of Fullerton, Nance county, Nebraska.

[220] Long had crossed from a point a little further up the Loup fork, estimating his distance to the Platte at twenty-five miles. See *idem*, xv, 233 ff. Ashley probably reached the Platte between the stations Clarke and Thummel on the Union Pacific, Merrick county, Nebraska.

reached that point (their usual crossing place) on their route to the wintering ground on the Arkansas river.[221] At two or three of my encampments previous to arriving at Plumb point, I was visited by small parties of young warriors, who were exceedingly troublesome to my party and committed several thefts before leaving us, but on my arrival at the encampment, the chiefs and principal men expressed much friendship and manifested the same by compelling the thieves to return the articles stolen from me.[222] From our encampment of the 24th to this place our hunters supplied us plentifully with provisions, and the islands and valleys of the Platt furnished a bountiful supply of rushes and firewood, but I was here informed by the Indians that until I reached the vicinity [of] the mountains, I should meet with but one place (the forks of the Platt) where a plentiful supply of fuel could be had, and but little

[221] Plumb point is the southernmost point of the Platte river a few miles south of Kearney, Buffalo county, Nebraska. There are a number of trails by which the Pawnees crossed to the Arkansas. Fremont on the map accompanying his *Report of the exploring expedition to the Rocky mountains* indicates such a route running southwest from the lower end of Grand island, while Long, who camped, june 19, 1820, in the vicinity of Vroman, Lincoln county, twenty-seven miles below the forks of the Platte, was informed by his guides that he was at a place where the "Pawnees often crossed the Platte," James, *op. cit.*, XV, 233; XVII, 256.

The Grand Pawnees, or Chaui, were one of the four tribes making up the Pawnee confederacy. The others were Republican Pawnee, Papage Pawnee, and Loup Pawnee. All belonged to Caddoan stock and had moved into the region bounded on the north by the Niobrara and on the south by Prairie Dog creek at a very early and hence traditional date. The population of the Grand Pawnees was estimated by Long in 1820 at three thousand five hundred souls, *idem*, XVII, 152; by Henry Atkinson in 1825 at five thousand five hundred souls, of whom one thousand one hundred were warriors, U.S. House, *Executive documents*, 19 cong., 1 sess., VI, no. 117. Speaking of their migratory habits Atkinson says, "They leave their villages in the spring and fall and go far into the plains south-west and north-west in pursuit of buffalo."

[222] Zebulon Pike had had a similar experience with several young Pawnee bucks in 1806 on the Republican fork. See Coues, *Expedition of Zebulon Montgomery Pike*, etc., II, 418.

food of any description for our horses.[223] They urged me to take up winter quarters at the forks of the Platt, stating that if I attempted to advance further until spring, I would endanger the lives of my whole party. The weather now was extremely cold, accompanied with frequent light snows. We advanced about eight miles further up the river, where we fell in with the tribe of Loup Pawneys and travelled in company with them to the forks of the Platt (their usual wintering place) where we arrived on the 12th day of december,

[223] Beckwourth had left a record of his remarkable contributions to the larder by his rare skill as a shot. Deer, elk, duck, bear, buffalo, geese, all fell before his unfaltering aim. On one occasion his pangs of appetite got the better of his conscience. Ashley had issued orders for the best hunters to sally out and try their luck. Beckwourth instantly complied. About three hundred yards from camp he saw two teal. "I levelled my rifle," he relates, "and handsomely shot one. This was a temptation to my constancy; and appetite and conscientiousness had a long strife as to the disposal of the booty." Appetite won the strife, although says Beckwourth, "a strong inward feeling remonstrated against such an invasion of the rights of my starving messmates," with whom he was in honor bound to share whatever he could procure. "But if," he argues, "by fortifying myself, I gained ability to procure something more substantial than a teal duck, my dereliction would be sufficiently atoned, and my overruling appetite, at the same time, gratified." Acting on this rather sensible conclusion, he built a fire, roasted, and ate the duck. Amazingly refreshed and strengthened, he then continued his hunting operations with very gratifying success. He bagged a large buck, a white wolf, and three large elk. Returning to camp, he summoned his comrades to help bring in the booty, after which, "the fame of Jim Beckwourth was celebrated by all tongues." "Amid all this gratulation," however, says Beckwourth, "I could not separate my thoughts from the duck which had supplied my clandestine meal in the bushes. I suffered them to appease their hungers with the proceeds of my toil before I ventured to tell my comrades of the offense I had been guilty of. All justified my conduct, declaring my conclusions obvious." Altogether, Beckwourth seems to have derived moral as well as physical strength from the incident. He never killed a teal duck thereafter without thinking of his "clandestine meal in the bushes," and "since that time," he told his biographer, "I have never refused to share my last shilling, my last biscuit, or my only blanket with a friend, and I think the recollection of that 'temptation in the wilderness' will ever serve as a lesson to more constancy in the future."—Bonner, *Beckwourth,* 38 ff.

There are a number of islands in the Platte between this point and the mouth of the Loup fork, the principal, of course, being Grand island.

and had so far found the Indians' information in relation to fuel and horse food to be correct. At this time
my men had undergone an intense suffering from the
inclemency of the weather, which also bore so severely
on the horses as to cause the death of many of them.
This, together with a desire to purchase a few horses
from the Loups and to prepare my party for the privations which we had reason to anticipate in travelling
the next two hundred miles (described as being almost
wholly destitute of wood), induced me to remain at the
forks until the 23d december, the greater part of which
time, we were favoured with fine weather, and, notwithstanding the uplands were still covered with from
eighteen to twenty-four inches of snow, the valleys
were generally bare and afforded a good range for my
horses, furnishing plenty of dry grass and some small
rushes, from the use of which they daily increased in
strength and spirits.

The day after our arrival at the forks, the chiefs and
principal men of the Loups assembled in council for
the purpose of learning my wants, and to devise means
to supply them.[224] I made known [to] them that I

224 The Pawnee Loups, or more properly the Skidi (more probably Tskiri,
a wolf) linguistically and according to their own tradition, are more closely
related to the Arikara branch of the Caddoan stock than are the other
Pawnee tribes. They had been united with the Arikaras at one time, they
believed, but in the course of the general northerly movement of all the
tribes of this stock, the Arikaras had continued up the Missouri while the
Pawnee Loups had been shunted off into the valley of the Platte. Their customs and their political affiliations were common to the other Pawnee
tribes, although Long found that "they appeared unwilling to acknowledge
their affinity." See James, op. cit., XVII, 153. The white settlers of New Mexico became acquainted with the Pawnees early in the seventeenth century by
the horse-stealing raids which these Indians frequently conducted into the
Spanish country. The Pawnee Loups, according to Long, numbered in 1820
one hundred dirt lodges, making five hundred families, or approximately
two thousand souls. Henry Atkinson in his report to Major-general Brown,
basing his calculations apparently on information derived from Ashley,

wished to procure twenty-five horses and a few buffalo robes, and to give my men an opportunity of providing more amply for the further prosecution of the
journey, I requested that we might be furnished with
meat to subsist upon while we remained with them, and
promised that a liberal remuneration should be made
for any services they might render me. After their
deliberations were closed, they came to this conclusion:
that, notwithstanding they had been overtaken by
unusually severe weather before reaching their wintering ground, by which they had lost a great number of
horses, they would comply with my requisition in
regard to horses and other necessaries as far as their
means would admit. Several speeches were made by
the chiefs during the council, all expressive in the
highest degree of their friendly disposition towards
our government, and their conduct in every particular
manifested the sincerity of their declarations.

On the 23d december, having completed the purchase of twenty-three horses and other necessary things,
I made arrangements for my departure which took
place on the next morning. The south fork of the river
being represented as affording more wood than the
north, I commenced ascending that stream. The weather
was fine, the valleys literally covered with buffaloe, and
everything seemed to promise a safe and speedy movement to the first grove of timber on my route, supposed
to be about ten days' march. The Loup Pawneys were
not at this time on very good terms with the Arapahoe
and Kiawa Indians, and were anxious to cultivate a
friendly understanding with them, to accomplish which,
they concluded to send a deputation of five men with

wrote, "The Pawnee Loups are estimated at 3500 souls of which 700 are warriors." See U.S. House, *Executive documents,* 19 cong., 1 sess., VI, no. 117.

me to meet those tribes and propose to them terms of peace and amity.[225] This deputation overtook me on the afternoon of the 25th.

Having now reached a point where danger might be reasonably apprehended from strolling war parties of Indians, spies were kept in advance and strict diligence observed in the duty of sentinels.

The morning of the 26th was cloudy and excessively cold. At 3 o'clock in the afternoon it began to snow and continued with violent winds until the night of the 27th. The next morning (28th) four of my horses were so benumbed with cold that they were unable to stand, although we succeeded in raising them on their feet. A delay to recruit them would have been attended with great danger, probably even to the destruction of the whole party. I therefore concluded to set forward without them. The snow was now so deep that had it not been for the numerous herds of buffaloe moving down the river, we could not possibly have proceeded. The paths of these animals were beat on either side of the river and afforded an easy passage to our horses. These animals were essentially beneficial to us in another respect by removing (in their search for food)

[225] The Arapaho, of Algonquin stock, according to their tradition, moved northeast from the vicinity of the upper Arkansas. En route they divided. These, the southern group, were usually at peace with their neighbors, the Kiowa Indians, but had a long tradition of hostility to the Pawnees. James (*op. cit.*, xv, 157 ff) describes a battle between the Pawnees and Arapaho in 1820. Their feud was kept up until they were confined on reservations. The Kiowas, constituting a distinct linguistic stock, migrated from the vicinity of the Three Forks to the Canadian and Arkansas. Lewis and Clark reported them on the North Platte. They were the most bloodthirsty and predatory of all the prairie tribes and have probably killed more white men in proportion to their numbers than any other of the plains Indians. The Pawnees were also seeking to cultivate a better understanding with the Arapaho ten years later, Dodge, Henry, "Report of the expedition with dragoons to the Rocky mountains during the summer of 1835, etc.," in U.S. Senate, *Executive documents,* 24 cong., 1 sess., no. 209.

the snow in many places from the earth and leaving the grass exposed to view, which was the only nourishment our horses could obtain.[226]

We continued to move forward without loss of time, hoping to be able to reach the wood described by the Indians before all our horses should become exhausted. On the 1st january, 1825, I was exceedingly surprised and no less gratified at the sight of a grove of timber, in appearance, distant some two or three miles on our front. It proved to be a grove of cottonwood of the sweet-bark kind suitable for horse food, situated on an island, offering among other conveniences, a good situation for defence. I concluded to remain here several days for the purpose of recruiting my horses, and made my arrangements accordingly. My Indian friends of the Pawne Loup deputation, believing this place to be nearly opposite to the Arrapahoe and other Indian camps on the Arkansas determined to proceed hence across the country. They prepared a few pounds of meat and with each a bundle of wood tied to his back for the purpose of fuel, departed the following morning on their mission. Being informed by the Pawneys that one hundred of my old enemies (the Arikara warriors) were encamped with the Arkansas Indians, and my situation independent of that circumstance, being rendered more vulnerable by the departure of the Indians, who had just left us, I was obliged to increase my guard from eight to sixteen men.[227] This was much the most severe duty my men had to perform, but they did it with alacrity and cheer-

---

[226] Beckwourth comments on the number of buffalo encountered. See Bonner, *Beckwourth*, 45.

[227] Long found a solitary Arikara who had been residing among the Pawnees but had traveled as far south as the Arkansas, James, *op. cit.*, xv, 219.

fulness as well as all other services required at their hands; indeed, such was their pride and ambition in the discharge of their duties, that their privations in the end became sources of amusement to them. We remained on this island until the cottonwood fit for horse food was nearly consumed, by which time our horses were so refreshed as to justify another move forward. We therefore made arrangements for our departure and resumed our march on the 11th january.

The weather continued extremely cold, which rendered our progress slow and very labourious. We procured daily a scanty supply of small pieces of driftwood and willow brush, which sufficed for our fuel, but we did not fall in with any cottonwood suitable for horse food until the 20th, when we reached another small island [228] clothed with a body of that wood sufficient for two days subsistence. From this last mentioned island, we had a clear and distant view of the Rocky mountains [229] bearing west, about sixty miles distant.[230]

---

228 This may very well be the same island on which Fremont found one Chabonard camped in july 1842, about nine miles above the mouth of Bijou fork. It is interesting to note that on the day Fremont first sighted the mountains, in 1842, he met a party of three men, one of whom was Jim Beckwourth, who were hunting for a band of horses which had strayed from Chabonard's camp. Near here, almost certainly, Beckwourth camped seventeen years before with Ashley, Fremont, *op. cit.*, 30.

229 The exact location of the point at which Ashley first sighted the mountains can be pretty definitely determined. Long, who traveled this route in june 1820, obtained his first glimpse two days after passing a creek he called Cherry creek, identified by Thwaites as Pawnee creek, Logan county, Colorado, James, *op. cit.*, xv, 260, 264. This would be from a point near the town of Cooper, Morgan county, Colorado. Fremont, who traveled this route in 1842 and again in 1843, sighted the mountains on the former expedition near the mouth of Beaver fork, Fremont, *op. cit.*, 30. On the latter expedition he described, july 1, "a faint blue mass in the west as the sun sank behind it," at approximately the same point, camping that night a few miles farther up the Platte at the mouth of Bijou creek, Fremont, *op. cit.*, 110. In both instances he sighted the mountains from a point near the confluence of Beaver fork with the South Platte, closely corresponding with Long's "first view." Rufus B. Sage obtained a distinct view of the main ridge in august 1842 a

Believing from the information of the Indians that it was impracticable to cross them at this time, I concluded to advance to their base with my whole party, and, after fortifying my camp, to proceed with a part of my men into the mountains, to ascertain if possible the best route to cross over, and at the same time, endeavour to employ my men advantageously until a state of things would allow me to proceed on my journey.

We advanced slowly to the point proposed, and had the good fortune to find on our way an abundance of wood for fuel as well as for horse food. On the 4th february, we approached near to the base of the mountain and encamped in a thick grove of cottonwood and willows on a small branch of the river Platt. Our situation here was distant six or eight miles north of a conspicuous peak of the mountains, which I imagined to be that point described by Major Long as being the highest peak and lying in latitude 40 N., longitude 29 W.[231] On my route hither from our encampment of the 20th january, I was overtaken by

few miles *above* Beaver fork, Sage, *Rocky mountain life*, 206. Ashley also, in all probability, secured his first view of the mountains very near Beaver fork.

[230] Near the boundary of Weld and Morgan counties. Compare Dodge, *op. cit.*, 20.

[231] On Big Thompson creek or the Cache la Poudre, probably the latter. Ashley estimates his distance at six to eight miles north of Long's peak, which would place him on Big Thompson, but like Pike and Long before him, he probably failed to make a correction for the deceptiveness of distances in the rare Colorado atmosphere. The Cache la Poudre is the larger stream, up whose course ran an Indian trail which later became a well-defined road. It was followed by Fremont in 1843, Fremont, *op. cit.*, 122. The best maps for this portion of Ashley's journey are the sheets of *Geological and topographical atlas* accompanying the *Report of the geological exploration of the fortieth parallel*, commonly known as the "King survey." These sheets, though abounding in inaccuracies in detail, show very graphically the general features of the topography. The map accompanying Fremont's *Report*, while serviceable, must be used with caution.

three Arapahoe Indians. They stated to me that they had been informed by the Indians of the Pawney deputation (whom they had received and treated with friendship) of my journey up the Platt, and that they with 60 or 70 other warriors had started from their encampment on the Arkansas to join me, but the unusual depth of snow on the prairies had deterred all the party except themselves from proceeding further than their second day's encampment. I made them some presents, gave them advice in relation to the course of conduct they should pursue towards our citizens, and pointed out to them the advantages which a friendly understanding between them and the Pawneys would produce to both tribes. They acknowledged the correctness of my admonition and promised in future to pursue the line of conduct I had advised them to adopt. They then thanked me for the presents I had made them and departed to rejoin their tribe.

We were busily [engaged] on excursions in different directions from our camp until the 25th february. Although the last ten days had been pleasant weather partly accompanied with warm suns, the scene around us was pretty much the same as when we arrived, everything being enveloped in one mass of snow and ice, but, as my business required a violent effort to accomplish its object, notwithstanding the mountains seemed to bid defiance to my further progress, things were made ready, and on the 26th we commenced the doubtful undertaking.[232] Our passage across the first range of mountains, which was exceedingly difficult and dangerous, employed us three days, after which the country presented a different aspect. Instead of

---

[232] Ashley is the first white man, so far as is known, to undertake the crossing of the Front range near this latitude.

finding the mountains more rugged as I advanced towards their summit and everything in their bosom frozen and torpid, affording nothing on which an animal could possibly subsist, they assumed quite an altered character. The ascent of the hills (for they do not deserve the name of mountains) was so gradual as to cause but little fatigue in travelling over them. The valleys and south sides of the hills were but partially covered with snow, and the latter presented already in a slight degree the verdure of spring, while the former were filled with numerous herds of buffaloe, deer, and antelope.[233]

In my passage hither I discovered from the shape of the country, that the range of mountains twenty or thirty miles to the north of my route, was not so lofty or rugged and in all probability would afford a convenient passage over them.[234] From here I pursued a W.N.W. course with such variations only as were necessary in selecting the smoothest route. The face of the country west and northwardly continued pretty much the same. Successive ranges of high hills gradually ascending as I advanced, with detached heaps of rock and earth scattered promiscuously over the hills several hundred feet higher than the common surface.[235] On

[233] The divide over the Front range is only about two thousand feet above the level of the plain to the east and of easy ascent in summer, but, in the dead of winter, it is surprising that Ashley succeeded in crossing at all. His description of the hills is accurate. Fremont called the divide "a range of buttes," Fremont, *op. cit.,* 122. Ashley after crossing the Front range (called by him the first range) passed from the watershed of the South Platte to that of the North Platte.

[234] The Medicine Bow range, the southern spurs of which are the higher. Compare Beekly, "Geology and coal resources of North Park, Colorado," in U.S. Geological survey *bulletin 596,* 12 ff.

[235] Pursuing a westward and northerly course, he paralleled the Medicine Bow range. His description of the broken country between the upper tributaries of the Cache la Poudre and Laramie rivers is unmistakable.

the south there appeared at the distance of fifteen or twenty miles a range of lofty mountains bearing east and west, entirely covered with snow and timbered with a thick growth of pine.[236] We were able to procure but a scanty supply of fuel till we arrived on the 10th march at a small branch of the north fork of the Platte, where we found an abundance of wood.[237] This stream is about one hundred feet wide, meandering north-eastwardly through a beautiful and fertile valley, about ten miles in width. Its margin is partially wooded with large cottonwood of the bitter kind.[238] The sweet cottonwood, such as affords food for horses, is nowhere to be found in the mountains; consequently our horses had to subsist upon a very small allowance of grass, and this, too (with the exception of a very inconsiderable proportion) entirely dry and in appearance destitute of all nutriment. Yet my horses retained their strength and spirits in a remarkable degree, which, with other circumstances, confirms me in the opinion that the vegetation of the mountains is much more nourishing than that of the plains.

On the 12th, I again set out and in the evening encamped at the foot of a high range of mountains covered with snow and bearing N.N.W. and S.S.E., which, as

[236] Hague peak, Long's peak. Mount Richthofen, Park View mountain, and other peaks in the vicinity would give the appearance of an east to west range. He was probably forty miles from the nearest of them.

[237] Laramie river. After flowing northwardly from its source in the Medicine Bow range, Big Laramie cuts a longitudinal valley through the mountains, and then, turning sharply to the east, emerges into the Laramie plains, flowing northeastwardly to the site of the town of Laramie, Albany county, Wyoming, where it turns north again.

[238] The *populus angustifolia* or narrow-leaf cottonwood. Unlike the other variety, the *populus angulata,* or round-leaf (sweet) cottonwood, it is not eaten by horses. It has a smoother trunk and more slender and flexible branches than the *populus angulata.* Lewis and Clark described the two varieties, which they identified as *populi,* Thwaites, *Original journals of the Lewis and Clark expedition,* VI, 145, 146.

they appeared to present the same obstructions to my passage as far north as the eye could reach, determined me (after a day's examination) to attempt the continuation of my course W.N.W., hoping to be as successful as I had been in crossing the first range. My attempt, however, proved unsuccessful.[239] After an unremitting and severe labour of two days, we returned to our old encampment with the loss of some of my horses, and my men excessively fatigued. We found the snow to be from three to five feet in depth and so firmly settled as to render our passage through it wholly impracticable. This mountain is timbered with a beautiful growth of white pine and from every appearance is a delightful country to travel over in the summer season. After remaining one day longer at the camp to rest my men and horses, I left it a second time and travelled northwardly along the base of the mountains. As I thus advanced, I was delighted with the variegated scenery presented by the valleys and mountains, which were enlivened by innumerable herds of buffaloe, antelope, and mountain sheep grazing on them, and what added no small degree of interest to the whole scene, were the many small streams issuing from the mountains, bordered with a thin growth of small willows and richly stocked with beaver.[240] As my men could profitably employ themselves on these streams, I moved slowly along, averaging not more than five or six miles per day and sometimes remained two days at the same encampment.

[239] Perhaps following up the Little Laramie, which emerges from a tempting opening in the Medicine Bow range.

[240] There are scores of streams issuing from the Medicine Bow range, tributary to the Medicine Bow and Laramie rivers, Cooke creek, Dutton creek, Rock creek, etc. The extensive growth of willows bordering these streams was noted by Fremont (*op. cit.*, 123).

On the 21st march, the appearance of the country justified another attempt to resume my former course W.N.W.[241] The principal or highest part of the mountain having changed its direction to east and west,[242] I ascended it in such manner as to leave its most elevated ranges to the south [243] and travelled north west over a very rough and broken country generally covered with snow. My progress was therefore slow and attended with unusual labour untill the afternoon of the 23d, when I had succeeded in crossing the range and encamped on the edge of a beautiful plain of a circular form and about ten miles in diameter.[244] The next day (24th) we travelled west across the plain, which terminated at the principal branch of the north fork of the river Platt, on which we encamped for the night.[245] On the two succeeding days we passed over an elevated

[241] On the twelfth he encamped at the foot of a high range which he undertook to cross. This is probably the northern section of the Medicine Bow range. After a day's "examination" (the thirteenth) he devoted two days of severe labor (the fourteenth and fifteenth) to crossing, but returned, baffled, to his camp at the foot of the mountain. Here he rested his men a day (the sixteenth) and on the seventeenth resumed his march. On the twenty-first (i.e., after five days' travel) he reached a point where he believed himself justified in essaying once more a west northwest course. He had advanced at the rate of only five or six miles a day and on one occasion, at least, laid over a day. Assuming that he averaged four miles a day for five days, he would, at a distance of twenty miles, be close to the point where the Medicine Bow river emerges from the Medicine Bow range, just to the east of Elk mountain. See U.S. Geological survey, *Fort Steele quadrangle* (topographic sheet).

[242] Elk mountain which terminates the Medicine Bow range on the north.

[243] The broken ranges to the south and west include Elk mountain and Sheephead mountain.

[244] Ashley crossed the divide by a route paralleling the line of the Union Pacific but to the south of it, and encamped probably on Pass creek near the confluence of Rattlesnake creek. A highway now follows this route. The circular plain to which Ashley refers lies south of Walcott, Carbon county, Wyoming. This is approximately the route followed by Fremont in 1843. See Fremont, *op. cit.*, 125 ff.

[245] In approximately latitude, 41°, 40 N., longitude, 106°, 54 W.

rough country entirely destitute of wood and affording no water save what could be procured by the melting of snow. We used as a substitute for fuel an herb called wild sage.[246] It resembles very much in appearance the garden sage but acquires a much larger growth and possesses a stock of from four to five inches in diameter. It burns well and retains fire as long as any fuel I ever used.

From the morning of the 27th to the night of the 1st april, we were employed in crossing the ridge which divides the waters of the Atlantic from those of the Pacific ocean.[247] The first two days, the country we met with was undulating with a gradual ascent to the west. Southwardly at the distance of twenty or thirty miles appeared a range of high mountains bearing east and west.[248] Northwardly, at an equal distance, were several mountains or high hills irregularly seated over the earth, which I afterwards ascertained to surround the sources of a branch of the Platt called Sweet Water.[249]

On the 3d, 4th and 5th days, we travelled over small ridges and valleys alternately, the latter much the most extensive and generally covered with water produced by the melting of the snow and which appeared to have no outlet.[250] This dividing ridge is almost entirely destitute of vegetation except wild sage with which the earth is so bountifully spread that it proved a considerable impediment in our progress. As my horses

[246] The characteristic *artemisia tridentata*.

[247] By the way of Bridger's pass. Ashley is the first white man to cross by this route. See U.S. War department, *Map of the military department of the Platte, Wyoming*.

[248] The Sierra Madre range of northern Colorado.

[249] Ferris mountains and Green mountains.

[250] Quite right; this was the Great Divide basin.

were greatly exhausted by the fatigue and hunger they had underwent, I advanced on the 2d april only two or three miles to a place where I had, on the preceding evening, discovered some grass. After my camp was arranged, I advanced with one of my men eight or ten miles on my route to a high hill for the purpose of taking a view of the adjacent country in the expectation of finding the appearance of water courses running westwardly. Nothing, however, was visible from which I could form an opinion with the exception of a huge craggy mountain, the eastern extremity of which, bearing from this hill due north, made nearly a right angle. The arm which extended northwardly divides (as I afterwards ascertained) the waters of the Yellow Stone and Bighorn from some of the headwaters of the Columbia, while the west arm separates the southern sources of Lewis's fork of the Columbia from what I suppose to be the headwaters of the Rio Colorado of the West. While on the mountain, I was discovered by a war party of Crow Indians, who were returning from an excursion against the southern Snake Indians. This party, unobserved by me, followed me to my camp and on the succeeding night stole seventeen of my best horses and mules.[251] This outrage reduced me to a dreadful condition. I was obliged to burden my men with the packs of the stolen horses, and, after making the necessary arrangements, they were directed to proceed to the hill where I had been discovered the day previous by the Indians, while I, with one man, pursued the fugitives, who travelled northwardly over the roughest parts

[251] Probably North Pilot butte from which an extensive view is obtainable of the Wind River and Gros Ventre ranges. Having crossed the continental divide, he quite naturally looked for westward flowing waters. Beckwourth, whose narrative jumps from the forks of the Platte to this point, calls it Pilot butte. He confirms the loss of the horses at this place, Bonner, *op. cit.*, 52 ff.

of the country and with all possible expedition. In the course of the day we recovered three of the stolen horses, which were left on the way, and rejoined our party that night. On the next morning I dispatched nine men on the trail of the Indians, and with the residue of my party I proceeded in search of a suitable encampment at which to await their return. On the 6th we reached a small stream of water running north west.[252] We deemed it about ten miles where it formed a junction with another rivulet of the same size, which headed northwardly in the range of mountains before described.[253] This stream is clothed with a growth of small willows and furnishes the only constant running water we have met with since the 24th march and also the first wood we have seen in the same space of time. We continued at this camp until the 11th inst., on which day, the men sent in pursuit of the Indians came back without success. They had ascertained, however, from the direction of the trace and other circumstances that they belonged to the Crow nation. On the 12th we again proceeded on our journey, pursuing the meanders of the creek last mentioned in a south west direction; but the weather was so exceedingly bad, snowing a greater part of the time, that we were unable to advance more than six or eight miles per day until the 18th inst., when we left the creek and traveled west

[252] According to Beckwourth (Bonner, *op. cit., loc. cit.*), it was he who discovered this stream at a distance of four or five miles from their camp of april 5. Beckwourth states that Ashley was ill at the time because of exposure and insufficient fare and consequently had to be conveyed in a litter. It is just such passages as these, the creations apparently of Beckwourth's egotistical mind, that have unfortunately discredited his entire biography.

[253] Morton creek, called White Horse creek on the maps of the eighties and nineties and as late as 1879 not even charted. Its course was to the east of the line of travel through the South pass. Ashley struck it ten miles above its confluence with Big Sandy. He here touches the trail used by his own men the previous spring and summer.

about fifteen miles to a beautiful river running south.[254]
This stream is about one hundred yards wide, of a bold
current, and generally so deep that it presents but few
places suitable for fording. Its margin and islands are
wooded with large long leafed (or bitter) cottonwood,
box-elder, willows, etc., and, judging from the quantity
of wood cut on its banks, and other appearances, it once
must have contained a great number of beaver, the
major part of which (as I have been informed) were
trapped by men in the service of the North West company some four or five years ago.[255]

The country in this vicinity and eastwardly fifty miles
is gently rolling. Some of the valleys afford a species
of fine grass, but the uplands produce but little vegetation of any kind except a small growth of wild sage.

I have hitherto said but little in relation to the fer-
tility of the soil on my route because that part of it
lying east [of] the mountains has in two or three instances been described by gentlemen who have travelled
over the country for that express purpose and further
because the perfect sameness in the quality of the soil
and its productions enabled me to describe them altogether and that in but few words. From this place to
Plumb point on the river Platt, the proportion of
arable land (which is almost entirely confined to the
valleys of the mountains) is so inconsiderable that the
whole country (so far as my observations extended) may
be considered of no value for the purpose of agriculture. The surface generally either exhibits a bed of sand

---

254 They left Big Sandy and, traveling west, came to the main stream of
Green river.

255 This must have occurred on the Snake expedition conducted by
McKenzie in 1819-1820, who traversed the region south of Lewis's fork to
the Blackfeet lake and perhaps as far as Soda springs. One of his letters was
dated, Black Bear's lake (Bear lake?), september 10, 1819, Ross, *Fur hunters,*
I, 227, 267.

or a light coloured barren earth, which is in many places wholly destitute of the least semblance of vegetation. In relation to the subsistence of men and horses, I will remark that nothing now is actually necessary for the support of men in the wilderness than a plentiful supply of good fresh meat. It is all that our mountaineers ever require or even seem to wish. They prefer the meat of the buffaloe to that of any other animal, and the circumstance of the uninterrupted health of these people who generally eat unreasonable quantities of meat at their meals, proves it to be the most wholesome and best adapted food to the constitution of man. In the different concerns which I have had in the Indian country, where not less than one hundred men have been annually employed for the last four years and subsist altogether upon meat, I have not known at any time a single instance of bilious fever among them or any other disease prevalent in the settled parts of our country, except a few instances (and but very few) of slight fevers produced by colds or rheumatic affections, contracted while in the discharge of guard duty on cold and inclement nights. Nor have we in the whole four years lost a single man by death except those who came to their end prematurely by being either shot or drowned. In the summer and fall seasons of the year, the country will afford sufficient grass to subsist any number of horses in traversing it in either direction and even in the winter season, such is the nutricious quality of the mountain grass that, when it can be had plentifully, although perfectly dry in appearance, horses (moderately used) that partake of it, will retain in a great degree their flesh, strength, and spirits. When the round leaf or sweet-bark cottonwood can be had abundantly, horses may be wintered with but little inconvenience. They are very fond of this bark, and, judging by the effect produced from feeding it to my horses last winter, I suppose it almost, if not quite, as nutricious as timothy hay.

On my arrival at the point last described,[256] I determined to relieve my men and horses of their heavy burdens, to accomplish which, I concluded to make four divisions of my party, send three of them by land in different directions, and, with the fourth party, descend the river myself with the principal part of my merchandise. Accordingly, some of the men commenced making a frame about the size and shape of a common mackinaw boat, while others were sent to procure buffaloe skins for a covering.[257] On the 21 april, all things being ready for our departure, I dispatched six men northwardly to the sources of the river; seven others set out for a mountain bearing s.s.w. and n.n.e., distant about thirty miles; and six others were sent in a southern direction.[258] After selecting one of the most intelligent and efficient of each party to act as partizans, I directed them to proceed to their respective points of destination and thence in such direction as circumstances should dictate for my interest.[259] At the same time they were

[256] He camped fifteen miles above the mouth of the Sandy.

[257] The craft would not technically be a mackinaw boat, which was a flat-bottomed vessel pointed at both ends and usually forty to fifty feet long with a twelve-foot beam. Ashley's boat was a bull-boat, the normal dimensions of which were a thirty-foot length by twelve-foot beam, with a draft of twenty inches.

[258] The twenty-first of april would make their sojourn here for the construction of the boat, three days. Beckwourth says they were encamped four or five days, Bonner, *Beckwourth,* 57. One division was sent to the upper course of Green river, a region familiar to Henry and Smith. The direction pursued by the party of seven is not clear but the passage seems to indicate that they moved toward the Bear River mountains. The division sent south must have advanced toward the Uintah mountains.

[259] James Clyman probably led one of the expeditions. He had been one

instructed to endeavor to fall in with two parties of men that were fitted out by me in the year previous, and who were then, as I supposed, beyond the range of mountains appearing westwardly.[260] The partisans were also informed that I would descend the river to some eligible point about one hundred miles below, there deposit a part of my merchandise, and make such marks as would designate it as a place of general rendezvous for the men in my service in that country, and where they were all directed to assemble on or before the 10th july following.[261]

After the departure of the land parties, I embarked with six men on thursday, the 21st april, on board my newly made boat and began the descent of the river. After making about fifteen miles, we passed the mouth of the creek which we had left on the morning of the 18th and to which we gave the name of *Sandy*.[262] At 4 o'clock in the afternoon we encamped for the remainder of the day and night at a place distant about forty miles from where we embarked, finding from the movement of our boat in its day's progress that she was too heavily burthened, we began the construction of another, which was completed and launched on the morning of the

of Smith's men who had preceded Fitzpatrick to Fort Atkinson in the early fall of 1824, Camp, *op. cit.,* 44; Bonner, *Beckwourth,* 62.

Beckwourth places the point of departure of the separate companies further down Green river near the mouth of Henry's fork. He is certainly mistaken, but his error may be due to his need for the setting of another rescue of General Ashley, the third time he saves the general's life within ten pages.

[260] This, of course, refers to the two parties, one under the command of Jedediah Smith, and the other probably headed by William Sublette. By this time both were presumably in Cache valley or at Great Salt lake.

[261] This is the second general rendezvous of the Ashley trappers. The first had been conducted the previous summer on the Sweetwater. Beckwourth says they were directed to gather at rendezvous the first of july. See Bonner, *op. cit.,* 62.

[262] This is the naming of the Sandy, famous for years in overland travel.

24th, when we again set out. As we advanced on our passage, the country gradually became more level and broken. The river bottom, which in point of soil, is but little better than the uplands, becomes narrower as we descended and has generally the appearance of being subject to inundation. Today we made 30 miles.

MONDAY, 25TH: the country today under our observation is mountainous on either side of the river for twenty miles, then it resumes its former appearance of elevated and broken heights. A beautiful bold running stream about fifty yards wide empties itself on the west side of the river bearing N.W. and S.E.[263] Below this junction the river is one hundred and fifty yards wide, the valley narrow and thinly timbered. We encamped on an island after making about twenty-five miles. Thence we departed on the succeeding morning and progressed slowly without observing any remarkable difference in the appearance of the river or surrounding country until the 30th inst., when we arrived at the base of a lofty rugged mountain, the summit of which was covered with snow and bearing east and west. Here also a creek sixty feet wide discharges itself on the west side.[264] This spot I selected as a place of general rendezvous, which I designated by marks in accordance with the instruction given to my men. So far, the navigation of this river is without the least obstruction. The channel in the most shallow places affords not less than four feet water. Game continues abundant, particularly buffaloe. There is no appearance of these animals win-

---

[263] Black's fork. Powell (*Exploration of the Colorado river of the west,* 10) camped below its confluence, march 25, 1869.

[264] Henry's fork. Powell cached his instruments here in 1869. The brothers Kolb camped very nearly at the site of Ashley's camp, september 13, 1911, Kolb, E. L., *Through the Grand canyon from Wyoming to Mexico,* 22.

tering on this river; but they are at this time travelling from the west in great numbers.

SATURDAY, MAY 2d: we continued our voyage about half a mile below our camp, when we entered between the walls of this range of mountains, which approach at this point to the waters' edge on either side of the river and rise almost perpendicular to an immense height. The channel of the river is here contracted to the width of sixty or seventy yards, and the current (much increased in velocity) as it rolled along in angry submission to the serpentine walls that direct it, seemed constantly to threaten us with danger as we advanced.[265] We, however, succeeded in descending about ten miles without any difficulty or material change in the aspect of things and encamped for the night.[266] About two miles above this camp, we passed the mouth of a creek on the west side some fifteen yards wide, which discharged its water with great violence.[267]

SUNDAY, 3RD: after progressing two miles, the navigation became difficult and dangerous, the river being

[265] Flaming Gorge canyon. Kolb mentioned the quickening of the current, Kolb, *op. cit.,* 24. The walls of the canyon rise to a height of one thousand five hundred feet, Powell, *op. cit.,* 14. F. S. Dellenbaugh (*A canyon voyage,* 20), locates the Green river "suck" at this point. See Bonner, *op. cit.,* 57. Powell (*op. cit.,* 14), says, "Entering Flaming Gorge, we quickly run through it on a swift current, and emerge into a little park. Half a mile below, the river wheels sharply to the left and we turned into another canyon cut into the mountain."

[266] This camp was probably near the two small islands at the point where the stream widens out within a little park just below the end of Kingfisher canyon. Three canyons had been passed this day, Flaming Gorge, Horseshoe, and Kingfisher. Dellenbaugh (*Canyon voyage,* 22), describes them as the gateway, the vestibule, and the ante-chamber, respectively. Ashley's estimate of their combined length, ten miles, is correct, Kolb, *op. cit.,* 29; Dellenbaugh, *op. cit.,* 22. Powell camped near this point may 30, 1869.

[267] Sheep creek, described by Powell (*op. cit.,* 14), and by Kolb (*op. cit.,* 28). This, the only stream of any size between Henry's fork and Red canyon, enters the main canyon through a fault.

remarkably crooked with more or less rapids every mile caused by rocks which had fallen from the sides of the mountain, many of which rise above the surface of the water and required our greatest exertions to avoid them. At twenty miles from our last camp, the roaring and agitated state of the water a short distance before us indicated a fall or some other obstruction of considerable magnitude. Our boats were consequently rowed to shore, along which we cautiously descended to the place from whence the danger was to be apprehended. It proved to be a perpendicular fall of ten or twelve feet produced by large fragments of rocks which had fallen from the mountain and settled in the river extending entirely across its channel and forming an impregnable barrier to the passage of loaded watercraft.[268] We were therefore obliged to unload our boats of their cargoes and pass them empty over the falls by means of long cords which we had provided for such purposes. At sunset, our boats were reloaded and we descended a mile lower down and encamped.[269]

[268] They here reached the dangerous Red canyon. For a map of this region, see U.S. Geological survey, *Marsh Peak quadrangle* (topographic sheet).

[269] Ashley falls in Red canyon. All who have navigated this dangerous passage have noted the ominous roar that greets the ear on approaching the defile, Powell, *op. cit.*, 16 ff; Dellenbaugh, *op. cit.*, 22. Powell and Kolb were obliged to resort to the use of lines to lower their boats before reaching this point, Powell, *op. cit.*, 15; Dellenbaugh, *op. cit.*, 24; Kolb, *op. cit.*, 31. One of Powell's boats upset in Red canyon on his second expedition, 1871. In the upper rapids Theodore Hook of Cheyenne, Wyoming, who attempted to follow Powell, was drowned in 1869. He and his party set out to descend the river in flat-bottomed boats. Hook was buried in the canyon, Dellenbaugh, *Canyon voyage*, 25; also, *Romance of the Colorado*, 249.

While encamped at this place, Ashley inscribed his name in paint on the cliffs by the river, "Ashley—1825." This inscription has had an interesting history and has given rise to much curious speculation. Powell (*op. cit.*, 17) found it in 1869 but could not make out the third figure, some of his party reading it "3," others "5." Powell (*op. cit.*, 27) relates the fate of Ashley thus:

MONDAY, 4TH : this day we made about forty miles.[270] The navigation and mountains by which the river is bounded continues pretty much the same as yesterday. These mountains appear to be almost entirely composed of stratas of rock of various colours (mostly red) and are partially covered with a dwarfish growth of pine and cedar, which are the only species of timber to be seen.

TUESDAY, 5TH : after descending six miles, the mountains gradually recede from the water's edge, and the river expands to the width of two hundred and fifty yards, leaving the river bottoms on each side from one to three hundred yards wide interspersed with clusters

Suffering a wreck further down the river in which all of his companions save one were drowned, Ashley and the other survivor "climbed the canyon walls and found their way across the Wasatch mountains to Salt Lake City, living chiefly on berries, as they wandered through an unknown and difficult country. When they arrived at Salt Lake, they were almost destitute of clothing and nearly starved. The Mormon people gave them food and clothing and employed them at the foundation of the temple, until they had earned sufficient to enable them to leave the country." The Powell party saw the inscription again in 1871. See Dellenbaugh, *Romance of the Colorado,* 112, where it is reproduced. William L. Manly, who came through the canyon in 1849, saw the inscription. In his narrative he writes, "While I was looking up toward the mountain top [at the site of Ashley's camp] and along down the rocky wall, I saw a smooth place about fifty feet above, where the great rocks had broken out there, painted in large black letters, were the words, 'Ashley, 1824.' This was the first real evidence we had of the presence of a white man in this wild place, and from this record it seems that twenty-five years before, some venturesome man had here inscribed his name. I have since heard there were some persons in St. Louis of this name, and of some circumstances which may link them with this early traveller."—Manly, W. L., *Death valley in 1849,* 80. Kolb (*op. cit.,* 39) says, "There were three letters, A-S-H, the first two quite distinct, and underneath were two black spots. It must have been pretty good paint to leave a trace after eighty-six years." This was in 1911.

[270] This is an exaggeration due perhaps to the velocity with which they traveled. The entire length of Red canyon is only twenty-five and two-thirds miles; judging from the distance made the following day in reaching Brown's Hole, they must have camped somewhere near the mouth of Park creek, where there is an excellent site. See Powell, *op. cit.,* 21 and map.

of small willows.[271] We remained at our encampment of this day until the morning of the 7th, when we descended ten miles lower down and encamped on a spot of ground where several throusand Indians had wintered during the past season.[272] Their camp had been judiciously selected for defence, and the remains of their work around it accorded with the judgment exercised in the selection. Many of their lodges remained as perfect as when occupied. They were made of poles two or three inches in diameter, set up in circular form, and covered with cedar bark.

FRIDAY, THE 8TH: we proceeded down the river about two miles, where it again enters between two mountains and affording a channel even more contracted than before. As we passed along between these

[271] Brown's Hole, afterwards a very famous valley. According to Dellenbaugh (*Romance of the Colorado*, 112), Ashley ended his journey at this point. "Here," says Dellenbaugh, "they discovered Provo encamped with an abundance of provisions, so their troubles were quickly over. The opening they had arrived at was probably Brown's Hole. There is only one other place that might be called an opening, and this is a small park-like break on the right side of the river, not far above Brown's Hole, previously called Little Brown's Hole and also Ashley park. The Ashley men would have had a hard climb to get out of this place, and it is not probable that Provo would have climbed into it, as no beaver existed there. It seems positive, then, that Ashley came to Provo in Brown's Hole. Thus he did not 'make his perilous way through Brown's Hole,' as one author says [Chittenden, *American fur trade*, I, 274], because he ended his journey with the beginning of that peaceful park . . . Provo had plenty of horses, and Ashley and his men joined him, going out to Salt Lake, where Provo had come from." Dellenbaugh's animadversion at Chittenden was probably occasioned by the latter's sneer at Powell's surmise regarding the identity of Ashley, Chittenden, *op. cit.,* I, 275. As a matter of fact, both Chittenden and Dellenbaugh are mistaken in their narratives of Ashley's movements, 1824-1825, including the descent of Green river, and in both cases the error is attributable to a too great confidence in Jim Beckwourth, who, as he himself says, did not accompany Ashley on this portion of his expedition.

Ashley camped twelve miles above the canyon of Lodore, near the present Bridgeport.

[272] Probably a band of Utes. The Utes are of Shoshonean stock and were frequently confused with the Snakes by early travelers.

massy walls, which in a great degree exclude from us the rays of heaven and presented a surface as impassable as their body was impregnable, I was forcibly struck with the gloom which spread over the countenances of my men; they seemed to anticipate (and not far distant, too) a dreadful termination of our voyage, and I must confess that I partook in some degree of what I supposed to be their feelings, for things around us had truly an awful appearance. We soon came to a dangerous rapid which we passed over with a slight injury to our boats.[273] A mile lower down, the channel became so obstructed by the intervention of large rocks over and between which the water dashed with such violence as to render our passage in safety impracticable. The cargoes of our boats were therefore a second time taken out and carried about two hundred yards, to which place, after much labor, our boats were descended by means of cords.[274] Thence we descended fifty (50) miles

[273] This is the first rapid of Lodore, really a series of four. Powell had difficulty here on his first expediiton, Powell, *op. cit.*, 22. On his second trip he ran the first rapid without difficulty, Dellenbaugh, *Canyon voyage*, 34. Kolb (*op. cit.*, 51) ran these without difficulty but in the month of september.

[274] Disaster falls, so named on his first voyage by Powell, who lost one of his boats here. Just below the falls Powell discovered a dutch oven, some tin plates, a part of a boat, and many other fragments, "which," says he, "denote that this is the place where Ashley's party was wrecked." As a matter of fact these articles were probably the remains of a camp made at this point in 1849. Some unknown party descended the river thus far, presumably en route to California. Says Manly (*Death valley in 1849*, 84), "We found a deserted camp, a skiff and some heavy cooking utensils with a notice posted on an alder tree saying that they had found the river route impracticable, and being satisfied that the river was so full of rocks and boulders that it could not be safely navigated, they had abandoned the undertaking and were about to start overland to make their way to Salt Lake. I put down the names of the party at the time in my diary, which has since been burned." The legibility of the sign, with the general description given by Manly, clearly indicates that these articles had been abandoned only recently. Powell saw these remains twenty-six years after.

Every expedition that has passed these rapids has had to use lines.

From this point, Ashley's narrative seems to be a summary of his journal,

to the mouth of a beautiful river emptying on each side, to which I gave the name of Mary's river.[275] The navigation continued dangerous and difficult the whole way; the mountains equally lofty and rugged with their summits entirely covered with snow. Mary's river is one hundred yards wide, has a rapid current, and from every appearance very much confined between lofty mountains. A valley about two hundred yards wide extends one mile below the confluence of these rivers, then the mountain again on that side advances to the water's edge.[276] Two miles lower down is a very dangerous rapid, and eight miles further the mountain withdraws from the river on the west side about a half mile. Here we found a luxurious growth of sweet-bark or round-leaf cottonwood and a number of buffaloe, and succeeded by narrow river bottoms and hills. The former, as well as several islands, are partly clothed with a luxuriant growth of round-leaf cottonwood and extend four miles down the river, where the mountains again close to the water's edge and are in appearance more terrific than any we had seen during the whole voyage.[277] They immediately produce bad rapids,

rather than a series of extracts quoted verbatim. Beginning with the words, "to which place," the writing continues in a different hand.

[275] Through the remainder of Lodore canyon, including the difficult and dangerous "Hell's Half-mile," which Ashley does not even mention. His journal reads "fifty miles," certainly a mistake. The copyist may have misread "fifteen," which would be very nearly correct. The total length of Lodore canyon is twenty and three-fourths miles; the drop in that distance four hundred twenty feet, Dellenbaugh, *Canyon voyage*, 48. Mary's river is the Yampa, known also to the early trappers as Bear river, the first tributary of any magnitude entering the Green river from the east, which very markedly increases the volume of that stream. On Fremont's map a hypothetical Mary's river joins Green river above Brown's Hole.

[276] A very accurate description of Echo park at the confluence of the Yampa with the Green. See Powell, *op. cit.*, 32; Dellenbaugh, *op. cit.*, 49.

[277] Whirlpool canyon, really a series of rapids, totaling fourteen miles, Kolb, *op. cit.*, 77. Powell was forced to resort to ropes at this point on his

which follow in quick succession for twenty miles, below which, as far as I descended, the river is without obstruction. In the course of our passage through the several ranges of mountains, we performed sixteen portages, the most of which were attended with the utmost difficulty and labor. At the termination of the rapids, the mountains on each side of the river gradually recede,[278] leaving in their retreat a hilly space of five or six miles, through which the river meanders in a west direction about (70) seventy miles, receiving in that distance several contributions from small streams on each side, the last of which is called by the Indians Tewinty river.[279] It empties on the north side, is about (60) sixty yards wide, several feet deep, with a bold current.

I concluded to ascend this river on my route returning, therefore deposited the cargoes of my boats in the ground near it, and continued my descent of the main river fifty miles to the point marked 5 on the topographical sketch sent you.[280] The whole of that distance

first expedition. The withdrawal of the mountains forms Island park, a charming enclosure, so called by Powell, who, like Ashley, noted the wooded islands, Powell, op. cit., 37, 38; Dellenbaugh, op. cit., 56. See Kolb, op. cit., 78. Kolb remarks the presence of the cottonwoods. According to Dellenbaugh the actual length of the valley is only about four miles, but the river meanders a course of nine.

278 These are the rapids of Split-mountain canyon. The Powell expedition used ropes to negotiate them on both journeys, Powell, op. cit., 40; Dellenbaugh, op. cit., 58 ff. The actual length of the canyon proper is only nine miles, Kolb, op. cit., 79. Island park and Split-mountain canyon total eighteen miles, which may be what Ashley had in mind when he said twenty miles.

279 Tewinty is the Uinta, which enters Green river, as Ashley says, about seventy miles, as the river flows, below Split-mountain canyon. One of the affluents mentioned by Ashley above the Uinta is called Ashley's fork. The town of Ouray, Utah, is at the mouth of the Uinta river.

280 All efforts to locate the topographical sketch, here referred to, have been in vain. None of the offices of the war department, to which it was undoubtedly transmitted, have any record of it.

the river is bounded by lofty mountains heaped together
in the greatest disorder, exhibiting a surface as barren
as can be imagined.[281] This part of the country is almost
entirely without game. We saw a few mountain-sheep
and some elk, but they were so wild, and the country
so rugged that we found it impossible to approach
them. On my way returning to Tewinty river, I met a
part of the Eutau tribe of Indians, who appeared very
glad to see us and treated us in the most respectful and
friendly manner. These people were well dressed in
skins, had some guns, but armed generally with bows
and arrows and such other instruments of war as are
common among the Indians of the Missouri. Their
horses were better than Indian horses generally are
east of the mountains and more numerous in proportion

[281] Desolation canyon. Just below the mouth of the Uinta Ashley passed
the mouth of White river entering from the east. He was now in a country
penetrated once or perhaps twice before by white men. Nearly fifty years
before Dominguez and Escalante, Spanish Franciscans, in their attempt to
pass by a northern route from Santa Fe to Monterey, crossed White river
some distance above its confluence with the Green, and then crossed Green
river itself, near the lower end of Split-mountain canyon. Escalante, in his
journal under date september 13, 1776 (printed in English translation in
Harris, *The Catholic church in Utah,* 164), in speaking of Green river (San
Buenaventura) says that it is "the same one that Fray Alonso de Posada says
in his report separates the Yuta nation from the Comanche, if we may judge
by Alonso de Posada" who was *custodio* of New Mexico, 1660-1664,
Twitchell, *Leading facts of New Mexican history,* I, 345. He wrote, about
1686, a report, *Informe a S. M. sobre las tierras de Nuevo Mejico, Quivira,
y Teguayo.* According to H. H. Bancroft (*History of Arizona and New
Mexico,* 21) his name has been misspelled Paredes. Harris (*op. cit.,* 60)
states that he was dispatched by Governor Tomas Veles Cachupin in 1763
to explore the country north of New Mexico. Cachupin was governor of
New Mexico 1749-1754 and again 1762-1767, a man much disliked by the
Franciscans. He did, to be sure, send expeditions northwest as far as the
Gunnison country in search of precious metals, but certainly not under
Alonso de Posada. Posada is not among the many sources utilized by Alexander von Humboldt, a list of which is given in his *Political essay on the
kingdom of New Spain,* translated by John Black, I, lvi-lxiv. Dominguez
and Escalante found the course of Green river to be southwest, and they
apparently followed it to the mouth of White river (Rio San Clemente).

to the number of persons. I understood (by signs) from
them that the river which I had descended, and which
I supposed to be the Rio Colorado of the West, continued its course as far as they had any knowledge of
it, southwest through a mountainous country.[282] They
also informed me that all the country known to them
from south to west from Tewinty river was almost entirely destitute of game, that the Indians inhabiting that
region subsist principally on roots, fish and horses. The
Eutaus are part of the original Snake nation of Indians.
They have no fixed place of residence but claim a district of country which (according to their representation) is about one hundred and fifty miles long by one
hundred miles wide, to which their situation at that
time was nearly central.[283].

I purchased a few horses of the Eutaus, returned to
Tewinty river and ascended to its extreme sources, distant from its mouth about seventy miles, in general
bearing W.N.W. and S.S.E.; [it] runs through a mountainous sterile country.[284] From the head waters of

---

[282] This, of course, disposes of the theory that Ashley was met in Green
River valley by Provot (Dellenbaugh, *Romance of the Colorado,* 112; Chittenden, *American fur trade,* I, 275) or that he met with shipwreck, or that
he surmised that he was on a stream that would conduct him back to St.
Louis. He knew that he was on the Rio Colorado of the West and he intended to return to his rendezvous after exploring it a bit. Chittenden says
(*op. cit.,* II, 779 footnote), "At the time that Ashley and his men entered the
valley of Green river in 1824, it was supposed to flow into the Gulf of
Mexico. Various hints in the correspondence of the times show this to be the
case, and it is even averred that General Ashley thought so when he started
to descend the river in a canoe in 1825. It is certain, however, that the
Astorians knew the identity of the stream, 1811-1812, for they called it the
Colorado, or Spanish river." So did Ashley.

[283] Ute Indians. The Utes occupied the region comprised within central
and western Colorado and eastern Utah. They obtained horses at an early
date and became famous for their skill in handling them. U.S. Bureau of
ethnology *seventh annual report* (1885-1886), 109.

[284] Ashley followed up the Uinta and its main affluent, the Duchesne. At
the forks, near the present Stockmore, he naturally selected the right-hand

Tewinty river, I crossed a range of lofty mountains nearly E. and W., which divide the waters of the Rio Colorado from those which I have represented as the Beaunaventura. This range of mountains is in many places fertile and closely timbered with pine, cedar, quaking-asp, and a dwarfish growth of oak; a great number of beautiful streams issue from them on each side, running through fertile valleys richly clothed with grass. I proceeded down the waters of the Beaunaventura about sixty miles bordered with a growth of willow almost impenetrable. In that distance I crossed several streams from 20 to 60 yards wide running in various directions. All of them, as I am informed, unite in one in the course of 30 miles, making a river of considerable magnitude, which enters a few miles lower down a large lake, represented on your sketch as Lake Tempagono.[285] This information was communi-

fork, as being the larger and affording the easier passage. He slightly over-estimated the distance to the headwaters of the Duchesne. Dominguez and Escalante followed this route up these streams, but at the site of the present town of Theodore, Wasatch county, Utah abandoned the main stream of the Duchesne to follow up the Strawberry and thence across the Wasatch range to Utah lake. At the confluence of the Duchesne and Uinta a trading-post was constructed by Antoine Robidoux, perhaps not long after Ashley's visit, Chittenden, *American fur trade*, III, 971. The Hudson's Bay company at a later period undertook to penetrate this country. Sir William Drummond Stewart in a letter to William L. Sublette, dated Head of Blue fork, august 27, 1838, writes, "The H. B. company have established a fort on the Wintey [Uinta] and Andy's people [the men in the employ of Andrew Drips, agent of the American Fur company] will be driven from here, if the government does not take some steps."—Sublette MSS., carton 12, Missouri historical society.

285 Ashley crossed the lofty Uintah range in the vicinity of Bald peak. The waters of the Buenaventura, on which he found himself after crossing the divide, are the tributaries of Weber river. The drainage area is indeed complicated, and he must have been confused by the various directions the streams pursued. Not all those that he crossed, however, united to form the Weber. Some of them are the head branches of Bear river, which, of course, only reaches Great Salt lake after a long and circuitous course. He may very well, too, have crossed the upper waters of Black's fork, a tributary

cated to me by our hunters who (as I before told) had crossed to this region in the summer of 1824 and wintered on and near the borders of this lake.[286] They had not explored the lake sufficiently to judge correctly of its extent, but from their own observations and information collected from Indians, they supposed it to be about eighty miles long by fifty broad. They represented it as a beautiful sheet of water deep, transparent, and a little brackish, though in this latter quality the accounts differ; some insist that it is not brackish.[287] I

---

of Green river, which he had just left. The mighty Buenaventura, which according to tradition entered the Pacific in the vicinity of San Francisco, has now dwindled to the rather insignificant Weber. Lake Tempagono (*sic*) is confounded with the Timpanogos of Dominguez and Escalante, who understood by that name the freshwater Utah lake of today. Chittenden (*American fur trade*, I, 275) is, of course, wrong in saying that, after meeting Provot in Green River valley, "the united parties now made their way westward across the Wasatch mountains into the Salt Lake valley." Ashley, however, had excellent reasons for calling the stream which he struck, the Buenaventura. *The map of the United States*, by William Darby (New York, 1818), shows the S. Buenaventura flowing into Lake Timpanogos. Carey [*General atlas* (Philadelphia, 1814), 29] shows the R. de Buenaventura entering not Lake Timpanogos (shown) but Great Salt lake, confusing it in part with the Sevier. C. V. Lavoisne [*Atlas* (Philadelphia, 1821), map 68, drawn by John Melish, and copied from an earlier map of 1816 by the same cartographer] shows the R. Buenaventura flowing into a large lake with an indeterminate western shore, out of which flows a hypothetical stream westward into San Francisco bay. John Thomson [*New and general atlas* (Edinburgh, 1817), map 58] shows the R. de S. Buenaventura rising in latitude 41°, longitude 108°, and flowing west into a large unnamed lake with an indeterminate western and southern shore line. Anthony Finley [*New and general atlas* (Philadelphia, 1826), map 31] shows the R. Buenaventura flowing into a Salt lake and out of it again at its southwest extremity, westward into San Francisco bay. To the north of this Salt lake he places Lake Tempanogos.

How far Ashley followed the upper Weber is uncertain, but he reached a point thirty miles below which these tributaries united and, a few miles lower down, entered a large lake. This would indicate that he advanced about to the Kamas Prairie, a charming mountain park, just east of Park City, Summit county, Utah.

286 See page 162 f.

287 Precisely. The reference here is to the descent of Bear river by James Bridger in a skin canoe. At the mouth of this stream the salinity of the

met several small parties of Eutaw Indians on this side
of the last mentioned range of mountains, 100 miles
long bearing about W.N.W. and S.S.E. [who said] that
a large river flowing out of it on the west end runs in a
western direction, but they know nothing of its discharge into the ocean or of the country any considerable
distance west of the lake. I also conversed with some
very intelligent men who I found with our hunters in
the vicinity of this lake and who had been for many
years in the service of the Hudson Bay Fur company.[288]
Some of them profess to be well acquainted with all
the principal waters of the Columbia, with which they
assured me these waters had no connection short of the
ocean. It appears from this information that the river is
not the Multnomah, a southern branch of the Columbia, which I first supposed it to be.[289] The necessity of

water varies with the season of the year. In the spring, when Bear river
is high, there is almost no trace of salt, but later in the season, Bear River
bay, as the northeastern arm of the lake is called, is noticeably salt, partly
due to the alkali in the lake itself and partly to the noxious waters of Malade
river, which joins Bear river a short distance above its mouth.

[288] The men who had been employed since 1819 on the Snake river expeditions of the Northwest and later the Hudson's Bay companies. For a
discussion of the extent of their explorations see page 42 ff. These are the
men who, at rendezvous, disposed of their furs to Ashley.

[289] According to the geographic ideas prevalent in Ashley's day, the
Multnomah was supposed sometimes to be a large tributary of the Columbia,
paralleling Snake river but a considerable distance to the south, entering the
Columbia below the mouth of the Snake. On the Carey map the Multnomah
rises in the Rockies and flows northwestward through the Sierras and into
the Columbia. On the Melish map the Multnomah rises in longitude 111°,
flows west, and is joined by a river from a large lake unnamed (corresponding to Lake Timpanagos of other maps) into the Columbia. The upper course
of the Multnomah is called R. de San Clementini on this map. Similarly,
Map 3 of *A complete historical, chronological, and geographical American
atlas,* intended as a companion to Lavoisne's edition of Le Sage's *Atlas*
(Philadelphia, 1822). "The Columbia and the Multnomah, its southern
branch, . . . after flowing toward each other, the one, a thousand, and the
other, nearly fifteen hundred miles, break through and find their way to the
sea, uniting their waters about sixty miles from it. The distance from the

my unremitted attention to my business prevented me
from gratifying a great desire to descend this river to
the ocean, which I ultimately declined with the greatest
reluctance.[290] The country drained by these waters,
which is about one hundred and twenty miles wide and
bounded on the north, east and south by three principal
and conspicuous mountains, is beautifully diversified
with hills, mountains, valleys, and bold running streams
and is in parts fertile. The northern part of it is well
supplied with buffaloe, elk, bear, antelope, and mountain-sheep. The country east and a considerable distance north of these lakes,[291] including the headwaters
of the Rio Colorado of the West and down the same to
Mary's river, is claimed by the Shoshone Indians. The
men in my employ here have had but little intercourse
with these people. So far they had been treated by them
in the most friendly manner. They had, however, some
time in the fall of 1824, attacked and killed several of
our citizens who had crossed from Taus and were
trading on the —— ——.[292]

---

sources of the Columbia to that of the Multnomah, which rises with the
Colorado of California, is not less than two thousand miles."—Brackenridge,
H. M., *Views of Louisiana*, 95. The non-existence of the Multnomah, or
rather, its identity (if identity it can really be called) with the Willamette
was shown on the Parker map of 1838, embodying data derived from
Jedediah S. Smith's explorations.

290 See footnote 285. Ashley, accordingly, did not "on this occasion" make
his explorations "south of Great Salt lake" and "as far as Sevier lake."—
Chittenden, *American fur trade*, I, 276. As a matter of fact, Ashley never
visited Great Salt lake but once, in the summer of 1826.

291 The first use of the plural in the narrative. Ashley must have been
advised of the existence of Utah lake and probably also Bear lake as well
as Great Salt lake.

292 This very probably refers to the attack on a party of men under
Joseph Robidoux alluded to in the *Missouri intelligencer* of april 19, 1825,
"William Heddest, who went to Santa Fe in one of the trading companies
last winter has just returned having left Taos, january twelfth. He says . . .
in August, he with fourteen others left Taos, to trap beaver and traveled
west thirty days," reaching Green river. Here the company separated, nine

On the 1st day of july, all the men in my employ or
with whom I had any concern in the country, together
with twenty-nine, who had recently withdrawn from
the Hudson Bay company, making in all 120 men, were
assembled in two camps near each other about 20 miles
distant from the place appointed by me as a general
rendezvous,[293] when it appeared that we had been

ascending the river. "Our informant was among those who remained and
in a few days they accidentally fell in with five other Americans among them,
Mr. Rubideau [sic]." Two days after, a party of Arapahos attacked them,
killed one man, Nowlin, and robbed the others. A party of six of them then
concluded to return to Taos, leaving Robidoux and his men in the mountains
without a single horse or mule. Compare also the report of William Gordon
to Lewis Cass, 1831, where occurs the following, "The same year [1824]
eight of Nolidoux [sic] men were killed by Comanches."—U.S. Senate,
Executive documents, 22 cong., 1 sess., 11, no. 90. According to Chittenden
(*American fur trade,* 11, 507) who summarizes the article in the *Missouri
intelligencer,* the Green river mentioned by Heddest (Huddart, the name
becomes in Chittenden) is the same which Ashley himself descended. The
origin of the name Green river, applied to the Rio Colorado of the West,
is uncertain. According to Bancroft (*History of Utah,* 21) it was so called
in honor of one Green, an employee of Ashley. Fremont (*op. cit.,* 129) says
that the Spanish early knew it by this name. In the *Missouri intelligencer,*
june 25, 1825, it is stated that Captain William Becknell left Santa Cruz in
november 1824 with nine men to trap on Green river, several hundred miles
from Santa Fe, and that on the way they met several parties of poor and
inoffensive Indians, who, however, it was afterward reported, had murdered
several of Provot's men and robbed the remainder. The reference here is
probably to the lower course of Green river, even below the lowest point
reached by Ashley. The probability that the attack on the party from Taos,
referred to by Ashley on a river *whose name was unknown to him,* actually
took place on the stream he had himself descended, is strengthened by the
fact that Robidoux is known to have trapped in the vicinity of the Gunnison and Uncompaghre, tributaries of the Green as early as 1825, having
left Fort Atkinson september 30, 1824. Kennerly, James, "Journal," Kennerly
MSS., Missouri historical society. The old Spanish trail (the route of Dominguez and Escalante) would have brought Robidoux into the drainage
area of Grand river. It was not unusual, a little later, to proceed thus from
Taos to the middle stretch of Green river, and the route was then thoroughly
familiar to Robidoux, Sage, *Rocky mountain life,* 228.

[293] Beckwourth states that the rendezvous was transferred from the place
selected at the "Suck," i.e. at the mouth of Henry's fork, *up* that stream to
a point where the Hudson's Bay people had agreed to meet them. He adds
that there were two hundred men present, Bonner, *op. cit.,* 73.

scattered over the territory west of the mountains in small detachments from the 38th to the 44th degree of latitude, and the only injury we had sustained by Indian depredations was the stealing of 17 horses by the Crows on the night of the 2nd april, as before mentioned, and the loss of one man killed on the headwaters of the Rio Colorado, by a party of Indians unknown.

Mr. Jedediah Smith, a very intelligent and confidential young man, who had charge of a small detachment, stated that he had, in the fall of 1824, crossed from the headwaters of the Rio Colorado to Lewis' fork of the Columbia and down the same about one hundred miles, thence northwardly to Clark's fork of the Columbia, where he found a trading establishment of the Hudson Bay company, where he remained for some weeks.[294] Mr. Smith ascertained from the gentleman [295] who had charge of that establishment, that the Hudson Bay company had then in their employment, trading with the Indians and trapping beaver on both sides of the Rocky mountains, about 80 men, 60 of whom were generally employed as trappers and confined their operations to that district called the Snake country, which Mr. Smith understood as being confined to the district claimed by the Shoshone Indians. It appeared from the account, that they had taken in the last four years within that district eighty thousand beaver, equal to one hundred and sixty thousand pounds of furs.[296]

You can form some idea of the quantity of beaver that country once possessed, when I tell you that some of our hunters had taken upwards of one hundred in the last spring hunt out of streams which had been trapped, as I am informed, every season for the last four years.

[294] Salish House.
[295] Peter Skene Ogden.
[296] See page 95.

It appears from Mr. Smith's account that there is no scarcity of buffalo as he penetrated the country. As Mr. Smith returned, he inclined — — west and fell on the waters of the Grand lake or Beaunaventura.[297] He describes the country in that direction as admitting a free and easy passage and abounding in salt. At one place particularly hundreds of bushels might have been collected from the surface of the earth within a small space. He gave me some specimens, which equal in appearance and quality the best Liverpool salt. Mr. S. also says the buffaloe are very plenty as far as he penetrated the country over it in almost any direction.

On the 2nd day of july, I set out on my way homewards with 50 men, 25 of whom were to accompany me to a navigable point of the Big Horn river, thence to return with the horses employed in the transportation of the furs.[298] I had forty-five packs of beaver cached

---

[297] It is uncertain in what month of the winter of 1824-1825 Bridger descended Bear river to Great Salt lake. Robert Campbell's claim of Bridger's discovery would seem to indicate that he reached it before Smith. If the latter's sojourn of "some weeks" at Flathead House means that he remained only till very early spring, it may indicate that Bridger and his companions descended Bear river in the late fall of 1824, after establishing themselves for the winter in Cache valley.

[298] According to Ashley rendezvous lasted only one day. He met his men on the first of july and departed on the second. Beckwourth says it lasted "about a week," Bonner, op. cit., 76. It is noteworthy that there is no definite entry of date in Ashley's narrative from the eighth of may to the first of july. Leaving Brown's Hole, may eighth, he had ample time to descend Green river to the Uinta, thence seventy miles farther down the Green and back to the Uinta, up that stream and the Duchesne, and across the divide to the waters of Weber river by the first of july. Beckwourth states that he was accompanied on his return by fifty men; twenty, including Beckwourth, himself, to continue the entire distance with Ashley, and thirty to act as a guard to the place of navigation, whence they were to return to the mountains with the horses, which, he adds, were borrowed from the Hudson's Bay people. Kearny states that Ashley descended the Missouri with twenty-two men, Kearny, S. W., "Journal," entry of august 27, Kearny MSS., Missouri historical society. Smith accompanied him.

a few miles east of our direct route.[299] I took with me 20 men, passed by the place, raised the cache, and proceeded in a direction to join the other party, but, previous to joining them, I was twice attacked by Indians, first by a party of Blackfeet about 60 in number. They made their appearance at the break of day, yelling in the most hideous manner and using every means in their power to alarm our horses, which they so effectually did that the horses, although closely hobbled, broke by the guard and ran off. A part of the Indians being mounted, they succeeded in getting all the horses except two, and wounded one man.[300] An attempt was also made to take our camp, but in that they failed. The following night, I sent an express to secure horses from the party of our men who had taken a direct route. In two days thereafter, I received the desired aid and again proceeded on my way, made about ten miles, and encamped upon an eligible situation. That night, about 12 o'clock, we were again attacked by a war party of Crow Indians, which resulted in the loss of one of the Indians killed and another shot through the body, without any injury to us.[301] The next day I joined my other

[299] This may have been the cache left by Thomas Fitzpatrick on his descent of the Platte in the summer of 1824.

[300] Presumably one of the attacks mentioned by Beckwourth, which he misdates by placing before rendezvous. While Beckwourth, acting under orders from Ashley, was conducting a detachment to rendezvous, he was attacked by Indians, soon after which he met another detachment of Ashley's men which had likewise been attacked. In the former Beckwourth distinguished himself, he says, receiving a wound in the left arm; but this is another perversion of the facts to the greater glory of Jim Beckwourth. If he can be accepted at all on this affair, the wounded man mentioned by Ashley was either Beckwourth himself or William Sublette. Beckwourth also mentions the loss of the horses, Bonner, *op. cit.*, 74.

[301] Beckwourth mentions the night attack by the Crows, giving the Indian casualties as one killed and one shot through the body. He also misdates this, however, by placing it previous to their departure from rendezvous.

party and proceeded direct to my place of embarkation just below the Big Horn mountain, where I arrived on the 7th day of august.

On my passage thither, I discovered nothing remarkable in the features of the country. It affords generally a smooth way to travel over. The only very rugged part of the route is in crossing the Big Horn mountain, which is about 30 miles wide. I had the Big Horn river explored from Wind River mountain to my place of embarkation.[302] There is little or no difficulty in the navigation of that river from its mouth to Wind River mountain.[303] It may be ascended that far at a tolerable

---

He adds a second, but bloodless, encounter with the Crows en route to the Big Horn. He further states that on the sixth day out, in the vicinity of the South pass, one of the party, named Baptiste, "having a portion of a buffalo on his horse, came across a small stream flowing near the trail, where he halted to get a drink." While stopping to drink, a grizzly bear sprang upon him and lacerated him in a shocking manner, Bonner, *op. cit.*, 76 ff. This story is confirmed by S. W. Kearny ("Journal," Kearny MSS., 50, Missouri historical society).

[302] On reaching the point of embarkation on the Big Horn, five days were spent constructing boats in which to descend the stream, Bonner, *op. cit.*, 81.

[303] Ashley followed the route of the Oregon trail, already traveled by Fitzpatrick, and, in part, by Bridger, Sublette, and Smith, through the South pass to the upper stretches of the Sweetwater, thence north, perhaps down the Little Popo Agie to its confluence with Wind river and down the latter to the point where it enters the Big Horn mountains to emerge on the other side as the Big Horn river. At the head of the canyon he dispatched a party to proceed down the stream by boat, while he, with the remainder of the company, crossed the mountains, rejoining his men just below the site of Thermopolis. The distance across the Big Horn mountains he places accurately at thirty miles. James Bridger may have been one of the party who navigated the canyon, for he told Lieutenant Raynolds in 1859 that he once went through on a raft, Raynolds, W. F., "Report on the exploration of the Yellowstone river" in U.S. Senate, *Executive documents,* 40 cong., 2 sess., no. 77. Ashley probably selected this route for his return in preference to the one he had followed coming out in order to avail himself of water transportation, which was more expeditious and secure *down stream,* and for which his men could construct their own boats. He might have gone down the North Platte in this manner, but Fitzpatrick's unfortunate mishap, the previous fall, together with his own experiences with canyons and rapids no doubt induced him to take no chances with torrential streams. He had with

stage of water with a boat drawing three feet water. The Yellowstone river is a beautiful river to navigate. It has rapids extending from above Powder river about fifty miles but I found about four feet water over the most.[304]

The Yellowstone expedition, under command of General Atkinson, had been dispatched to conclude a series of treaties with the tribes of the upper Missouri. On july 2, the day Ashley left his rendezvous, the expedition had reached the mouth of the Teton river. On august 7, the date of Ashley's embarkation on the Big Horn, they were just leaving the Mandan villages, and ten days later they camped a little beyond the mouth of the Yellowstone at the site of Henry's abandoned post.[305] On the nineteenth, as if by prearrange-

him, also, a very valuable collection of furs, which made safety the first consideration. At the Yellowstone it may have occurred to him that he could secure government protection for the remainder of the way by descending with the so-called Yellowstone expedition. "Aug. 20, Gen'l Ashley (who has determined to detain his party and furs 'til we go below in order to be sure of a safe passage) is with us," Kearny, "Journal," Kearny MSS., Missouri historical society. Last of all, his shortage of horses would induce him to select the water route. After the colossal difficulties encountered in bringing them in, he could scarcely afford to take many of them out again. The horses used to convey his furs to the Big Horn were sent back to the mountains for the use of his trappers or to be returned to the Hudson's Bay men, from whom he is said to have borrowed them.

[304] Ashley descended the Yellowstone, arriving at its mouth august 19 at noon, Kearny, "Journal," Kearny MSS., Missouri historical society; Reeves, L. U., *Life and military services of General William S. Harney*, 67. According to Beckwourth, while the party was attempting to land at the mouth of the Yellowstone, one of the boats was sunk, "on board which was thirty packs of beaver skins, and away they went as rapidly as though they had been live beaver." All was noise and confusion in a minute, the general in a perfect ferment, shouting to his men to save the packs. Fortunately there were good swimmers in the party, who recovered the precious cargo. It was the turmoil and shouting which attracted some of Atkinson's troops in their encampment not far distant and led consequently, to the meeting of the two parties, Bonner, *op. cit.*, 81. Ashley's narrative ends abruptly at this point.

[305] Kearny, "Journal," Kearny MSS., folio 31 ff, Missouri historical society.

ment, Ashley arrived in his keel-boat with a hundred or more packs of beaver skins, valued at from forty to seventy-five thousand dollars.[306] Stephen Watts Kearny, who accompanied the Yellowstone expedition, records his arrival thus

August 19 [1825] Gen'l. Ashley and party arrived today about noon with 100 packs of beaver skins from the mountains. He left Council Bluffs last november and wintered near the headwaters of the Platte. He has met with several nations of Indians and had his horses stolen and his party fired upon by the Blackfeet [sic] and one of his men is severely injured from the attack by the White Bear.[307]

Atkinson had been commissioned to conclude a treaty with the Blackfeet, who, according to Ashley, would probably be found above the Great Falls of the Missouri, in which case they could not be reached with the boats of the expedition. As other tribes might be encountered, however, it was decided to proceed some distance farther up stream. Ashley accompanied them. The party advanced about one hundred twenty miles to the mouth of the Porcupine. Finding, however, no trace of the Blackfeet or other tribes, they turned about and, by the twenty-sixth, were back again at the mouth of the Yellowstone. Next day Ashley embarked his beaver on three government vessels and proceeded down stream, accompanied by Jedediah Smith and a score of the men.[308]

[306] Eighty to one hundred packs, value forty thousand dollars, *Niles register,* november 5, 1825. One hundred thirty packs, value seventy-five thousand dollars, Letter of N. J. Wyeth, november 8, 1833, in Young, *Sources of Oregon history,* I, 74. One hundred packs, Kearny, "Journal," Kearny MSS., folio 50, Missouri historical society. L. U. Reeves (*op. cit.,* 67) gives the value as two hundred thousand dollars.

[307] Kearny, "Journal," Kearny MSS., folio 50, Missouri historical society. See also the reports of General Atkinson and Major O'Fallon to the secretary of war, in U.S. House, *Executive documents,* 19 cong., 1 sess., VI, no. 117.

[308] Atkinson, Henry, "Report," *idem;* Lyman, H. S., *History of Oregon,* III,

"No incident worthy of mention occurred on the way down except the wrecking of the Muskrat on a snag three miles above the mouth of James river. The boat was repaired and Ashley's fur was saved." [309] At Fort Look-out, ten miles above the present Chamberlain, South Dakota, they met Joshua Pilcher, who, according to Beckwourth, manifested his good-will toward Ashley by making him a present of a large grizzly bear for a plaything. Beckwourth states

And a pretty plaything we found him before we were done with him.[310] He was made fast with a chain to the cargo box on deck, and seemed to think himself captain; at any rate, he was more imperious in his orders than a commodore on a foreign station. He would suffer no one on deck, and seemed literally to apply the poet's words to himself,

> "I am monarch of all I survey,
>   My right there is none to dispute."

When they reached St. Louis and

After the peltry was all landed and stored, the bear still occupied his station. Hundreds were yet gazing at him, many of whom had never seen one of the kind before. The general said to me, "James, how, under the sun, are we to get that animal off the boat?" I, having a few glasses of "artificial courage" to back me, felt exceedingly valorous, and thought myself able to throw a mill-stone across the Mississippi. Accordingly, I volunteered to bring him ashore. I procured a light stick, walked straight up to the bear, and, speaking very sharp to him (as he had to us all the way down the river), deliberately unfastened his chain. He looked me in the eyes for a moment, and, giving a low whine, drooped his head. I led him off the boat along a staging prepared for the purpose, the crowd instantly falling back to a respectful distance. Landing him without accident, the general

61; De Bow, J. B., *Industrial resources*, III, 517; *Niles register*, november 6, 1830.

[309] Bonner, *op. cit.*, 83. The catastrophe occurred september 13, Kearny, "Journal," Kearny MSS., folio 54, Missouri historical society.

[310] Bonner, *op. cit.*, 85.

wished me to lead him to the residence of Major Biddle, distant a quarter of a mile from the landing. Courageous as ever, I led him on, though some of the time he would lead his leader, Bruin often looking round at the crowd that was following up at a prudent distance behind. I arrived safe at the residence, and made Grizzly fast to an apple-tree that stood there. I had scarcely got to the length of his chain, when he made a furious spring at me; the chain, very fortunately, was a strong one, and held him fast.

I then called at the major's house, and, delivering our general's compliments to him, informed him he had sent a *pet* for his acceptance. He inquired what kind of a *pet,* and, taking him to the tree where I had made fast the bear, I showed the huge beast to him. The major almost quaked with fear. While we stood looking at him, a small pig happened to pass near the bear, when Grizzly dealt him such a blow with his paw that he left him not a whole bone in his body, and piggy fell dead out of the bear's reach.

The major invited me in, and, setting out some of his *best,* I drank his health according to the custom of those days, and left to rejoin my companions.

On the nineteenth of september the combined companies reached Council Bluffs.[311] Three days later Ashley and Smith departed for St. Louis, where they arrived about the eighth of october. Twenty miles above the city, at St. Charles, Ashley dispatched a courier to his financial agents, Wahndorf and Tracy, informing them of his great success and of his imminent arrival. A veritable celebration greeted them. Beckwourth says,

We were saluted by a piece of artillery, which continued its discharges until we landed at the market-place. There were not less than a thousand persons present, who hailed our landing with shouts which deafened our ears.[312]

On disposing of his furs Ashley not only cleared himself of debt but was left with sufficient capital to set

---

311 Kearny, "Journal," Kearny MSS., folio 61, Missouri historical society.

312 Bonner, *op. cit.,* 86. For two days Beckwourth drank at the general's expense.

about preparing another expedition for the following spring, the last which he personally accompanied.[313] This expedition and his further connection with the fur-trade may be briefly summarized.

He left St. Louis in march 1826 with a hundred horses and mules and fifty men, accompanied by Jedediah Smith, Moses (Black) Harris, and William Sublette, the latter having come out of the mountains during the winter, probably by way of the Sweetwater and North Platte.[314] Following his trace of 1824 as far as the forks of the Platte, Ashley there turned up the North Platte, guided by Smith and Sublette, along the main road through the South pass. As spring was approaching, an ample supply of grass was available. Reports of their approach preceded them, and preparations were made by the men left in the mountains the previous year to conduct rendezvous at Great Salt lake.[315] Ashley's route from the South pass lay down the Sandys to Green river, which he followed some distance, and then, crossing the divide, "descended a river, believed to be the Buenaventura, about one hundred and fifty miles to the Great Salt lake." [316]

During his absence Ashley's men had spent the summer of 1825 in trapping on the waters of Salt river, Green river, Bear river, and the tributaries of these streams. Beckwourth, according to his own story, had been sent back by Ashley to the mountains in the late fall of 1825, rejoining the men just as winter was com-

313 Wyeth, N. J., Letter of november 8, 1833, in Young, *Sources of Oregon history*, I, 74.

314 Bonner, *op. cit.,* 96; *Niles register,* december 9, 1826. Among the men were some who later accompanied Jedediah Smith to California, including, perhaps, Harrison G. Rogers.

315 Called by Beckwourth "Weaver" (Weber) lake, Bonner, *op. cit.,* 101.

316 *Niles register,* december 9, 1826. Ashley's Buenaventura was the Weber.

ing on.[317] The parties had separated widely for the fall
hunt but had finally gathered in Cache valley for winter. For some unknown reason, however, William Sublette, who seems to have been in charge, ordered the
men to remove to Great Salt lake. They had, accordingly, moved to the mouth of Weber river, probably
near the site of the present city of Ogden, where they
established themselves for the winter, numbering, with
their Indian comrades, six to seven hundred souls. During the winter they had the misfortune to lose about
eighty horses, stolen by a marauding band of Bannock
Indians. As soon as the loss had been discovered, a party
of forty was selected to follow them on foot. Arriving
before the villages, the small force was divided, Fitzpatrick commanding one contingent and James Bridger
the other. Fitzpatrick's party charged the Indians,
while Bridger's men ran off the horses. With no losses
themselves, they managed to rout the enemy, whose
number Beckwourth placed at from three hundred to
four hundred, and stampeded two to three hundred
horses, some of which the Indians afterward recovered.
When the little force got back to winter quarters, they
still had, however, forty additional horses.

In the spring of 1826 the entire company, together
with the Indians, returned to Cache valley where the
furs were deposited.[318] It was very likely just before
their removal from Great Salt lake that a party of four
men was dispatched to make a closer examination of
the shores of the lake. They were sent to discover any
fur-bearing affluents and to locate the river which was
supposed to flow out of the western side of the lake into
the sea. It took them about twenty-four days to make
the circuit. "They did not exactly ascertain its outlet

[317] Bonner, *op. cit.*, 93 ff.
[318] *Idem*, 96.

but passed a place where they supposed it must have been." [319]

The spring hunt was conducted beyond the interior basin along the tributaries of Snake river as far west as Raft river and thence to Snake river itself and the Portneuf.[320] Here, on the ninth of april, a detachment of twenty-eight fell in with Peter Skene Ogden, commanding the Snake country expedition of the Hudson's Bay company, who recognized among the Americans some of the men who had deserted him the previous year.[321] After camping near each other for two days, the two companies separated, the Americans moving up the Portneuf, the English down the stream.[322] Returning to the interior basin again, Ashley's men were busily engaged on Sage creek, a tributary of Bear river, when they learned from Ashley's couriers of the latter's approach. Hastily packing up, they repaired to Great Salt lake, where they arrived just before Ashley and Sublette.[323]

---

[319] *Niles register,* december 9, 1826. Robert Campbell in a letter of april 4, 1857 to Lieutenant G. K. Warren says, "In the spring of 1826, some men went in skin boats around it [Great Salt lake] to discover if any streams containing beaver were to be found emptying into it, but returned with indifferent success.

"I went to Willow or Cache valley in the spring of 1826 and found the party just returned from the exploration of the lake."—Pacific Railroad *Report,* XI, 35.

This corresponds exactly with Beckwourth's narrative, Bonner, *op. cit.,* 101. Captain Bonneville professed to doubt the genuineness of this exploration, because the men were alleged to have suffered from thirst, although, as a matter of fact, objects Bonneville, there are a number of fine streams entering the lake, Irving, *Rocky mountain sketches,* I, 208 ff. J. H. Simpson (*Report of exploration across the great basin,* 16, note k) sufficiently answers Bonneville's objections, citing Howard Stansbury, *Expedition to the valley of the Great Salt lake of Utah,* 103.

[320] Ogden, "Journal," entry of march 20, 1826, Oregon historical society quarterly, X, 356; entry of may 21, 1826, *idem,* X, 361.

[321] Entry of april 9, 1826, *idem,* X, 359.

[322] Entry of april 11, 1826, *idem,* X, 360.

[323] Bonner, *Beckwourth,* 100, 101, 107.

This was Ashley's first and only visit to the Great Salt lake.[324] At the rendezvous, following his arrival, he sold his business to three of his former associates, Smith, Jackson, and Sublette, disposing of the Indian goods he had on hand at an advance of one hundred fifty per cent, the sum to be paid within five years in beaver skins at five dollars a pound or in cash, optional with the purchasers.[325] After the sale had been completed, Ashley, according to Beckwourth, delivered a touching farewell address to his men and at once set out for St. Louis.[326] Returning not by water, as in 1825, but by land, he reached the city seventy days after leaving rendezvous.[327] The supply of grass along the route was

[324] He is said to have built a fort on or near the shores of Utah lake, Chittenden, *American fur trade*, I, 279, III, 973. Chittenden places the erection of this fort in 1825. T. C. Elliott ("Peter Skene Ogden journals," Oregon historical society *quarterly*, XI, 365) suggests that he built a post on Sevier lake. That a fort was constructed somewhere in the vicinity of Great Salt lake is certain, but it was probably built by Ashley's men during the winter of 1825-1826 or, more probably, in 1826 by Ashley's successors, who purchased through him a four-pound cannon, which was dragged out the next year. The post seems to have been located near the Great Salt lake itself rather than on Utah lake. Peter Skene Ogden refers to the American post at "Salt lake" in 1827 and 1828, Ogden, "Journal," Oregon historical society *quarterly*, XI, 365, 368, 369. "Tullock, the American, who failed to get through the snow to Salt lake tried to engage an Indian to carry letters to the American deposit at Salt lake," *Idem*, XI, 372. It was from Great Salt lake, furthermore, that Smith set out on his expedition to the southwest in august 1826, MS. draft of a letter of W. H. Ashley, december 24, 1828, Ashley MSS., Missouri historical society.

[325] Ogden, "Journal," entry of january 5, 1828, Oregon historical society *quarterly*, XI, 368 ff; Letter of W. H. Ashley, december 24, 1828, Ashley MSS., Missouri historical society; Letter of Thomas Forsyth to the secretary of war, St. Louis, october 24, 1831, in U.S. Senate, *Executive documents*, 22 cong., 1 sess., II, no. 90; Pilcher, "Report," *idem*. N. J. Wyeth in a letter of november 8, 1833 says that Ashley sold out for thirty thousand dollars, Young, *Sources of Oregon history*, I, 74. Beckwourth states that arrangements had been made for this transaction before Ashley reached rendezvous, Bonner, *op. cit.*, 107. The original instrument is in the Sublette MSS., carton 11, Missouri historical society.

[326] Bonner, *op. cit.*, 111.

[327] *Niles register*, december 9, 1826.

more than ample for his horses. "The men also found an abundance of food; they say there was no day in which they could not have subsisted a thousand men, and often ten thousand." [328] He retired a rich man, having made a fortune in furs amounting to eighty thousand dollars, it is said. [329]

Ashley continued to retain an indirect interest in the trade, though he made no further visits to the mountains in person. Instead he furnished Smith, Jackson, and Sublette with goods from the states, accepting their furs in payment. For three years, at least, he sent such supply trains to the mountains. Later, after Smith, Jackson, and Sublette had sold out to Fitzpatrick, Sublette, and Bridger, he still acted as agent for the latter, receiving in a single year three thousand dollars as commission. [330]

For a time Ashley's successors continued to reap huge profits from the business. In the first year alone they cleared twenty thousand dollars, [331] while by 1828 the value of all furs brought out to that date either by

---

[328] *Idem.*

[329] Ogden, "Journal," in Oregon historical society *quarterly,* XI, 368 ff. Wyeth says that after his obligations were all settled, he was worth fifty thousand dollars, Young, *Sources of Oregon history,* I, 74.

[330] "Washington City, 24th february, 1833.

"Wm. L. Sublette, My account against Jackson and Sublette for commission on sales in 1831 to 1832 . . . $3000

(signed) W. H. Ashley."

Sublette MSS., carton 1, Missouri historical society.

"[Ashley] has sold out to Messers Jackson, Sublette, and Smith, and now has nothing more to do with the business either in hunting or trading about the mountains. He brings on goods etc. from the eastward to this city [St. Louis] and furnishes Jackson, Sublette, and Smith with all they require, and receives annually from them their furs in payment."—Biddle, Thomas, "Report," october 29, 1831, in U.S. Senate, *Executive documents,* 21 cong., 1 sess., I, no. 47. "I (with the exception of a small outfit made last year by Major Pilcher) have furnished every article during the period."—MS. letter of Ashley, december 26, 1828, Ashley MSS., Missouri historical society. In 1833 Maximilian speaks of the fur company of Messrs. Ashley and Sublette. See Thwaites, *Early western travels,* XXII, 250.

[331] Ogden, "Journal," Oregon historical society *quarterly,* XI, 368 ff.

Ashley himself or his successors totaled, by Ashley's estimate, two hundred twenty thousand dollars.[332] But this fortunate state of affairs could not endure. Until 1827 no other American company had penetrated the interior basin, so that the only competition which the Ashley and post-Ashley companies had to face was that of the Hudson's Bay company. When, however, in 1830, the firm of Fitzpatrick, Sublette, and Bridger, operating under the name of the Rocky Mountain Fur company, succeeded Smith, Jackson, and Sublette, the conditions of the trade had materially altered.[333] Competition had begun. Joshua Pilcher, representing the old Missouri Fur company interests, had entered the field in 1827, while the great American Fur company, the most dangerous of all competitors, had already begun to undermine the virtual monopoly enjoyed by Ashley's successors west of the mountains. The American Fur company, in fact, had a half interest in the supply train which Ashley dispatched to the mountains in the spring of 1827.[334]

[332] MS. draft of a letter of Ashley, december 26, 1828, Ashley MSS., Missouri historical society.

[333] Smith, Jackson, and Sublette "followed it up with equal good fortune for a time, but it was not to be expected that such a series of rich returns would fail to command the attention of others."—Pilcher, "Report," december 1, 1831, in U.S. Senate, *Executive documents,* 22 cong., 1 sess., I, no. 90. Pilcher was one of those who entered the field against them. "It is to be observed, finding themselves alone, they [Smith, Jackson, and Sublette] sold their goods one third dearer than Ashley did, but have held out a promise of reduction in price this year. What a contrast between these young men and myself. They have been only six years in the country and without a doubt in as many more will be independent men."—Ogden, "Journal," Oregon historical society *quarterly,* XI, 369.

[334] "What the Rocky mountains will produce cannot be known for months to come, but by the accounts from Ashley's district, it seems probable that he will be quite as successful as last season. You will have learned that we hold a half interest in Ashley's expedition and that profits are fair."—Letter of Ramsay Crooks to J. J. Astor, St. Louis, april 13, 1827, Crooks MSS. (copy), Missouri historical society. The American Fur company was probably deal-

This left St. Louis in march 1827, conducted by sixty men. Included with the usual goods was a piece of artillery, a four-pounder, mounted on a primitive carriage drawn by mules.[335] Despite his resolve of the previous summer Ashley accompanied the expedition as far as the frontier, where, it is said, he was compelled to return on account of sickness, leaving the command in other hands. The expedition selected the now familiar route by way of the North Platte and South pass to Green river and thence to the vicinity of the Great Salt lake, drawing along as they went the first wheeled vehicle to cross the mountains, although two years before Ashley had recognized the perfect feasibility of using even wagons.[336] Arrived at rendezvous, which seems to have been conducted this year not at Great Salt lake or Cache valley but at Bear lake, they found Jackson and Sublette in charge and Jedediah Smith but lately returned from his first visit to California, full of the details of his hardships and of the strange civilization of the Pacific coast, which he was the first American to approach by land. The supplies, including the four-pounder, were left with the company and on july 17 the train started back for the states. Ashley seems to have met them at Lexington, relieved them of their furs, one hundred thirty packs in all, and started them back for the mountains with the same outfit.[337] Reaching the

ing through Bernard Pratte and company. Compare Chittenden, *American fur trade*, I, 280, 322.

[335] Letter of Ashley to General A. Macomb, Washington, march 1829, in U.S. Senate, *Executive documents*, 21 cong., 2 sess., I, no. 39.

[336] Compare Atkinson, "Report," Louisville, Kentucky, november 23, 1825, in U.S. House, *Executive documents*, 19 cong., 1 sess., VI, no. 117. Compare *Niles register*, december 9, 1826: "Wagons and carriages could go with ease as far as General Ashley went, crossing the Rocky mountains at the sources of the North fork of the Platte, and descending the valley of the Buenaventura toward the Pacific ocean." See also *St. Louis reveille*, march 1, 1847.

[337] Chittenden (*American fur trade*, I, 279) states that "he took a six-

Rockies late in november, they found their way blocked by snow and were unable to get through to Great Salt lake that winter.[338]

Although Ashley continued to send outfits of supplies to the mountains, his chief interest and occupation from this time was politics. Elected lieutenant-governor of Missouri in 1821, three years later, on the expiration of his term, he ran for governor but was defeated by Frederick Bates.[339] In the course of the campaign Ashley's friends made much of his daring, the romantic character of his business, and his ambitious enterprise in pushing the trade into the unknown wilds of the far west. On his retirement from active business with a considerable fortune, he was in a position to give more serious attention to politics. In 1829 he sought election to the United States senate but was defeated.[340] Shortly after, however, his opportunity came. In 1831 Spencer Pettis, congressman from Missouri, was killed in a duel by Thomas Biddle, and Ashley was at once selected as

pounder wheeled cannon through to Utah lake and installed it in his post there (1826)." The fact of the matter is that Ashley, as he himself says, sent the cannon, a four-pounder, but in the year 1827. "In the month of march, 1827, I fitted out a party of 60 men, mounted a piece of artillery (a four-pounder) on a carriage which was drawn by two mules; the party marched to or near the grand Salt lake, beyond the Rocky mountains, remained there one month, stopped on their way back 15 days, and returned to Lexington in the western part of Missouri in september, where the party was met with everything necessary for another expedition, and did return (using the same horses and mules) to the mountains by the last of november in the same year."—Letter of Ashley to Macomb, Washington, march 1829, in U.S. Senate, *Executive documents*, 21 cong., 2 sess., I, no. 39.

[338] Ogden, "Journal," entry of february 16, 1828, in Oregon historical society *quarterly*, XI, 374.

[339] Switzler, W. F., "General William Henry Ashley," in *American monthly magazine*, XXXII, 323 ff; Davis, W. B. and D. S. Durrie, *Illustrated history of Missouri*, 86; *Edwards's great west*, 337. Switzler erroneously states that Lafayette was entertained by Ashley on his visit to St. Louis, april 1825. Ashley was, of course, in the mountains at that time.

[340] Switzler, W. F., "Historical sketch of Missouri," in Barnes, *Commonwealth of Missouri*, part ii, 222.

a candidate for the remainder of Pettis's term. Though actively supported by the anti-Jackson men in the western part of the state, his friends were not over sanguine of his success. He was, nevertheless, elected.[341] He had been a member of congress only a year when he was forced to undertake another political campaign to secure his reelection. Again he won by a close margin. In 1835 he ran again, this time as an anti-Van Buren man, and was again elected, his term expiring with the last session of the twenty-fourth congress in the spring of 1837.[342]

During his career in congress Ashley showed himself an active and determined champion of the west. Henry Dodge, writing to George W. Jones, delegate from Michigan territory, spoke of him as a man, who, like Benton and Linn, could invariably be counted on to support western interests.

I have been on the most intimate and friendly terms with General Ashley for thirty years, and I have never had a more true and consistent friend. If I were to make a selection of my personal friends, three in whom I have as much confidence as any on earth, it would be Dr. Linn, Gen. Ashley, and yourself.[343]

Ashley's intimate knowledge of so large a section of the far west entitled his opinions in matters touching Indian affairs and the economic and fiscal problems of the

---

[341] "The anti-Jackson men in this quarter are almost to a man in favor of Gen. Ashley for congress. We expect a small majority for him in this country, although the caucus men are making powerful exertions in favor of Wells. I expect these four upper counties [Lafayette, Jackson, Clay, and Ray] will give a small, very small majority for Wells. . . I think the general must be elected."—MS. letter of James Aull to George C. Sibley, Lexington, Missouri, october 22, 1831, Sibley MSS., II, Missouri historical society.

[342] Davis and Durrie, *Illustrated history of Missouri,* 101, 105, 108, 109; Switzler, "General William Henry Ashley," *American monthly magazine,* XXXII, 325.

[343] Fort Leavenworth, january 28, 1836, in *Annals of Iowa,* third series, III, 295 ff.

west to respectful attention. He served as member of the house committee on Indian affairs and always used his influence in support of what he believed to be the best interests of both races. He had small patience with the sentimentalists in congress who habitually exaggerated the Indian sense of honor and who were ever ready to attribute to the savage mind concepts of government and of law which Ashley well knew were completely and utterly foreign to it. He opposed excessive appropriations for the Indian department, including remuneration for special service rendered by the Indian agents in the pursuit of their duties. He had, he said, "been exposed to great dangers and losses from the Indians and never in all that time had he found more than two agents at their stations."[344] He was, in fact, utterly opposed to the existing Indian policy of the government. He believed in abolishing the Indian office altogether and having all Indian agents appointed by the president with the approval of the senate. He saw the danger both for the whites and the Indians if the two races were brought into too close proximity and advocated the creation of a neutral strip thirty miles wide between the last white settlements and the Indian tribes. He saw that this would prevent the Indians from too readily molesting the whites and at the same time would make it more difficult for them to secure spirituous liquors, which he frankly recognized as the most dangerous influence among them.[345] He was emphatically opposed to "buying" peace with the Indians, as he called it, which meant the awarding of money "to such friendly Indians as may take refuge on our frontier during the existing difficulties with other Indian tribes." [346]

344 Gales and Seaton, *Register of debates*, VIII, part 2, 2317, march 30, 1832.
345 *Idem*, VIII, part 2, 2329, 2358, march 31, 1832, april 3, 1832.
346 *Idem*, VIII, part 3, 3238, june 1, 1832; X, part 3, 4080, may 5, 1834.

No one ever questioned his loyalty to his constituents. One of his first speeches in congress was in support of an amendment to the Apportionment bill which would give his state additional representation in congress.[347] The amendment, however, was lost. All measures that looked to public improvements in Missouri naturally had his heartiest sanction. On may 5, 1832 he secured an amendment to the Internal Improvement Appropriation bill, expending fifty thousand dollars for the improvement of navigation of the Missouri river.[348] All measures for improving western waterways he supported vigorously.[349] In june 1834 he tried to secure an appropriation of twenty-five thousand dollars to improve the harbor of St. Louis, which was in danger of being destroyed by a sand bar, but in vain.[350] In march 1835 he tried to tack an appropriation of twenty thousand dollars to the Lighthouse bill for a similar object, but was induced to withdraw his amendment.[351] Similarly with roads. He proposed an amendment to the Internal Improvement Appropriation bill, may 5, 1832, providing for the extension of the National highway from Vandalia, Illinois, to Jefferson City, Missouri.[352] In 1836 he tried an amendment to the Fortification bill for the same purpose but again without success.[353] One of his last speeches, february 11, 1837, was a violent arraignment of the proposal to receive in congress petitions from slaves.[354]

With the dissolution of the twenty-fourth congress,

[347] *Idem*, VIII, part 2, 1778, march 10, 1832.

[348] *Idem*, VIII, part 2, 2804, may 5, 1832.

[349] *Idem*, X, part 3, 4137 ff., may 17, 1834; X, part 4, 4544, june 18, 1834; X, part 4, 4569, june 19, 1834; XII, part 4, 4390, june 22, 1836.

[350] *Idem*, X, part 4, 4694 f., june 23, 1834.

[351] *Idem*, XI, part 2, 1642, march 3, 1835.

[352] *Idem*, VIII, part 2, 2804, may 5, 1832.

[353] *Idem*, XII, part 4, 4175, june 4, 1836.

[354] *Idem*, XIII, part 2, 1710, february 11, 1837.

Ashley retired from public life. In 1836 he had run for governor of Missouri but had been defeated by Lilburn W. Boggs of anti-Mormon fame.[355] After Ashley's return to St. Louis from Washington, Daniel Webster paid a visit to the city. At a public festival given in his honor in a grove of trees just west of Ninth street, General Ashley presided. The chronicler of the event in describing the celebration says, "A sumptuous dinner plentifully supplied with choice liquors soon put the whole company on the most sociable footing, and speeches and complimentary toasts were made and drank with all the zest of happy feeling and festive enjoyment." At the close of the dinner Mr. Webster delivered a speech of more than an hour's duration.[356]

Ashley had built a magnificent house in what is now North St. Louis. It was surrounded by about eight acres of land, which he had purchased on his retirement from the fur-trade. In 1838, however, because of failing health, he abandoned this home to retire to the country, occupying the house of his father-in-law, Dr. James Wynne Moss, near the mouth of Lamine river, Cooper county. But even the change of environment and a physician's care were incapable of restoring him and on march 26, 1838 he succumbed to a sudden attack of pneumonia. "Just previous to his death, he sent in haste for Benjamin Thompkins, then a young lawyer of Boonville, to visit him at once to draw up his will. He obeyed the summons; but the testament was not completed, for when about half written, General Ashley died." [357] A widow survived him.[358]

---

[355] Davis and Durrie, *Illustrated history of Missouri*, 109.

[356] *Edwards's great west*, 362.

[357] Switzler, "General William Henry Ashley," in *American monthly magazine*, XXXII, 321 ff.

[358] Ashley was married three times. His second wife was Miss Eliza

Ashley's opinions were widely sought on matters relating to the fur-trade, Indian affairs, and the west in general. He prepared reports on such matters for Colonel Henry Atkinson,[359] Thomas Hart Benton,[360] General Macomb,[361] Colonel Gratiot of the corps of engineers,[362] Albert Gallatin,[363] and others.[364]

Christy whom he married october 26, 1825. She died june 12, 1830. In october 1832 he married Mrs. Elizabeth Moss Wilcox, daughter of Dr. James W. Moss, of Boone county, Missouri. Compare Switzler, *op. cit.*, 327 ff., and "Collections of newspaper excerpts," Missouri historical society.

[359] U.S. House, *Executive documents,* 19 cong., 1 sess., VI, no. 117.

[360] U.S. Senate, *Executive documents,* 20 cong., 2 sess., I, no. 67.

[361] U.S. Senate, *Executive documents,* 21 cong, 2 sess., I, no. 39.

[362] Draft of a letter by Ashley, Ashley MSS., Missouri historical society.

[363] Gallatin, Albert, "Synopsis of Indian tribes," in American antiquarian society *transactions,* II, 140.

[364] *Missouri intelligencer,* july 8, 1832; drafts of Ashley's letters, Ashley MSS., Missouri historical society; McCoy, Reverend Isaac, "Journal," december 23, 1835, folio 67, McCoy MSS., Kansas historical society.

Jedediah Strong Smith

Jedediah Strong Smith, unlike most of his contemporaries in the fur-trade, came of pioneer New England stock. His father, plain Jedediah Smith, a native of New Hampshire, following that first stream of emigration into the Mohawk valley settled in Chenango county, New York, toward the close of the eighteenth century. Here, on june 24, 1798, in the town of Bainbridge, his son, Jedediah Strong, was born, being one of fourteen children.[365] Subsequently his parents pushed farther west, living for a time in Erie, Pennsylvania, and finally in Ashtabula, Ohio.

During his childhood Smith acquired from a friendly physician, Doctor Simons, "the rudiments, of an English education, and a smattering of Latin," and a fair hand.[366] All through his life Smith retained a warm affection and respect for this gentleman, whose daughter later married one of Smith's brothers. It may very well have been he who first suggested to Smith the utility of making a careful geographical study of the far west,

[365] Smith, E. D., "Jedediah Smith and the settlement of Kansas," in Kansas historical society *collections,* XII, 252 footnote. Compare "Captain Jedediah Strong Smith: an eulogy," *Illinois magazine,* june 1832, reprinted as an appendix in Sabin, *Kit Carson days,* 512 ff. Smith was not born in King's county, Ireland, as stated by Hugh Quigley (*Irish race in California*), nor in Connecticut, as stated by J. M. Guinn ("Captain Jedediah S. Smith," Southern California historical society *publications,* III, part 4, 46). For a portrait of Smith see Sullivan, *Travels of Jedediah Smith,* frontispiece.

[366] There is still extant a shipper's manifest made out by Smith at the age of fourteen for a cargo of goods shipped on Lake Erie, "written in a clear and distinct hand."—Guinn, *op. cit., loc. cit.*

an object which Smith had seriously in mind during the last years of his life. In 1830, Smith wrote one of his brothers

I am indebted to Doctor Simons for his epistle dated, march 15, 1830, and I wish you to express my gratitude in becoming terms of respect. I fear that Doctor Simons thinks I only feel bound where I sign my name, but, if so, he to whom I am under so many obligations is much mistaken. How happy I should consider myself if I could *again* be allowed the privilege of spending some time with my much esteemed friend. I think the doctor recollects this excellent precept, "If you have one friend, feel or think yourself happy." I hope I have one *friend*. On my arrival at the settlements (should I be so fortunate as to gain that point), I intend writing to Doctor Simons.[367]

It may have been he, too, who gave Smith that deep religious sentiment which marked him off from the mass of men with whom he was associated. Before he left home Smith became a member of the Methodist church and, though most of his life far from the ministrations of religion, remained a devout christian.[368] Finally, in making arrangements to expend the small fortune he had accumulated in the fur-trade, he wrote, "In the first place, my brother, our parents must receive of our benefaction, and if Doctor Simons is in want, I wish him to be helped." [369]

At the age of thirteen Smith secured a clerical posi-

[367] Letter of Smith to his brother Ralph, dated Blue fork, Kansas river, september 10, 1830, Smith MSS., Kansas historical society. Again he writes, "I wish to consult Dr. Simons on the method of educating our brothers as it is my wish to carry them into some of the higher branches of education."— *Ibid.* to *ibid.,* dated Wind river, east of the Rocky mountains, december 24, 1829, Smith MSS., Kansas historical society.

[368] Waldo, William, "Reminiscences," Waldo MSS., Missouri historical society; Smith, *op. cit.,* XII, 254. The "Eulogy,"however, states that "without being connected with any church, he was a christian."—Sabin, *Kit Carson days,* 517.

[369] Letter of Jedediah S. Smith to Ralph Smith, december 24, 1829, Smith MSS., Kansas historical society.

tion on one of the freight boats of the Great lakes, where he soon had occasion to meet traders and trappers of the English fur companies, who were ever passing back and forth between Montreal and the interior country. A natural roving disposition, which has so frequently characterized the stock of which he came, with a determination to better himself, attracted Smith to this occupation, which seemed to offer so much in the way of adventure and profit.

Having spent the summer and fall of 1821 in northern Illinois and the winter of 1821-1822 near Rock Island, Smith came down to St. Louis early in 1822 where, hearing of Ashley's expedition for which the latter had advertised for men, he engaged himself as a hunter. Accompanying the original party which had left St. Louis on may eighth, he recorded in his journal the wreck of their boat, the "Enterprise," at the mouth of Sinabar creek and Ashley's resourcefulness in fitting out a second expedition which he accompanied himself. On reaching the Arikara villages, Ashley, as noted earlier, purchased a supply of horses and proceeded overland to join his partner, Andrew Henry, at the mouth of the Yellowstone, returning immediately to St. Louis. Smith, who remained at the post, joined one of the parties sent up the Yellowstone to procure a supply of meat and to take such beaver as might incidentally be encountered. On his return to the fort from this foray he joined a party that followed along the banks of the Missouri to a point near the mouth of the Musselshell, where he spent the winter. In the spring it appears to have been Smith who hastened down country to advise Ashley of the need for additional horses.[370]

---

[370] For incidents in Smith's career during the period 1821 to the winter of 1822, see Sullivan, *Travels of Jedediah Smith*, 1-10.

The next incident in this period of Smith's career that can be fixed beyond question is his participation in the engagement with the Arikaras in 1823. He was with the detachment that camped on land with the horses at the time of the first encounter. He and David E. Jackson, after having fought bravely round the animals till most of them were dead, made their way to the shore, leaped into the river, and managed to swim to the boats unscathed by the shower of shot and arrows concentrated upon them. When, after the battle was over and before the arrival of the relief party under Colonel Leavenworth, it became necessary to send word to Major Henry, it was Jedediah Smith who volunteered for that service. Accompanied only by a Frenchcanadian hunter and traversing nearly a thousand miles of unfamiliar country swarming with vigilant and hostile Indians, he pushed through in excellent time, found Henry on the Yellowstone, gave an account of the battle and of the urgent need of support, and immediately turned back with the relief detachment.

The first battle had been fought june third. By late june or early july Smith was back at Ashley's camp, now removed to the mouth of the Cheyenne river. From this point he was dispatched to St. Louis with furs which Henry had brought down. Arrived at the city he had an interview with General Atkinson, in which he related the incidents of the first Arikara fight and the departure of the Leavenworth relief expedition, and then hastening back, rejoined Ashley in time to take command of one of the companies in the battle of the tenth of august.[371]

After the conclusion of peace with the Arikaras, Smith returned to the mountains as one of Ashley's men,

[371] See page 78 ff.

spending the fall in the Crow country and in winter quarters on Wind river and the Sweetwater. In the late winter or early spring of 1824 he crossed South pass to the upper reaches of Green river. In the summer or fall of that year, as noted above, he headed the party of Ashley's men which crossed to Snake river and Clark's fork of the Columbia, met Alexander Ross, accompanied him to Flathead post, and from that point returned in the winter to the Great Salt lake and Cache valley. In the spring of 1825 he was with the united trapping parties that met Ashley at the appointed rendezvous near Green river. From rendezvous he accompanied Ashley to the Big Horn, continued down that stream to the Yellowstone, and the remainder of the distance to St. Louis.

Leaving St. Louis in the spring of 1826, along with Ashley, Smith entered on the first stage of a journey which was to carry him, the first white man, from the Mississippi to the Pacific over the midland route. As Lewis and Clark discovered the northern route, so Smith, utilizing the discoveries and experiences of Ashley between the Missouri and the Great Salt lake, traced the southwestern and central routes to the coast. Though the Great Salt lake was to terminate the expedition for Ashley, it marked only a half-way station for Smith and many of the men who had accompanied them thus far, for from this point Smith continued his outward journey to California, approximating the course of the San Pedro, Los Angeles, and Salt Lake railroad, returning, next spring, across the state of Nevada by the central Pacific route. Before leaving St. Louis Smith and Ashley had presumably come to an agreement regarding the transfer of the latter's business to Smith in company with the two other Ashley

men, David E. Jackson and William L. Sublette.[372]
On their arrival at rendezvous, the transfer was concluded.[373]

Smith, Jackson, and Sublette now undertook to operate in the field opened up by Ashley's men two years
before. It was still immensely rich in beaver and capable
of continued trapping for a number of years and was
also untouched by competition. But the ambitious young
men who succeeded Ashley had visions of pushing their
trapping parties even farther west. Aware that a vast
area must lie between the Great Salt lake and the Pacific ocean, but ignorant of its barren and beaverless
nature, they resolved to penetrate this new field at once.
The first step, however, was naturally one of exploration and survey. To turn a large division of the company into this unworked field before its business possibilities had been determined would be folly. It was
decided, accordingly, that two of the partners, Sublette
and Jackson,[374] should remain in the mountains with
the main company, while Smith should set out with a
few men to investigate the new area to the west. Besides
determining the fur-bearing resources of the new country, Smith may also have had in view the possibility of

---

[372] Beckwourth says that Ashley's men, who had been left in the mountains
in 1825, "learned previous to the arrival of the general, that General Ashley
had sold out his interest to Mr. Sublette, embracing all his properties and
possessions."—Bonner, *Beckwourth*, 107.

[373] According to E. D. Smith (*op. cit.,* XII, 257) Smith had bought out
Henry's interest in the business on the latter's withdrawal in the fall of
1824. J. J. Warner refers to him as the direct successor of Andrew Henry
and speaks of the firm name, "Ashley and Smith."—Warner, "Reminiscences
of early California," in Southern California historical society *publications,*
VII, 186. Compare Thwaites, *Early western travels,* XIX, 237 footnote.

[374] It should be said of David E. Jackson that, through the entire life of
the firm of Smith, Jackson, and Sublette, he was the resident partner, remaining continually in the mountains, while Sublette returned regularly to
the states. This is one reason why so little is known of him. Compare Victor,
F. F., *River of the west,* 48.

shipping furs from one of the Californian ports. He would thus revive the project of John Jacob Astor, fifteen years earlier, but with a central or southern Pacific port. Ashley himself had had such a project in mind and it was, as he said, with the greatest reluctance that he abandoned it. In the draft of a letter written soon after his return in 1825, he stated that it was "reasonable to suppose the whole of the fur trade west of the mountains will take that direction [to the Pacific] to market as soon as any place on the sea coast may be established to a trade operated about the 43rd degree of latitude." [376] Later, however, he wrote to Thomas Hart Benton, "I should myself prefer transporting my furs from the vicinity of the Grand lake to St. Louis in preference to taking them to the Pacific." [377] Perhaps also, like Brigham Young twenty years later, Smith intended to explore the Colorado as a possible waterway from Utah to the sea.

Smith, moreover, was selected to command this exploring expedition because he already knew more about the country than anyone else in the company. He had met Alexander Ross and Peter Skene Ogden at Flathead House in the fall and winter of 1824 and, as Ashley himself testified, used his opportunities to find out all that he could about the country in which the Hudson's Bay company was operating and the extent of its business. He had talked also with their trappers, men who, for years, had been employed on the Snake country expeditions and who, consequently, would be well informed about the country south of the Columbia and the Snake. Whatever they may have told him, if they were truthful, was probably disheart-

[376] *American monthly magazine,* XXXII, 329.
[377] December 28, 1828, Ashley MSS., Missouri historical society.

ening, though it is not unlikely that Smith took their descriptions of that truly barren country with reservations, knowing their anxiety to keep Americans out of it. Smith, furthermore, was the best educated of the three partners and consequently better able to handle the affairs of the company among the Mexican population of California. Last of all, he was a man of recognized character and courage.

On Smith's return to rendezvous in the summer of 1827, he dispatched the following letter to William Clark, superintendent of Indian affairs, in which he briefly sketched his course and summarized the more important incidents of his sojourn in California.

LITTLE LAKE OF BEAR RIVER,[378] july 12th, 1827. GENL. WM. CLARK,[379] Supt. of Indian affairs

Sir, My situation in this country has enabled me to collect information respecting a section of the country which has hitherto been measurably veiled in obscurity to the citizens of the United States. I allude to the country s.w. of the Great Salt lake west of the Rocky mountains.

I started about the 22d of august 1826, from the Great Salt lake,[380] with a party of fifteen men,[381] for the pur-

[378] Rendezvous was usually conducted at the southern or upper end of the lake near Laketown, Randolph county, Utah.

[379] This letter, probably a copy of the original, is contained in Superintendent of Indian affairs, Letter book, Kansas historical society MSS. It was printed in full in the *Missouri republican,* october 11, 1827. There is a French version of it in Eyriés, de Larénaudière, et Klaproth, *Les nouvelles annales des voyages,* second ser., VII, 308-312.

[380] He probably started from the trading-post built this year, to which Ashley sent the four-pounder the year following. On august 22, 1826, presumably the date of his departure, Smith presented a number of useful articles to the Utah Indians and a few days later made another and more generous gift. In addition to these articles bestowed at the start, he carried with him a stock of merchandise to be distributed en route.

[381] The names of some of the men are recoverable from the Harrison G. Rogers journal, which contains, interspersed with the narrative, memoranda

pose of exploring the country S.W. which was entirely
unknown to me, and of which I could collect no satisfactory information from the Indians who inhabit this
country on its N.E. borders.

My general course on leaving the Salt lake was S.W.
and W. Passing the Little Uta lake [382] and ascending
Ashley's river, which empties into the Little Uta lake.[383]
From this lake I found no more signs of buffalo; there
are a few antelope and mountain sheep, and an abundance of black tailed hares. On Ashley's river, I found
a nation of Indians who call themselves *Sampatch;*
they were friendly disposed towards us.[384] I passed
over a range of mountains running S.E. and N.W. and
struck a river running S.W. which I called Adams river,
in compliment to our president.[385] The water is of a

---

of allowance to the employees. Among the names occurring in these accounts
are the following: Harrison G. Rogers, James Reed, Silas Gobel, Arthur
Black, John Gaiter, Robert Evans, Manuel Lazarus, John Hanna, John Wilson, Martin McCoy, Daniel Ferguson, Peter Ranna (or Ransa) (colored),
and Abraham Laplant. This makes a total of thirteen.

[382] The first indication of the name applied to this body of water, now
Utah lake. He probably followed the Salt Lake valley, east of the lake, the
route of the Denver and Rio Grande railroad. This is the course assigned
to him on Chittenden's "Map of the Trans-Mississippi territory," accompanying his *American fur trade,* III, and by I. B. Richman on his "Map of
twenty-two Spanish and American trails, etc.," accompanying his *California
under Spain and Mexico.* Bancroft says twice that he *crossed* Utah lake,
Bancroft, *History of California,* III, 152, 154, footnote. This lake is marked
Ashley L. on the Gallatin map but without connection with Great Salt lake.

[383] Ashley's river is presumably the Sevier, which, however, does not
empty into Utah lake but into Sevier lake. Smith's mistake in this matter
may be due to the fact that he seems to have reached the Sevier only after
"passing" Utah lake.

[384] Sanpete Indians, a branch of the Ute tribe of Shoshonean stock, living
in the Sanpete valley and along the Sevier river.

[385] Smith's route is difficult to trace from his confused and inadequate
directions. Following up the Sevier he evidently crossed west by the gap
later known as Fremont's pass to the neighborhood of Parowan, Utah, thence
westerly still, reaching before october first a point on the present Utah-
Nevada line near where the Los Angeles and Salt Lake railroad now crosses,
and so to the headwaters of Muddy river. Assuming this river, which he

muddy cast, and is a little brackish. The country is mountainous to east; towards the west there are sandy plains and detached rocky hills.

Passing down this river some distance, I fell in with a nation of Indians who call themselves *Pa-Ulches* [386] (those Indians as well as those last mentioned, wear rabbit skin robes) who raise some little corn and pumpkins. The country is nearly destitute of game of any description, except a few hares. Here (about ten days march down it) the river turns to the south east. On the S.W. side of the river there is a cave,[387] the entrance of which is about 10 or 15 feet high, and 5 or 6 feet in width; after descending about 15 feet, a room opens out from 25 to 30 in length and 15 to 20 feet in width; the roof, sides and floor are solid rock salt, a sample of which I send you, with some other articles which will be hereafter described. I here found a kind of plant of the prickly pear kind, which I called the cabbage pear, the largest of which grows about two feet and a half high and 1½ feet in diameter; upon examination I found it to be nearly of the substance of a turnip, altho' by no means palatable; its form was similar to

named Adams river, to be the main stream, he followed it "southwest," perhaps missing its confluence with the Virgin (named for Thomas Virgin), which he apparently assumed to be a tributary rather than the main stream itself. See Meriam, C. H., "Earliest crossing of the deserts of Utah and Nevada to southern California," in California historical society *quarterly*, II, 229. Either this year or the next he seems to have learned of Sevier lake. Says Albert Gallatin, "The discoveries south and west of that place [Great Salt lake] appear to belong to others and principally to J. S. Smith. Another river, known by the name of Lost river, coming also from the coast, falls into another lake without outlet situated in 38°N. latitude and the same longitude as L. Timpanogo."—American antiquarian society *transactions*, II, 141.

[386] Paiutes, a name applied at one time or another to most of the Shoshonean tribes of western Utah. They were confined to the area of southwestern Utah, southwestern Nevada, and northwestern Arizona.

[387] There are a number of such caves in this area. It is impossible to identify this particular one.

that of an egg, being smaller at the ground and top than in the middle; it is covered with pricks similar to the prickly pear with which you are acquainted.[388]

There are here also a number of shrubs and small trees with which I was not acquainted previous to my route there, and which I cannot at present describe satisfactorily, as it would take more space than I can here allot.

The *Pa Ulches* have a number of marble pipes, one of which I obtained and send you, altho' it has been broken since I have had it in my possession; they told me there was a quantity of the same material in their country. I also obtained of them a knife of flint, which I send you, but it has likewise been broken by accident.

I followed Adams river [389] two days further to where it empties into the Seedskeeder a south east course.[390] I crossed the Seedskeeder, and went down it four days a south east course; I here found the country remarkably barren, rocky, and mountainous; there are a good many rapids in the river, but at this place a valley opens out about 5 to 15 miles in width, which on the river banks is timbered and fertile.[391] I here found a nation of Indians who call themselves *Ammuchabas;* they cultivate the soil, and raise corn, beans, pumpkins, watermelons and muskmelons in abundance, and also a little wheat and cotton.[392] I was now nearly destitute

---

[388] Of the genus *echinocactus.*

[389] Meadow Valley wash? Meriam suggests that he may have reached this stream near Panaca or Pioche.

[390] His course was south-southwest. He reached the Colorado, which he recognized as the Seedskedee, or Green river, by october 5. There is now a ferry across the river at this point. See U.S. Geological survey, *St. Thomas quadrangle* (topographic sheet). He followed the same route the next year.

[391] The Mojave valley.

[392] The Mojave Indians, the most populous and warlike of the Yuma tribes. They have lived in this valley, chiefly on the eastern side of the Colorado, for centuries.

of horses, and had learned what it was to do without food; I therefore remained there fifteen days and recruited my men, and I was enabled also to exchange my horses and purchase a few more of a few runaway Indians who stole some horses of the Spaniards. I here got information of the Spanish country (the Californias) and obtained two guides, recrossed the Seedskadeer, which I afterwards found emptied into the Gulf of California about 80 miles from this place by the name of the Collarado; many render the river *Gild* from the east.[393]

I travelled a west course fifteen days over a country of complete barrens, generally travelling from morning until night without water.[394] I crossed a salt plain about 20 miles long and 8 wide; on the surface was a crust of beautiful white salt, quite thin. Under this surface there is a layer of salt from a half to one and a half inches in depth; between this and the upper layer there is about four inches of yellowish sand.[395]

On my arrival in the province of Upper California, I was looked upon with suspicion, and was compelled to appear in presence of the governor of the Californias residing at San Diego, where, by the assistance of some American gentlemen (especially Capt. W. H. Cunningham,[396] of the ship Courier from Boston) I was enabled to obtain permission to return with my men the route I came, and purchased such supplies as I

---

[393] He was still on the Colorado as late as the fifth of october. He crossed at the Needles. The reference to the Gila is not clear.

[394] He followed presumably the present route of the Atchison, Topeka, and Santa Fe railroad, identical with what was presently to be the Santa Fe-Los Angeles trail. Compare Richman, *op. cit.*, 289.

[395] The Mojave desert. The route indicated on the Chittenden map is incorrect. According to the Gallatin map he followed the Mojave river, which is fittingly called "Inconstant" river. He entered California via Cajon pass.

[396] For a reference to W. H. Cunningham, see page 203 f.

stood in want of. The governor would not allow me to trade up the sea coast towards Bodaga.[397] I returned to my party and purchased such articles as were necessary, and went eastward of the Spanish settlements on the route I had come in. I then steered my course N.W. keeping from 150 miles to 200 miles from the sea coast.[398] A very high range of mountains lay on the east.[399] After travelling three hundred miles in that direction through a country somewhat fertile,[400] in which there was a great many Indians, mostly naked and destitute of arms, with the exception of a few bows and arrows and what is very singular amongst Indians, they cut their hair to the length of three inches; they proved to be friendly; their manner of living is on fish, roots, acorns and grass.

On my arrival at the river which I named the *Wim-mul-che* (named after a tribe of Indians which resides on it, of that name) I found a few beaver, and elk, deer, and antelope in abundance.[401] I here made a small hunt,

[397] They arrived at the mission of San Gabriel november 27, 1826. For a discussion of the principal events during their sojourn here, see the Harrison G. Rogers journal, page 194 ff.

[398] He overestimates his distance from the sea. As he goes north, he keeps at an average of about one hundred miles from the coast.

[399] The Sierra Nevada range. The directions jotted down by Rogers (see footnote 424). "Two days above Saint Fernando (?), plenty of beaver at a lake. . . Three days above Santa Clare river, Pireadero, Two Larres or Flag lake" give some indication of their route. They crossed the Santa Clara river north of San Gabriel, whence they proceeded to Tulare lake, and so northwest.

[400] Three hundred miles would bring Smith a little beyond the San Joaquin river at the point where it emerges from the mountains to the east, but his route was naturally circuitous, and there is an indication that he slightly overestimated distances. Compare Warner, "Reminiscences of early California," in Southern California historical society *publications,* VII, 180 ff.

[401] The Wimilche Indians, a Yokuts (Mariposan) tribe, formerly living north of King's river. The stream which Smith reached and which he named from the tribe dwelling on it, I take to be the Stanislaus. The Wimilche never lived much farther north.

and attempted to take my party across the [mountain] which I before mentioned, and which I called *Mount Joseph,* to come on and join my partners at the Great Salt lake. I found the snow so deep on Mount Joseph that I could not cross my horses, five of which starved to death; I was compelled therefore to return to the valley which I had left, and there, leaving my party, I started with two men, seven horses and two mules, which I loaded with hay for the horses and provisions for ourselves, and started on the 20th of may, and succeeded in crossing it in eight days, having lost only two horses and one mule.[402] I found the snow on the top of

[402] Smith left the vicinity of San Gabriel some time after january 27. J. M. Guinn says that he did not leave until february. He adds, however, that the party had removed their camp to Mission San Bernardino. See Southern California historical society *publications,* III, part 4, 48. After traveling three hundred miles they reached a river where they made a small hunt, attempted to cross the mountains, failed, returned to the valley, and established a camp. In his first attempt to cross the mountains he followed the American fork, for on february 20, 1828, a year later, while on his return from California, he says, "I went with the trappers within a mile of the place where I struck the river on the last ap'l. . . The river was quite rapid and the rushing of the water brought fresh to my remembrance the cascades of Mount Joseph and the unpleasant times I had passed there when surrounded by the snow which continued falling. My horses freeze, my men discouraged, and our utmost exertion to keep from freezing to death" (Sullivan, *op. cit.,* 63). This attempt had failed, and Smith returned to his camp site. In other words, he essayed first to make the crossing with his entire party. Failing in this, he took the outfit back to the Stanislaus, where he established a permanent camp. "And there," says he, "leaving my party, I started with two men, seven horses and two mules, which I loaded with hay for the horses and provisions for ourselves." By the latter part of may he "found the snow on the top of the mountain from 4 to 8 feet deep, but it was so consolidated by the heat of the sun that my horses only sunk half a foot to one foot deep." C. H. Meriam, who erroneously asserts that Smith's base camp was near the site of Folsom, assumes that the crossing was made by the same route as the first attempt, basing his conclusion largely on his belief that Gallatin wrote north*west* when he meant north*east* (Gallatin was simply following Smith's own statement), or the highly inaccurate work of T. S. Cronise, or a somewhat confused statement in Warner's "Reminiscences," and on the assumption that the Wimilche Indians did *not* live north of King's river as stated by Hodge. Meriam first propounded this theory in the *Bulletin* of the Sierra club, 1923,

this mountain from 4 to 8 feet deep, but it was so consolidated by the heat of the sun that my horses only
sunk from half a foot to one foot deep.[403]

After travelling twenty days from the east side of
Mount Joseph, I struck the S.W. corner of the Great
Salt lake, travelling over a country completely barren
and destitute of game. We frequently travelled without

was sufficiently answered by F. L. Fletcher in the june 1924 issue of the
Quarterly of the California historical society but returned to the fray with
the distortions noted above in the april 1924 issue of the same publication. A
further reason for assuming that Smith crossed by the Stanislaus is his statement, quoted by Gallatin, that "he crossed some streams coming from the
south, which may either be lost in the sands, or breaking through the mountains,
north of Mount Joseph, unite with the River Benaventura" (Gallatin, *op. cit.*,
141). Smith's actual route can be fairly accurately determined. Richman takes
him up the Mokelumnes river, Chittenden up the Merced, but it seems more
probable that he followed the Stanislaus, starting eastward along the route
followed in the opposite direction by the Bartleson-Bidwell party of 1841
through the Sonora pass. The evidence for this is the fact that he named the
stream the Wimilche, from the tribe of Indians dwelling on it. The Wi-
milches live north of King's river. On the Stanislaus river he was in the
midst of a Mariposan area and he was not far north of King's river. Again,
orders were issued in october 1827 to bring into San Francisco the trappers
on the Rio Estanislao (Governor's orders of august 3, september 14, october
1 and 16 in Departmental records MSS., V, 78, 88, 94, 102, cited in Bancroft,
California, III, 158 footnote. Compare Bojorges, Recuerdos, MSS., 12-14, cited
in *idem*). In the third place, Smith states that he traveled north three hundred miles from San Gabriel, which would bring him approximately to the
Stanislaus. Finally, the Burr map of 1839 shows Smith's route as following up
a river whose mouth was nearly due east of San Jose, and we have Smith's
own statement that the encampment where he left his men and from which
he started east was seventy miles from that place.

[403] Assuming that, in continuing his journey, he followed up the middle
fork of this river, he would pass to the south of Mount Stanislaus (11,202
feet), and on the other side of the Sierras would strike the upper reaches
of the West Walker river, which he would follow down into the plains to the
east, presumably passing to the south of Walker lake. Thence he proceeded
northeast to Great Salt lake. A highway follows this route today. See U.S.
Geological survey, *California-Nevada, Jackson, Big Tree, Sonora, Yosemite,
Dardanelles, Bridgeport, Pyramid, Peal, Wellington, Carson,* and *Wabuska
quadrangles* (topographic sheets). For the Bidwell route see Richman,
"Map," *loc. cit.,* and Bidwell, "First emigrant train to California," *Century
magazine,* XIX, 106 ff. See also F. N. Fletcher, "Eastbound route of Jedediah
S. Smith, 1827," in California historical society *quarterly,* II, 344 ff.

water sometimes for two days over sandy deserts, where there was no sign of vegetation and when we found water in some of the rocky hills, we most generally found some Indians who appeared the most miserable of the human race having nothing to subsist on (nor any clothing) except grass seed, grass-hoppers, etc. When we arrived at the Salt lake, we had but one horse and one mule remaining, which were so feeble and poor that they could scarce carry the little camp equipage which I had along; the balance of my horses I was compelled to eat as they gave out.

The company are now starting, and therefore must close my communication. Yours respectfully,
(signed) JEDEDIAH S. SMITH, of the firm of Smith, Jackson and Sublette.

During Smith's sojourn in California, both he and Harrison G. Rogers, the clerk of the company, kept a record of daily occurrences. Rogers's journal has been preserved. Like Smith, Harrison G. Rogers was a man of deep religious sentiment, a stalwart Calvinist. From the entire absence of all mention of him prior to 1826, it would seem not unlikely that he made his first trip to the mountains in company with Ashley and Smith in the spring of that year. Two bits of philological evidence suggest a possible New England or Canadian origin for him. The mission of San Gabriel reminded him of the "British barracks," which he presumably had seen. Again, black raspberries he calls by the name, "Scotch cap," an Americanism. He was killed july 14, 1828, with eleven other of Smith's men, at the massacre on the Umpqua.

Two of his journals, both of them fragments, have survived. The first covers the period from november 27 to december 20, 1826 and from january 1 to january

27, 1827. The second runs from may 10 to july 13, 1828. What became of the remainder of these journals is unknown. It is possible that the first part of the first journal, i.e., the portion covering the march from Great Salt lake to San Gabriel was handed over to the Mexican authorities at San Diego. Governor Echeandía, writing december 20, 1826 to the minister of war, stated that he was enclosing Smith's diary.[404] He may, of course, have referred to Smith's own journal, but the abrupt fashion in which the Rogers narrative begins with their arrival at San Gabriel may indicate that Smith took the first section of this with him to San Diego as evidence of his purely pacific and commercial intentions, and that it there came into Echeandía's hands, and was by him forwarded as noted above. Efforts to locate it, however, have been futile. The portions of the journals that have survived [405] were carried about by Rogers from his first arrival in California.

With Smith's return to California in the winter of 1827, and the resumption of the journey northward in the spring of 1828, Rogers continued his diary. Day by day, during the tedious and dangerous march through northern California and southern Oregon, he diligently recorded the distance made and the direction pursued, taking pains to make his log as perfect and accurate in detail as the difficulties of an unnamed and unknown wilderness would permit. Nothing escaped his attention, from the size of the raspberries to the shape and character of the Indian lodges and the peculiarities of their dialects. Occasionally he indicted a little prayer for preservation against the perils and dangers of the way, until, at last, on the thirteenth of

[404] St. Pap. Sac. MSS., XIX, 37, 38, cited by Bancroft, *California*, III, 155, footnote 6.
[405] They fill one hundred twelve pages, 30 cm. by 10 cm.

july, having arrived at the Umpqua, he sets down in his book with an apparent sigh of relief, "Those Inds, tell us after we get up the river 15 or 20 miles, we will have good travelling to the Wel Hammet or Multe-nomah, where the Callipo Inds. live." After nearly two years of almost constant danger, they were then within easy distance of the friendly Kalapoo Indians, the Willamette river, and Fort Vancouver, the Hudson's Bay company's post at its mouth. For the first time the outlook was bright. This, however, was the last entry in Rogers's journal. Next morning after breakfast, he and all the company save three were brutally mas-sacred by the Umpqua Indians, into whose hands fell all the property of the little band, including the furs, the outfit, and the journals themselves. Three refugees only, Smith, Black, and Turner, made their way amid terrible hardships to Fort Vancouver, where they se-cured assistance from the British in recovering their property.

For many months the journals were in the Indians' possession. Why they did not destroy them is a mystery. Perhaps they regarded them as an unknown and pow-erful medicine. Finally recovered, however, by Smith himself in the late fall of 1828, they were brought out by him from the mountains in the fall of 1830. The following summer, after having eluded constant danger and even having escaped the massacre on the Umpqua, Smith was at length shot down on his way to Santa Fe. Ashley, who had been made the executor of his will, took possession of his papers, including the Harrison G. Rogers journals. Instead of returning them to Smith's relatives, who, perhaps, would have scarcely appreciated their value, he retained them. With his death they passed to the administrator of his estate and so to the hands of Mrs. Benjamin F. Gray of St. Louis, Ashley's grand-niece, by whom they were deposited with the Missouri Historical society, where they are now preserved.

[FIRST] JOURNAL OF HARRISON G. ROGERS [406]
member of the company of J. S. Smith

Merchandise taken by Jedediah S. Smith for the Southwest expedition, august 15th, 1826.

4 dozen B. knives	10 lbs. lead
1 paper tax. 2 lbs. beads	55 lbs. powder
1½ dozen looking glasses	55 lbs. tobacco
2, 3pt. Am. blanketts	6 Frenchen chisaels
3. 2½ pt. Am. blanketts	1 fuzie
1 road shawl	

Merchandise presented to the Eutaw Indians, by J. S. Smith, august 22nd, 1826.

3 yards red ribbon	1 brass handle knife
10 awls	40 balls, arrow points
1 razor. 1 dirk knife	½ lb. tobacco

August 27th, 1826. Indian presents.

1 tin kettle	2 dozen rings
3 yards red stranding	1 dozen combs

[406] Interspersed with the narrative are memoranda of issues of soap, tobacco, Indian goods, etc., to the men. From these accounts the following data regarding their itinerary are obtainable:

Muddy river, october 1, 1826
    "   "   "   2, "
Siskadee   "   5, "
    "   "   24, "
    "   november 5, "
Rainy encampment, october
Rock creek encampment, november 25, 1826.
Saint Gabriel, december 1, 1826.
    "   "   "   5, "
    "   "   "   31, "
    "   "   january 4, 1827.

4 razors, 2 durk knives	4 hawk bells
2 butcher knives	2 stretch needles
50 balls, 1 lb. powder	2 doz. awls, buttons
3 looking glasses	1 large green handle knife

Broad, handsomely stripped, the cattle differ from ours; they have large horns, long legs, and slim bodies; the beef similar to ours. The face of the country changes hourly, handsome bottoms covered with grass similar to ours. Blue grass; the mou. goes lower and clear of rock to what they have been heretofore.

[MONDAY, NOVEMBER] 27TH. We got ready as early as possible and started a W. course, and traveled 14 m. and enc. for the day, we passed innumerable herds of cattle, horses and some hundred of sheep; we passed 4 or 5 Ind. lodges, that their Inds. acts as herdsmen. There came an old Ind. to us that speaks good Spanish, and took us with him to his mansion,[407] which consisted of 2 rows of large and lengthy buildings, after the Spanish mode, they remind me of the British barracks. So soon as we enc. there was plenty prepared to eat, a fine young cow killed, and a plenty of corn meal given us; pretty soon after the 2 commandants of the missionary establishment come to us and had the appearance of gentlemen. Mr. S. went with them to the mansion and I stay with the company, there was great feasting among the men as they were pretty hungry not having any good meat for some time.[408]

28TH. Mr. S. wrote me a note in the morning, stating that he was received as a gentleman and treated as such,

---

407 *Sic* for mission (?).

408 The arrival in the vicinity of the mission of San Gabriel to which reference is here made. San Gabriel, the fourth of the Alta California missions, was originally established on San Pedro bay in 1771. Subsequently it was removed inland to its present site near Los Angeles. Smith's men stayed this night near an Indian farmhouse about four miles northeast of the mission. See entry of january 18, page 221.

and that he wished me to go back and look for a pistol
that was lost, and send the company on to the missionary
establishment. I complyed with his request, went back,
and found the pistol, and arrived late in the evening,
was received very politely, and showed into a room and
my arms taken from me. About 10 o'clock at night
supper was served, and Mr. S. and myself sent for. I
was introduced to the 2 priests over a glass of good old
whiskey and found them to be very joval friendly gentlemen, the supper consisted of a number of different
dishes, served different from any table I ever was at.
Plenty of good wine during supper, before the cloth
was removed sigars was introduced. Mr. S. has wrote
to the governor,[409] and I expect we shall remain here
some days.

29TH. Still at the mansion. We was sent for about
sunrise to drink a cup of tea, and eat some bread and
cheese. They all appear friendly and treat us well,
although they are Catholicks by profession, they allow
us the liberty of conscience, and treat us as they do their
own countrymen, or brethren.

About 11 o'clock, dinner was ready, and the priest
come after us to go and dine; we were invited into the

[409] José Maria de Echeandía, sometime director of the College of Engineers
in Mexico City and lieutenant-colonel in the army, was the second governor
of Alta California under Mexican rule. He was appointed in january 1825
but did not formally assume office until november. His term ended january
31, 1831. He established his official residence at San Diego, some five or six
miles from the present city of that name, thereby giving offense to the people
of Monterey and the north, which resulted in the Solis revolt. At the same
time he made himself unpopular with the missions by proposing in 1830 an
enlightened scheme of secularization. A successor was appointed in 1830, but
Echeandía, placing himself at the head of an insurrectionary movement, retained his hold as *jefe politico* and *jefe militar* over southern California till
january 1833, when, at last, a successor arrived from Mexico. He left California in the spring of that year, retiring to Mexico, where he died before
1871, Richman, *California under Spain and Mexico,* 243 and *passim;*
Thwaites, *Early western travels,* XVIII, 290 ff; Bancroft, *California,* II, 788.

office, and invited to take a glass of gin and water and
eat some bread and cheese; directly after we were seated
at dinner, and every thing went on in style, both the
priests being pretty merry, the clerk and one other
gentleman, who speaks some English. They all appear
to be gentlemen of the first class, both in manners and
habbits. The mansion, or mission, consist of 4 rows of
houses forming a complete square, where there is all
kinds of macanicks at work; the church faces the east
and the guard house the west; the N. and S. line comprises the work shops. They have large vineyards, apple
and peach orchards, and some orrange and some fig
trees. They manufacture blankets, and sundry other
articles; they distill whiskey and grind their own grain,
having a water mill, of a tolerable quality; they have
upwards of 1,000 persons employed, men, women, and
children, Inds. of different nations. The situation is
very handsome, pretty streams of water running through
from all quarters, some thousands of acres of rich and
fertile land as level as a die in view, and a part under
cultivation, surrounded on the N. with a high and lofty
mou., handsomely timbered with pine, and cedar, and
on the S. with low mou, covered with grass. Cattle —
this mission has upwards of 30,000 head of cattle, and
horses, sheep, hogs, etc. in proportion. I intend visiting
the iner apartments to-morrow if life is spared. I am
quite unwell to-day but have been engaged in writing
letters for the men and drawing a map of my travels
for the priests. Mr. Smith, as well as myself, have been
engaged in the same business.[410] They slaughter at this
place from 2 to 3,000 head of cattle at a time; the mission lives on the profits. Saint Gabriel is in north lati-

---

410 Unfortunately these maps have not come to light.

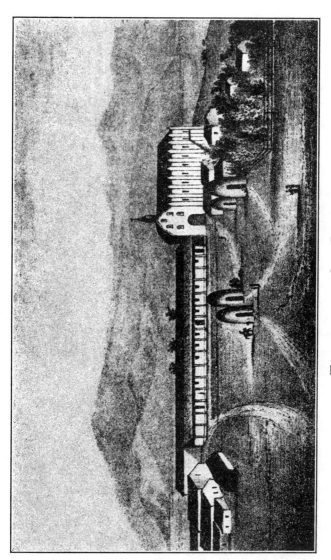

THE MISSION OF SAN GABRIEL
From a contemporary woodcut

tude 34 degrees and 30 minutes.[411] It still continues warm; the thermometer stands at 65 and 70 degrees.

30TH. Still at Saint Gabriel; everything goes on well; only the men is on a scanty allowance, as yet. There was a wedding in this place today, and Mr. S. and myself invited; the bell was rang a little before sun rise, and the morning service performed; then the musick commenced serranading, the soldiers firing, etc., about 7 o'clock tea and bread served, and about 11, dinner and musick. The ceremony and dinner was held at the priests; they had an ellegant dinner, con-sisting of a number of dishes, boiled and roast meat and fowl, wine and brandy or ogadent, grapes brought as a dessert after dinner. Mr. S. and myself acted quite independent, knot understanding there language, nor they ours; we endeavored to appoligise, being very dirty and not in a situation to shift our clothing, but no excuse would be taken, we must be present, as we have been served at there table ever since we arrived at this place; they treat [us] as gentlemen in every sense of the word, although our apparel is so indifferent, and we not being in circumstances at this time to help our-selves, being about 800 m. on a direct line [412] from the place of our deposit. Mr. S. spoke to the commandant this evening respecting the rations of his men; they were immediately removed into another apartment, and furnished with cooking utensils and plenty of provisions, they say, for 3 or 4 days. Our 2 Ind. guides were imprisoned in the guard house the 2nd. day after we arrived at the missionary establishment and remain confined as yet. Mr. S. has wrote to the commandant of

[411] 34° 6' N. latitude, 118° 6' w. longitude, to be exact.

[412] Really only a little over six hundred miles in a direct line from Great Salt lake.

the province, and we do not know the result as yet, or
where we shall go from this place, but I expect to the
N.W. I intended visiting the iner apartments to-day,
but have been engaged in assisting Mr. S. in making a
map for the priest and attending the ceremonies of the
wedding.

DECEMBER 1ST, 1826. We still remain at the mansion
of St. Gabriel; things going on as usual; all friendship
and peace. Mr. S. set his blacksmiths, James Reed and
Silas Gobel, to work in the B.S. shop, to make a bear
trap for the priest, agreeable to promise yesterday. Mr.
S. and the interpreter went in the evening to the next
mission, which is 9 m. distance from St. Gab. and called
St. Pedro,[413] a Spanish gentleman from that mission
having sent his servant with horses for them. There
came an Itallian gentleman from Port Sandeago today
by the name of John Battis Bonafast who speaks good
English, and acts as interpreter for all the American
and English vessels that arrives in ports on the coast,
quite a smart and intelligent man.[414] The men all appear satisfied since there was new regulations made
about eating. Mr. S. informed me this morning that
he had to give Read[415] a little floggin yesterday evening, on account of some of his impertinence; he ap-

---

413 The port of San Pedro is thirty-four miles from the mission of San
Gabriel via the Pueblo of Los Angeles. Rogers seems to have confused this
distance with that to Los Angeles.

414 Juan Bautista Bonifacio, an Italian or Austrian, landed in California
in 1822 from the ship "John Begg," Bancroft, *California,* II, 478. In 1829 he
married and two years later became naturalized, Bancroft, *op. cit.,* II, 723.
According to Bancroft, he was an illiterate honest fellow, but his intelligence
impressed Rogers; and he had at least sufficient to become second officer or
lieutenant of the *Compañía Extranjera de Monterey* in 1832. Later he seems
to have become a commander of this organization, Bancroft, *op. cit.,* III, 221,
223. He died about 1834, leaving a widow and three children.

415 James Read, a troublesome fellow, who later abandoned Smith's employ.

peared more complasant to-day than usual. Our fare at table much the same as at first, a plenty of everything good to eat and drink.

2ND. Much the same to-day as yesterday, both being what the Catholicks call fast days; in the morning after sun rise, or about that time, you have tea, bread and cheese, at dinner fish and fowl, beans, peas, potatoes and other kinds of sauce, grapes as a desert, wine, gin and water plenty at dinner. I could see a great deal of satisfaction here if I could talk there language, but, as it is, I feel great diffidence in being among them knot knowing the topic of there conversation, still every attention is paid to me by all that is present, especially the old priest. I must say he is a very fine man and a very much of a gentleman.[416] Mr. S. has not returned from the other mission as yet. This province is called the Province of New California; this mission ships to Europe annually from 20 to 25 thousand dollars worth of hides and tallow, and about 20 thousand dollars worth of soap. There vineyards are extensive; they make there own wine, and brandy; they have orranges and limes growing here. The Inds. appear to be much altered from the wild Indians in the mou. that we have passed. They are kept in great fear; for the least offense

---

[416] José Bernardo Sanchez. Born september 7, 1778 at Robledillo, Spain, he joined the Franciscan order in 1794 and ten years later arrived in California. He served at San Diego from 1804-1820, at Purisima 1820-1821, and finally at San Gabriel 1821-1833. He was regarded by his superiors as a man of distinguished merit and ability. He was by no means a friend or sympathizer of Echeandía, the governor, whose policy of secularization he strenuously opposed. From 1827-1831 he held the high office of president of the Alta California missions, performing its difficult duties with much tact and credit. He is described as fair and fat, of lively disposition, generous, and hospitable, with a multitude of friends among all classes. He was an able manager of the temporal affairs of his mission and was proud of its prosperity. His declining years were harassed by a painful and incurable malady, Bancroft, *California*, III, 642 footnote.

they are corrected; they are compleat slaves in every sense of the word. Mr. S. and Laplant [417] returned late in the evening, and represents there treatment to be good at the other mission. Mr. S. tells me that Mr. Francisco, the Spanish gentleman that he went to visit, promises him as many horses and mules as he wants.[418]

DECEMBER 3RD., SUNDAY. About 6 o'clock the bell rang for mass, and they poured into church from all quarters, men, women and children; there was none of us invited therefore we all remained at our lodgings. The fare to-day at table much as usual; there was an additional cup of tea in the afternoon. The Inds. play bandy [419] with sticks, it being the only game I have seen as yet among them. They play before the priests door. I am told they dance, both Spanyards and Inds., in the course of the evening.

4TH. Still at St. Gabriel; things much as usual. The priest presented Mr. S. with two pieces of shirting containing 64 yards for to make the men shirts, all being nearly naked. Mr. Smith gives each man 3½ yards and kept the same number for himself, each man getting enough to make a shirt. The weather still continues to be moderate, the thermometer stands at 60 and 63 in the day, and 50-53 in the night. The thermometer hangs within doors, etc.

5TH. We are still remaining at the mansion of St. Gabriel, waiting the result of the governor's answer to a letter that Mr. S. addressed him on the 27th of no-

[417] Abraham Laplant, one of Smith's men, who apparently accompanied him to San Pedro. He was also a member of the expedition of 1828.

[418] Francisco Martinez (see entry of december 7), a Spanish gentleman, who had been residing in California for some time but who was obliged to leave by the law of 1827, ordering the expulsion of all Spaniards from Mexican territory. He is said to have sailed on the "Thomas Nowlan" from San Pedro. See Bancroft, *California*, III, 51 footnote; IV, 733.

[419] I.e. hockey.

vember. We expect the courier some time today with letters. It still continues moderate.

6TH. Early this morning I presented the old priest with my buffalo robe and he brought me a very large blankett and presented me, in return, about 10 o'clock. Nothing new. Things going on as they have been heretofore; no answer from the governor as yet; we are waiting with patience to hear from the governor.

11TH [7TH]. No answer as yet from the governor of the province. Mr. S. and all hands getting impatient. There was a Spanish gentleman arrived yesterday evening named Francis Martinnis,[420] a very intelligent man, who speaks pretty good English, and appears very friendly; he advises Mr. S. to go an see the governor in case he does not receive an answer in a few days. He is a man of business and is well aware that men on expenses and business of importance should be presservering; he appears anxious as respects our well fare. Mr. S. has some idea of going in company with him to Sandiego, the residence of the governor.

8TH. Nothing of importance has taken place today. Mr. S. was sent for to go to Sandiego to see the governor. Capt. Cunningham, commanding the ship Courier, now lying in port at Sandiego, arrived here late this evening.[421] The captain is a Bostonian, and has been trading on the coast for hides and tallow since june last; he informs me that he is rather under the impression

---

420 Francisco Martinez.

421 William H. Cunningham of Boston, who came to California as master of the "Courier" in 1826. Although on the California coast for several years, he seems to have spent much of his time on shore. He befriended J. O. Pattie on his arrival in California. By 1831 he was back in Boston. He seems to have spent the remainder of his life in Massachusetts, dying after 1880, Bancroft, *California,* II, 772; III, 146; Pattie, James O., *Personal narrative,* in Thwaites, *Early western travels,* XVIII, 245. It seems to have been Cunningham who brought Echeandía's message to Smith.

that he shall be obliged to remain untill some time in the succeeding summer in consequence of so much opposition, as there is a number of vessels on the coast trading for the same kind of articles. He says that money is very scarce, amongst the most of the people. Mr. Martinas tells me that there is between 16 and 17,000 natives that is converted over to the Catholic faith and under the control of the different missions, the white population he estimates at 6,000, making 22 or 23,000 souls in the province of New Callifornia.

9TH. Mr. Smith and one of the men, in company with Capt. Cunningham, left San Gabriel, this morning for Sandiego, the governor's place of residence. I expect he will be absent for eight or ten days. The weather still keeps moderate, things much the same, friendship and peace as yet.

10TH. SUNDAY. There was five Inds. brought to the mission by two other Inds, who act as constables, or overseers, and sentenced to be whiped for not going to work when ordered.

Each received from 12 to 14 lashes on their bare posteriors; they were all old men, say from 50 to 60 years of age, the commandant standing by with his sword to see that the Ind. who flogged them done his duty. Things in other respects similar to the last sabbath.

11TH. Nothing of consequence has taken place today more than usual, only the band of musick consisting of two small violins, one bass violin, a trumpet and triangle was played for 2 hours in the evening before the priests door by Inds. They made tolerable good music, the most in imitation to whites that [I] ever heard. Directly after the musick would cease, there was several rounds of cannon fired by the soldiers in commemoration of some great saints day or feast day. They keep at this place 4 small field pieces, 2 6-pounders and 2 2-pounders to protect them from the Inds. in case they should rebel, and, from the best information I can get from the soldiers, they appear at times some what alarmed, for fear the Inds. will rise and destroy the mission.

12TH. About sun rise, the bell rang and mass called; men women and children attended church; they discharged a number of small arms and some cannon while the morning service were performing. There main church is upwards of 200 feet in length and about 140 in breadth made of stone and brick, a number of different apartments in it. They hold meeting in the large church every sunday; the Spanyards first attend and then the Inds. They have a room in the iner apartment of the mission to hold church on their feast days. There religion appears to be a form more than a reality. I am in hopes we shall be able to leave here in five or six days at most, as all hands appear to be anxious to move on to the north. Things in other respects much the same; the weather still continues to be good. In the evening there was kind of procession, amongst both Spanyards and Inds. I enquired the reason, I was told by a Mr. David Philips, an Englishman, that this day, a year ago, the Virgin Mary appeared to an Ind. and told him that the 12th day of december should always be kept as a feast day and likewise a holliday among them and both Spaniards and Inds. believe it.[422]

13TH. I walked through the work shops; I saw some Inds. blacksmithing, some carpentering, others making the wood work of ploughs, others employed in making spining wheels for the squaws to spin on. There is

---

[422] David Philips, according to Bancroft, was an English cooper. He places the date of his arrival in 1834 [*sic* for 1824 (?)] and says that he was in San Diego in 1836, living with a Mexican wife, Bancroft, *California*, IV, 776.

upwards 60 women employed in spining yarn and others weaving. Things much the same, cloudy and some rain today. Our black smith[s] have been employed for several days making horse and nails for our own use when we leave here.

14TH. I was asked by the priest to let our black smiths [423] make a large trap for him to set in his orrange garden, to catch the Inds. in when they come up at night to rob his orchard. The weather clear and warm. Things in other respects much the same as they have been heretofore; friendship and peace prevail with us and the Spanyards. Our own men are contentious and quarrelsome amongst themselves and have been ever since we started the expedition. Last night at supper for the first time the priest questioned me as respected my religion. I very frankly informed him that I was brought up under the Calvinist doctrine, and did not believe that it was in the power of man to forgive sins. God only had that power, and when I was under the necessity of confessing my sins, I confessed them unto God in prayer and supplication, not to man; I further informed him that it was my opinion, that men ought to possess as well as profess religion to constitute the christian; he said that when he was in his church and his robe on, he then believed he was equal unto God, and had the power to forgive any sin, that man was guilty of, and openly confessed unto him, but when he was out of church and his common waring apparel on he was as other men, divested of all power of forgiving sins.

[DECEMBER] 15TH. I went out fowling with the commandant of the mission. I killed 7 brant and one duck, and the commandant killed 2 brants and a duck; the priest furnished me with shot. Two of our men

---

[423] James Read and Silas Gobel presumably.

went to work today, Arthur Black and John Gaiter; they are to get a horse a piece for 3 days work. Times much the same as they have been some time back; nothing new occurs.

16TH.[424] Late this morning a Mr. Henry [Edwards?], owner of a brig now lying in port, arrived at the mission; he appears to be a very much of a gentleman, and quite intelligent. His business here is to buy hides, tallow and soap, from the priest. Nothing new has taken place. Things much the same about the mission; the priest administered the sacrament to a sick Indian today, and he thinks he will die.

17TH. The sick Indian that the priest administered the sacrament too yesterday, died last night, and was entered in there graveyard this evening; the proceedings in church similar to the last sabbath. Sunday appears to be the day that the most business is transacted at this mission; the priest plays at cards both sunday a[nd] weak a days, when he has company that can play pretty expert.

18TH. I received a letter from Mr. S. informing me that he rather was under the impression that he would be detained for some time yet,[425] as the general did [not] like to take the responsibility on himself to let

424 Inserted at this point are the following directions: "Two days above Saint Francisco, plenty beaver at a lake. Three days above Santa Clare river, Piscadaro, Two Larres or Flag lakes. Plenty of beaver as we are informed by Mr. Martinos." The first lake referred to is probably Buena Vista lake, Kern county, about seventy-five miles northwest of the mission of San Fernando Rey. The Santa Clara river rises in the mountains north of San Gabriel and flows westward, entering the Santa Barbara channel, sixty miles north of San Pedro. The Two Larres lake is, of course, the Tulare, discovered and named by Pedro Fages in 1773 from *los tules* (flags, rushes).

425 "The Spaniards throughout looked upon him [Smith] with much suspicion, he underwent a thousand cross-examinations but they never could believe that his sole object was to hunt beaver, an animal they scarcely knew by name, altho' some of the rivers within a few miles of their settlement abounded therewith," Simpson, "Report," in Sullivan, *op. cit.,* 145.

us pass until he received instructions from the general in Mexico; under those circumstances I am fearful we will have to remain here some time yet. Our men have been employed fitting out a cargo of hides, tallow, and soap for a Mr. Henry Edwards, a German by birth, and the most intelligent man that I have met with since I arrived at this place; he is what they term here a Mexican trader.[426]

Mr. S. also wrote to me for eight beaver skins, to present to the Spanish officers to face there cloaks with; I complied with his request, and selected eight of the best and sent to him.

19TH. Still remaining at San Gabriel; things much the same. I went out with my gun to amuse myself, killed some black birds and ducks. The express left here this morning for Sandiego. I sent the eight beaver skins to Mr. Smith to present to the Spanish officers to face their cloaks, by him. The old father continues his friendship to me; it does not appear to abate in the least. I still eat at his table. This mission, if properly managed, would be equal to [a] mine of silver or gold; there farms is extensive; they raise from 3 to 4000 bushels of wheat annually, and sell to shippers for $3. per bushel. There annual income, situated as it is and managed so badly by the Inds., is worth in hides, tallow, soap, wine, ogadent, wheat, and corn from 55 to 60,000 dollars.

20TH. Nothing new has taken place; all peace and friendship. I expect an answer from Mr. Smith in six or eight days if he does not get permission to pass on. My situation is a very delicate one, as I have to be

426 Henry Edwards is unidentifiable. All trade with Mexico proper was still conducted by sea. Shortly after this the term, "Mexican trader," was applied to those who journeyed overland between Santa Fe and Alta California.

amongst the grandees of the country every day. My clothes are [illegible] the clothing of blanketts [illegible] pantaloons, two shirts and [illegible] read cap. I make a very grotesque appearance when seated at table amongst the dandys with there ruffles, silks, and broad clothes, and I am [427]

---

[427] There is a break in the manuscript at this point.

Smith, meantime, had reached San Diego, where he was presented to Echeandía. He explained that he had been compelled to enter Mexican territory because of his lack of provisions and horses. Echeandía seems to have been impressed with Smith's honesty and to have been confirmed in this impression when, december 20, Smith produced the following document as an attestation of his character and good faith:

"We, the undersigned, having been requested by Capt. Jedediah S. Smith, to state our opinions regarding his entering the province of California, do not hesitate to say that we have no doubt but that he was compelled to for want of provisions and water, having entered so far into the barren country that lies between the latitudes of forty-two and forty-three west [sic], that he found it impossible to return by the route he came, as his horses had most of them perished from want of food and water, he was therefore under the necessity of pushing forward to California—it being the nearest place where he could procure supplies to enable him to return.

"We further state as our opinion that the account given by him is circumstantially correct, and that his sole object was the hunting and trapping of beaver and other furs. We have also examined the passports provided the United States of America, and do not hesitate to say we believe them perfectly correct.

"We also state that, in our opinion, his motives for wishing to pass by a different route to the Columbia river on his return is solely because he feels convinced that he and his companions run great risks of perishing if they return by the route they came.

"IN testimony whereof we have herewith set our hands and seals this 20th day of december, 1826.

WM. G. DANA,	JAMES SCOTT.
Capt. Schooner, Waverly.	THOMAS M. ROBINSON,
WM. H. CUNNINGHAM,	Mate, Schooner, Waverly.
Capt. Ship, Courier.	THOMAS SHAW,
WM. HENDERSON,	Supercargo, Ship, Courier."
Capt. Brig Olive Branch.	

The above is published in Southern California historical society *publications*, III, parts 4, 47, 48, and in Cronise, *Natural wealth of California*, 43.

New Years address by Harrison G. Rogers to the
Reverend Father of San Gabriel mission
January 1st. 1827

REVEREND FATHER, Standing on the threshold of a New Year, I salute you with the most cordial congratulations and good wishes.

While the sustaining providence of God has given us another year of probation, every thing seems to remind me that is for probation.

Many, very many, during the past year have, doubtless, been called throughout the different parts of the tractless globe, to weep over friends now sleeping in their graves, many others have personally felt the visitations of sickness, and probably many more, ere another year ushers in, will be called from time into eternity.

While revolving seasons, while sickness, disappointment, and death raise their minatory voice, remember, reverend sir, that this world is not our home. It is a world of trial. It is the dawn of an immortal existence.

Therefore my advice is, to all the human family, to be faithful, be devoted to God, be kind, be benevolent to their fellow sufferers, to act well their part, live for eternity; for the everlasting destinies of their souls is suspended upon their probation, and this may close the present year.

Our Savior, sir, after having spent his life in untrying [untiring] benevolence, and before he ascended to his native heavens, probably in allusion to the twelve tribes of Israel, elected twelve apostles or missionaries.

To these, after having properly qualified and instructed them, he left a part of his legacy, a world to be converted.

He directed that "repentance and remission of sins should be preached in his name among all nations, beginning at Jerusalem" – Agreeably to his command the first church was founded at Jerusalem.

But, reverend father, remember the whole world was missionary ground. Before the days of Christ Jesus, our Saviour, we never heard of missionaries to the heathen with a solitary exception.

The exception to which I allude is the case of Jonah, who was sent to preach to the heathen at Nineveh about 800 years before Christ.

It was not till several years after the ascension of our Saviour that a single gentile was converted. But now the door was opened. The apostles hesitated, delayed no longer. It is said by ancient history that the world was divided among them by lot.

Be this as it may, it is certain that they soon seperated and went from village to village.

To this little number of missionaries we are informed that Paul was soon added.

With the exception of this man, the missionaries were not learned in the arts and sciences; were ignorant of books and of men, yet they went forth unsupported by human aid, friendless and opposed by prejudices, princes, laws, learning, reasonings of philosophy, passions and persecutions.

And what was the result of their labors? We know but a little; we can trace only a few of their first steps. Yet we know enough to astonish us. We know by the labors of those missionaries there are mentioned in the New Testament, sixty-seven different places in which christian churches were established by them, several of which places contained several churches.

Paul informs us that in his time the gospel had been preached to every [race] which is under heaven. Justin Martyr tells us that in the year 106, "There was not a nation either Greek or barbarian or of any other name even of those who wander in tribes and live in tents, among whom prayers and thanksgivings are not offered to the Father and Creator of the universe, by the name of the Crucified Jesus." We know, assuredly, that at this time that there were churches in Germany, Spain, France, and Brittain. Besides the apostles, there were at least eighty-seven evangelists in this age, so that the whole number of active missionaries in the Apostolic age, was ninety-nine or one hundred. Of the apostles we have reasons to believe, nine at least suffered martyrdom. On the whole, then, we have no reason to doubt, on the testimony of history and tradition, that the last command of Christ was so obeyed, that in the Apostolic age, the gospel was preached in every part of the globe which was then known.

MONDAY, JANUARY 1ST, 1827. This morning church was held before day; men, women and children attended as usual; after church, musick played by the Inds. as on sunday; wine and some other articles of clothing given out to the Inds. The priest keeps a memorandum of all articles issued to them. The fare at the table the same as other days, if any difference, not so good. Some rain last night and to-day; weather warm; showers alternate through the day like may showers in the states, and equally as pleasant; things in other respects much the same; no news from Mr. S. and I am at a loss how to act in his absence with the company, as he left no special instructions with me when he left here.

TUESDAY 2ND. Still at the mission of San Gabriel; nothing new has taken place to-day; the men commenced work again this morning for the old padre; no news from Mr. S; friendship and peace still prevail. Mr. Joseph Chapman,[428] a Bostonian by birth, who is married in this country and brought over to the Catholic faith, came here about 10 oclock A.M. to superintend the burning of a coal pitt for the priest. He is getting wealthy, being what we term a Yanky; he is jack of all trades, and naturally a very ingenious man; under those circumstances, he gets many favours from the priest, by superintending the building of mills, black smithing, and many other branches of mechanicism.

W. 3RD. There was five or six Inds. brought to the mission and whiped, and one of them being stubbourn and did not like to submit to the lash was knocked down by the commandant, tied and severely whiped, then chained by the leg to another Ind who had been guilty of a similar offence. I rec'd a letter from Mr. S. this morning informing me that he had got his passports signed by the governor, by the intercession of the gentlemen officers, and that he would join me in a few days; he intended embarking on board Capt. Cun-

---

[428] Joseph Chapman, one of the most picturesque figures in the California of this period. A Bostonian, he had come to California in 1818 as a carpenter and blacksmith. He was at Sta. Ines in 1820, constructing a grist mill, and a year later at San Gabriel, engaged in a similar task. In 1822 he was baptized at San Buenaventura, being known henceforth as José Juan, and soon after married a Mexican lady. From 1824 to 1826 he owned a house at Los Angeles and sufficient land for a vineyard of 4000 vines. He still continued to do odd jobs about the mission, however, which no doubt accounts for his arrival at San Gabriel during Smith's sojourn there. He was a jack-of-all-trades, indeed, being able, apparently, to repair or to construct anything, having built a schooner, and even having served, on one occasion, as a surgeon. "He was a great favorite with the friars, especially Padre Sanchez, who declared it a marvel that one, so long in the darkness of the Baptist faith, could give such an example of true Catholic piety to older christians." He was naturalized in 1831. A few years later he removed to Santa Barbara, where he seems to have lived until his death, about 1848. He was survived by his wife and a number of daughters, Bancroft, *California*, II, 757; Bryant, Edwin, *What I saw in California*, 421; Thompson and West, *History of Los Angeles county, California*, 24.

ningham's ship, and coming to St. Pedro, which is forty-five miles distant from San Gabriel.[429]

THURS. 4TH. Still at the mission; nothing new; four of our men, Robert Evans, Manuel Lazarus, John Hannah,[430] and John Wilson went with Mr. Joseph Chapman, to cut wood for the coal pitt, and assist him in erecting it, and burning the coal. Myself and Mr. McCoy went up in the mountains to see if we could find some dear; I saw two and wounded one, killed a wolf and two ducks; Mr. McCoy saw two dear, and got one shot but missed. We passed through a great abundance of oak timber, some trees heavy laden with acorns, the land, rich, and easy cultivated, some large springs, or lagoons, which offered a great quantity of water, which is brought in all directions through the

---

[429] Echeandía had issued the desired papers, thanks to the intervention of the American ship-masters in the port of San Diego. Smith then sailed for San Pedro on board the "Courier." Captain Cunningham's account of his dealings with Smith is as follows:

"There has arrived at this place Capt. Jedediah Smith with a company of hunters, from St. Louis, on the Missouri. These hardy adventurers have been 13 months travelling their route and have suffered numerous hardships. They have often had death staring them in the face, sometimes owing to the want of sustenance; at others to the numerous savages which they have been obliged to contend with. Out of 50 horses which they started with, they brought only 18 in with them; the others having died on the road for want of food and water.

"Does it not seem incredible that a party of fourteen men, depending entirely upon their rifles and traps for subsistence, will explore this vast continent, and call themselves happy when they can obtain the tail of a beaver to dine upon? Captain Smith is now on board the Courier, and is going with me to St. Pedro to meet his men: from thence he intends to proceed northward in quest of beaver, and to return, afterwards, to his deposits in the Rocky mountains.

"(St. Diego and St. Pedro are ports in California, w. coast of America. near 3,000 miles from Boston)." Letter dated San Diego, december 1826, in *Missouri republican*, october 25, 1827.

[430] John Hannah was slain at the Umpqua. His estate brought suit for the recovery of his wages, which the court allowed, final payment being made in october 1830, Sublette MSS., carton 10, Missouri historical society.

mission farm as they have to water their orchards, gardens, and farms.

FRIDAY 5TH. Still remaining at the mission of San Gabriel, waiting the arrival of Mr. S. Five men went with Mr. Chapman, this morning, to cut cord wood for the coal pitt. I walked over the soap factory and find it more extensive than I had an idea; it consists of 4 large cisterns, or boilers, that will hold from 2000 to 2500 hundred gallons each; the cistern is built in the shape of an sugar loaf made of brick, stone, and lime; there is a large iron pott, or kittle, fixed in the bottom where the fire strikes them to set them boiling, lined around the mouth of the cisterns and the edge of the potts with sheat iron 8 or 10 inches wide; the potts, or kittles, will hold from 2 to 250 gallons each, and a great many small ones, fixed in like manner. Things in other respects much the same about the mission as usual, friendship and peace with us and the Spaniards.

6TH, SATURDAY. This being what is called Epiphany or old Christmas day, it is kept to celebrate the manifestation of Christ to the gentiles, or particularly the Magi or wise men from the East. Church held early as usual, men, women, and children attend; after church the ceremonies as on sundays. Wine issued abundantly to both Spanyards and Inds., musick played by the Ind. band. After the issue of the morning, our men, in company with some Spanyards, went and fired a salute, and the old padre give them wine, bread, and meat as a treat. Some of the men got drunk and two of them, James Reed and Daniel Ferguson, commenced fighting, and some of the Spanyards interfered and struck one of our men by the name of Black, which

come very near terminating with bad consequence.[431]
So soon as I heard of the disturbance, I went among
them, and passified our men by telling what trouble
they were bringing upon themselves in case they did
not desist, and the most of them, being men of reason,
adheared to my advice.

Our black smith, James Reed, come very abruptly
into the priests dining room while at dinner, and asked
for argadent; the priest ordered a plate of victuals to
be handed to him; he eat a few mouthfuls, and set the
plate on the table, and then took up the decanter of
wine, and drank without invitation, and come very
near braking the glass when he set it down; the padre,
seeing he was in a state of inebriety, refrained from
saying anything.

SUNDAY 7TH. Things carried on as on former sab-
aths, since I have been at the mission, church services

---

[431] James Reed was the blacksmith whom Smith flogged and who seems to
have been a troublesome fellow. Nothing is known of his subsequent history.

Daniel Ferguson, confused by Bancroft (*California*, II, 526) with Joseph
Daniel Ferguson, came to California with Smith but, on the departure of the
expedition from San Gabriel, was nowhere to be found. See page 223. He
remained concealed until they had gone far enough to eliminate the possibility of recapturing him. Probably his loss was not grievously felt. The
California authorities knew of his presence in may, and his testimony was
sought as to the character and intentions of Smith's men, Bancroft, *California*, III, 156, citing Departmental records MSS., V, 45. Later he seems to have
settled in or near Monterey. His name appears with that of Bonifacio on the
Compañía Extranjera de Monterey, su organización en 1832, which was
formed to support Zamorano in his insurrection against Echeandía. By 1836
he was residing in Los Angeles and was then thirty-eight years old, not
thirty, as stated by Bancroft (*California*, III, 736). He seems to have come
north again in 1839 or 1840. In july 1841 he was murdered in Salinas valley,
perhaps by José Antonio Arana, the paramour of Ferguson's wife, Maria
del Carmen Ruiz, Bancroft, *California*, III, 736; IV, 653 footnote; Thompson
and West, *History of Los Angeles county, California*, 33.

Arthur Black remained loyal to Smith, accompanied him north in 1828,
and was one of the three to escape the massacre on the Umpqua. He is said
never to have returned to the states, Bancroft, *History of the Northwest coast*,
II, 454 footnote.

morning and evening, issues to the Inds. of wine and clothing; the priest in the evening threw oranges among the young squaws to see them scuffle for them, the activest and strongest would get the greatest share. Mr. Smith has not joined us yet.

MONDAY 8TH. Last night there was a great fandago or dance among the Spanyards; they kept it up till nearly day light from the noise. The women here are very unchaste; all that I have seen and heard speak appear very vulgar in their conversation and manners. They think it an honnour to ask a white man to sleep with them; one came to my lodgings last night and asked me to make her a blanco Pickanina, which, being interpreted, is to get her a white child, and I must say for the first time, I was ashamed, and did not gratify her or comply with her request, seeing her so forward, I had no propensity to tech her. Things about the mission much the same. No news of Mr. S., and I am very impatient, waiting his arrival.

9TH, TUESDAY. Business going on about the mission as usual. About 8 or ten boys employed gathering orranges overseed by the commandant and the steward of the mission, old Antonio, a man of 65 years of age, who is intrusted with the keys of all the stores belonging to the mission; he generally is served at the priests table, and, from appearance, is very saving and trusty. I went out in company with Mr. McCoy this evening with our guns to amuse ourselves; I killed one brant and Mr. McCoy killed nothing. Mr. S. still absent from the company.

WEDNESDAY, 10TH. About noon Mr. S., Capt. Cunningham, Mr. Shaw, and Thos. Dodges [432] come to the

---

[432] Thomas Shaw, supercargo of the "Courier," and one of the signers of the testimonial to Smith's character. Like Cunningham a native of Massachu-

mission from the ship Courier, and I was much rejoiced to see them as I have been waiting with anxiety to see him. Nothing new has taken place to-day; things much the same, about the mission. Mr. S. intends going back in the morning to the ship.

THURSDAY, 11TH. Mr. S. in company with Capt. Cunningham, Mr. Shaw, and Chapman, left the mission this morning for the sea shore. About noon, Capt. Cunningham returned to the mission, and informed me that Mr. S. wished me to go to the parbalo to buy horses, which is 8 miles distance from San Gabriel.[433]

I complied with his request went, and met Mr. S. there, and purchase two horses for our trap, and Mr. S. made an agreement for 10 more, for which he is to give merchandise at the ship in exchange.

FRIDAY, 12TH. I got the two horses we bought last evening, from Mr. Francis St. Abbiso,[434] and returned to the mission about the middle of the day; just as I arrived the priest from San whan [435] arrived on a visit

---

setts, he was employed from 1826-1828 as clerk and supercargo on the ships, "Courier" and "Waverly." In 1830 he was supercargo of the "Pocahontas," John Bradshaw, master. The following year he contracted with Juan Bandini, the insurrectionary leader, to transport Governor Victoria to Mazatlan, sailing january 1832. *The marine list* of 1833-1835 shows him as supercargo and master of the "Volunteer," the "Harriet Blanchard," and the "Lagoda," all of them engaged in the Hawaiian trade. He is said to have been in Boston in 1836, with no intention of returning to California. By 1839-1840, however, he was back again as supercargo of the "Monsoon," remaining on the coast for some time apparently. He died in Boston, presumably about 1866. See Bancroft, *California,* III, 146, 148, 210 ff., 382 ff., 410 ff; IV, 105 footnote; V, 718.

Thomas Dodge is unidentifiable, presumably an officer or passenger on the "Courier."

433 The pueblo, or town of Los Angeles, the second municipality founded in Alta California, at this time consisting of about eighty houses and seven hundred inhabitants.

434 Francis St. Abbiso is unidentifiable.

435 The mission of San Juan Capistrano, founded midway on the road between San Gabriel and San Diego. The priest referred to is probably Padre José Barona, at this time sixty-two years of age, a native Spaniard who had

with his carriage, and Indian servants. He is a man about 50 years of age, upwards of six feet high, and well made in proportion, and, from his conduct, he appears to be a very good man, and a very much of a gentleman. I had a branding iron made by our blacksmith so soon as I returned, and branded the two horses that we bought, with J.S.; things in other respects at the mission much the same.

SATURDAY, 13TH. This morning I set the men to work to put the traps in order for packing; one of the horses I bought yesterday got loose last night and ran off, and I have not got him yet or heard anything of him. Today at dinner I was asked a great many questions by the priest who came here yesterday, respecting our rout and travels; I give him all the satisfaction I could and informed him as respects the situation of the country I have traveled through, also the United States, and their laws. Things about the mission much as usual.

SUNDAY, 14TH. As agreeable to promise I sent Arthur Black, John Gaiter,[436] and Peter Ranne [437] to the parbalo to meet Mr. Smith to get horses, which he is purchasing at that place. Time is passing off swiftly and we are not under way yet; but I am in hopes we shall be able to start in three or 4 days from here. Church as usual; wine issued, etc. In the evening, four Inds. who had been fighting and gambling was brought before the guard house door, and sentenced to be whiped; they received from 30 to 40 lashes each on their bare posteriors.

come to California in 1798. He served in San Diego 1798-1811 and at San Juan Capistrano 1811-1831. After 1827, however, he spent most of his time at San Luis Rey, being described as a man in broken health. Here he died, Bancroft, *California*, III, 625.

[436] John Gaiter continued in Smith's employ and was killed at the Umpqua in july 1828.

[437] Peter Ranne, a negro.

MONDAY [JANUARY] 15TH. About noon Capt. Cunningham and Mr. Chapman arrived at the mission from the ship. Mr. S. still remain in the parbalo, purchasing horses. Mr. Chapman informed me that there is a natural pitch mine north of the parbalo, 8 or 10 miles, where there is from 40 to 50 hogsheads of pitch throwed up from the bowels of the earth, daily; the citizens of the country make great use of it to pitch the roofs of their houses;[438] he shew me a piece which have the smell of coal, more than any other thing I can describe. Business about the mission much the same as it has been heretofore. I went in their church to-day for the first time and saw their molten images; they have our Savior on the cross, his mother and Mary, the mother of James, and 4 of the apostles, all as large as life. They appropriate the room, where the images stand, to a sugar factory.

TUESDAY, 16TH. Mr. S. returned from the parbelo, with 41 head of horses, which he purchased at that place; he got 8 new saddles from the padra and set the men to work to fix them; nothing new has taken place about the mission; things much the same.

WEDNESDAY, 17TH. All hands are busily employed fixing their things ready to start tomorrow morning; the old father has given a great deal to Mr. Smith, and some of the men, and continues giving. I expect we shall be able to get off early in the morning. Things about the mission much the same.

THURSDAY, 18TH. All hands were up early this morning, and went to the farm, where we had our horses, 68 in number, and got them packed, and under way in pretty good season. After we got ½ mile off the mis-

---

438 Perhaps Devil's gate, Los Angeles county, California. Compare De Mofras, *Exploration du territoire de l'Oregon,* 357 ff.

sion, our unpacked horses, together with those that had packs on started to run 8 or 10 miles before we stoped them; one of the pack horses lossed 12 dressed skins, that Mr. Smith had got, from our old father of San Gabriel mission, Joseph Sances. We traveled a direct course N.E. about 4m. and we [arrived] at an Ind. farm house where we stayed on the 27th november, when we first reached the Spanish inhabitants.[439] Mr. S. and myself intends returning to the mission, this evening.

FRIDAY, 19TH. Mr. S. and myself returned to the mission, late last evening and took supper with old Father Sancus, for the last time, and our farwell. The old father give each of us a blankett, and give me a cheese, and a gourd filled with ogadent. All hands being ready early in the morning, we started and travelled, and had an Ind. guide, a N.E. course about 25 m. and enc. at St. Ann, an Ind. farm house, for the night;[440] our wild horses created us considerable trouble during the day.

SATURDAY, 20TH. Still at St. Ann; Mr. S. commands to lie by to-day, as there is five of our best horses missing, and hunt them, and brake some other horses; a number of the men are employed hunting horses and others haltering and brake more. The horse hunters returned without finding them; and he intends leaving them and proceeding on his journey early tomorrow morning.

SUNDAY, 21ST. All hands were up early and getting their horses packed; we were under way in pretty good season in the morning, and had an Ind. boy as a pilot; we started and travelled a N.E. and by east course, 25 or

---

439 See footnote 408. In the vicinity of Santa Anita, a station on the Atchison, Topeka and Santa Fe railroad. See U.S. Geological survey, *Pasadena quadrangle* (topographic sheet).

440 At some point north of Pomona, perhaps on Live Oak creek. See U.S. Geological survey, *Cucamonga quadrangle* (topographic sheet).

30 m. and reached an Ind. farm house about 4 m. distant from San Bernado, and enc. where we have an order from the governor, and our old Father Joseph Sanchus, at the mission of San Gabriel, for all the supplyes we stand in need of. The country quite mountainous and stoney.

MONDAY, 22ND. Mr. S. and the interpreter started early this morning up to San Bernardano for to see the steward, and get supplys. We intend killing some beef here and drying meat. I expect we shall remain here two or three days. All hands get milk this morning. We have killed two beeves and cut the meat, and drying it. Mr. S. has got corn, peas, parched meal, and flour of wheat. Old Father Sanchus has been the greatest friend that I ever met with in all my travels, he is worthy of being called a christian, as he possesses charity in the highest degree, and a friend to the poor and distressed. I ever shall hold him as a man of God, taking us when in distress, feeding, and clothing us, and may God prosper him and all such men; when we left the mission he give Mr. S. an order to get everything he wanted for the use of his company, at San Bernandino. The steward complyed with the order so soon as it was presented by Mr. S.

TUESDAY, 23RD. Still at the Ind. farm 3 m. from San Burnandeino; some of the men are employed in braking horses, and others makeing pack saddles and riggin them; Mr. S. sent a letter back this morning to old Father Sanchius concerning the horses, we lossed at Saint Ann, six in number; he will wait the result of his answer.

WEDNESDAY, 24TH. We are still remaining at the Ind. farm waiting the result of the priests answer, and drying meat, and repairing saddles for our journey.

Some of the men are kept employed braking wild horses. Daniel Ferguson, one of our men, when leaving the mission on the 18th inst. hide himself, and we could not find him; the corporal who commands at the mission promised to find him, and send him on to us. But I expect we shall not see him again.[442] The weather continues fine.

THURSDAY, 25TH. No answer from the priest this morning, and we are obliged to remain here another day. The men still keep at work, braking young horses. Mr. S. discharged one of the men, John Wilson, on the 17th inst., and he could not get permission to stay in the country, therefore we obliged to let him come back to us; he remains with the company but not under pay as yet; I expect he will go on with us.[443] The weather still continues beautiful. Things about our camp much as usual. Inds. traveling back and forward from the mission steady. The Inds. here call themselves the Farrahoots.[444]

FRIDAY, 26TH. Early this morning we collected our

---

[441] They camped near Rialto. San Bernardino was on the frontier of Spanish settlement in California. Here, until a period shortly before Smith's arrival, there had been only a ranch or two, cultivated by Indians. In 1819 the gentiles of the Ranchería Guachana, also called by the Spanish, San Bernardino, voluntarily asked for the introduction of agriculture and stock-raising. No station was established or buildings erected prior to 1822. About that time, a church was erected as a branch of the mission of San Gabriel, *Illustrated history of southern California,* 409.

[442] See footnote 431.

[443] John Wilson, however, did not go on with them. In may he was a prisoner in the hands of the Mexican authorities at Monterey. The government ordered proceedings to be instituted against him. Departmental records, MSS., V, 45; Archivo del Arzobispado, MSS., V, part 1, 28-33, cited by Bancroft, *California,* III, 156. He is mentioned in the account book of Thomas O. Larkin in 1838 and 1839. In 1841 he was given a license to marry Maria F. Mendoza of San Carlos, Bancroft, *op. cit.,* V, 777.

[444] A tribe of Shoshonean (?) stock. See Latham, R. G., "On the languages of the northern, western, and central Americas," in London philological society *transactions,* 85.

horses and counted them; and two was missing. Mr. S. sent a man in search of them; he returned with them about 10 o'clock. We are still at the Ind. farm house, waiting an answer from the priest at San Gabriel. I expected we shall remain here to-day, if the courier does not arrive. In the evening James Reed and myself concluded we would go into the cowpen and rope some cows and milk them, after the Ind. fashion, accordingly we made ready our rope, and haltered four cows, and tied their heads up to a steak, and made fast their hind feet and milked them, but did not get much milk on account of not letting their calves to them; so soon as we were done Capt. Smith and Silas Gobel followed our example. This country in many respects is the most desirable part of the world I ever was in, the climate so regular and beautiful; the thermomater stands daily from 65 to 70 degrees, and I am told it is about the same in summer.

Mr. S. swaped six of our old horses off for wild mares.

SATURDAY, 27TH. Still at the Ind. farm house waiting the answer from the priest. 20 of our horses missing this morning and four men sent in search of them. Mr. S., and Laplant is gone up to San Burnandeino to see the old steward on business.[445]

Having left his men encamped for the summer in the valley of the Stanislaus with Harrison G. Rogers in charge, Smith with his two companions, Silas Gobel, his blacksmith, and Richard Evans, crossed the Sierras (Smith's Mount St. Joseph) and the deserts of Nevada, reaching Great Salt lake june 27, 1827.

Smith's route from the crossing of Mount St. Joseph

---

445 The first Harrison G. Rogers journal ends abruptly at this point.

till he "struck the S.W. corner of the Great Salt lake" was across one of the most barren stretches in western America where, as he states, he frequently journeyed for as much as two days without water. His courage and dogged will alone kept him and his companions going. Frequently ascending the high points along the way, he saw little ahead to encourage his party and, as he wrote in his journal, "I durst not tell my men of the desolate prospect ahead, but framed my story so as to discourage them as little as possible." [446] Almost within reach of their goal near the present Nevada-Utah boundary, one of his companions, Richard Evans, gave out completely and had to be left behind, almost certainly to die of thirst, while Smith and his other companion pushed ahead in a desperate search for water. Said Smith, "We could do no good by remaining to die with him and we were not able to help him along, but we left him with feelings only known to those who have been in the same situation and with the hope that we might get relief and return to save his life." [447] Fortunately they were near the Stansbury range and after a few miles travel reached a fine stream of water. Filling a kettle with several quarts of the precious fluid, Smith hastened back to succor Evans, whom he found far gone and scarcely able to speak. Revived and refreshed, he was soon able to proceed with Smith's aid to a spring where Gobel had made camp. Continuing south of Great Salt lake and at length much restored in spirits and encouraged, the three of them, although encountering considerable difficulty crossing the swollen Jordan river, outlet of Utah lake, finally reached the plain beyond, rounded the tip of Great Salt lake,

[446] Sullivan, *op. cit.,* 20.
[447] *Ibid.,* 21.

and on the third of july 1827, much to the surprise of
the latter, rejoined Smith's partners and their assembled trappers at the rendezvous on the shores of Bear
lake,[448] "one of the most beautiful lakes in the West and
therefore in the world." From the east shore, bare hills
of burnt sienna rise sheer from the water's edge, culminating in the gentle domes of the Bear river divide,
while, to the west, beyond a narrow hem of gently slop-
ing arable land, rise sparsely covered hills of hock and
quaking asp, topped by the dark timber of the main
Wasatch ridge. At the north end of the lake is the outlet to Bear river, which, at this point, swings in from
the hills to the east, flows diagonally across the lower
valley, rounds the hills to the west, not far from Soda
springs, marking the main highway from the South
pass to the Columbia and Oregon. The valley of Bear
lake was a sort of siding on the main line of travel, a
convenient spot, where trappers could withdraw from
the beaten way and find seclusion and safety for the
conduct of their business.

Here Smith met his partners, Jackson and Sublette,
delivered the few furs he had managed to convey across
the Sierras, wrote a report to William Clark summar-
izing the results of his explorations, and prepared to
start back again to join his men in California.

He rested only ten days, however, for on july 13 he
set out again with nineteen men, including at least one
of the men who had just accompanied him from California.[449] His companions were Thomas Virgin,
Charles Swift, Toussaint Marichall, John Turner, Jo-

---

[448] For Smith's fragmentary account of his return to rendezvous, covering
the period, june 22 to july 3, see Sullivan, *op. cit.,* 19-26.

[449] Silas Gobel returned with him. Compare draft of a letter of Ashley to
Benton (?), St. Louis, december 24, 1828, in Ashley MSS., Missouri historical
society. Richard Evans, who had so nearly perished of thirst, did not return.

seph Palmer, Joseph Lepoint, Thomas Daws, Silas Gobel, David Cunningham, Francis Deramme, William Campbell, Boatswain Brown, Gregory Ortaga, John B. Ratelle, Pale, Polite, Robiseau,[450] and Isaac Galbraith.[451] Two Indian women also accompanied the expedition.[452]

Smith had learned enough about the direct route west to know that it would be impossible to cross the deserts with so large a body of men and animals. Consequently he followed in general the same route he had pursued the previous year. Leaving rendezvous the party headed southeast to upper Bear river, which they ascended, crossed to the headwaters of the Weber, thence by way of Salt Lake valley to Utah lake, which they reached in six days. As in the previous year, Smith ascended the Sevier (Ashley's river) where he discovered traces of an unknown party which the Indians related had crossed that way the year previous en route to Taos. Instead of crossing the mountains at the head of the Sevier, he apparently followed the Santa Clara river, crossing by a low divide to Beaver Dam wash (called by Smith, Pautch creek) coming out on the Virgin (Smith's Adams) river. Stopping at the salt caves near St. Thomas, Nevada, he replenished his supply and moved on to the confluence of the Virgin with the Colorado, which he crossed as in the previous year,

---

[450] These ten were killed by the Indians while attempting to cross the Colorado river. Casualty list, furnished by Smith, Jackson, and Sublette to William Clark, Superintendent of Indian affairs, Letter book, 299 ff, Kansas historical society MSS.

[451] Isaac Galbraith was discharged in California, december 27, 1827, Sublette MSS., carton 10, Missouri historical society.

[452] Brief sketch of accidents, misfortunes, and depredations committed by Indians on the firm of Smith, Jackson, and Sublette, Indian traders on the east and west side of the Rocky mountains, since july 1, 1826, to the present, 1829, Kansas historical society MSS.

descending along the left bank to the Mojave villages near Needles.

Allayed by the apparently friendly attitude of these Indians, Smith began crossing his goods over the Colorado on rafts, but, as soon as the party was divided, some of them on either bank and some of them still on the rafts, the Indians, "who in large numbers and with most perfect semblance of peace and friendship were aiding the party to cross the river, suddenly rose upon them and surrounding the party in a most unexpected moment and manner" began an attack.[453] The company being divided was taken at a great disadvantage. Those already across, including Smith, seemed to have suffered least. Those on the river were very likely all killed as were also, most, at least, of those on the eastern bank. Out of nineteen men who had left rendezvous a month earlier only ten survived. The two Indian women who accompanied them were taken prisoners. Rallying the little force about him, Smith told his men that their only hope lay in trying to cross the deserts to the mission stations near the coast. Scattering his stores on the sand spit where they had temporarily halted, Smith allowed each man to pick what he would to take along with him, knowing that once the Indians had crossed they would spend some time quarreling over this loot and thus be delayed in pursuit. With no horses or supplies of any kind save fifteen pounds of dried meat they started westward. They had not gone more than half a mile, however, when the Indians closed in upon them. Fortunately, they were still near

---

[453] The Indians had probably been warned by the Mexican government not to allow Americans to cross the river and enter California. News of the disaster did not reach St. Louis till a year later. "I have recently heard of the loss of eight men," etc., Draft of a letter of Ashley to Benton (?), december 24, 1828, Ashley MSS., Missouri historical society.

the river and, selecting a thick clump of cottonwoods, cut down such trees as they could to form a slight breast-work. They only had five guns for nine men, but by fastening each of their knives to the end of a light pole made what Smith called "a tolerable lance." With these inadequate weapons they prepared to sell their lives as dearly as possible. Fortunately their first shots were well directed. Two Indians were killed and a third wounded, whereupon the entire body ran off, as Smith says, "like frightened sheep." There were no further attacks and just before nightfall they resumed their journey, traveling mostly by night, since the days were intolerable, from water-hole to water-hole, following in general the same course that Smith had taken the previous year across the Mojave sinks and up the dry bed of the Mojave river toward its upper reaches and thence directly to Cajon pass from which, nine and a half days after leaving the Colorado, he emerged in the vicinity of San Bernardino ranch, familiar to Smith from his previous journey.[454]

In dire need of food he killed three of the mission cattle and dried the meat, reporting what he had done to the overseer of the mission farm. The latter received Smith well, presented him and his men with little luxuries and in exchange for sufficient horses to provide the entire party with mounts accepted such little effects as Smith and his men had been able to pack across the desert on their backs.[455] After resting five days, Smith, having written a report of his entry into California to Father Sanchez at San Gabriel and leaving two of his men, Isaac Galbraith,[456] a free trapper attached to his

---

[454] Near the present site of Redlands.

[455] "Draft of a letter," etc. Ashley MSS., Missouri historical society.

[456] "On october 8, Galbraith asked for an interview with Echeandía wishing a license to remain in the country or to rejoin his leader. He also corrects

party, and Thomas Virgin,[457] who had been wounded in the affray with the Mojave Indians, started north to join his men at their camp on the Stanislaus. He arrived on the eighteenth of september within two days of the final date he had set for his return.

During Smith's absence the men had been in difficulties with the Mexican authorities. Even before his departure in may the head of the Mission of San Jose, Padre Duran, had accused the men of enticing his neophytes to desert. Although this charge had been dismissed by the commandant at San Francisco, orders were issued may 18 to find out who the strangers were, what their business was, and to demand their passports, in short, to detain them till further orders.[458] It was too late, however, to secure Smith, for, on the twentieth, he had set out for Great Salt lake, having the previous day written Padre Duran as follows:

Reverend Father: I understand through the medium of one of your christian Indians that you are anxious to know who we are, as some of the Indians have been at the mission and informed you that there were certain white people in the country. We are Americans, on our journey to the river Columbia. We were in at the mission of San Gabriel, january last. I went to San Diego and saw the general and got a passport from him to pass on to that place. I have made several efforts to pass the mountains, but the snow being so deep, I

an impression that Smith is a captain of troops, stating that he is but a hunter of a company of Smith, Jackson, and Sublette."—Bancroft, *California,* III, 158 footnote, citing Departmental state papers, MSS., II, 36, 37. Galbraith was not dismissed at this time but accompanied Smith north and did not withdraw from his service till december 27, 1827, Sublette MSS., carton 10, Missouri historical society.

[457] Thomas Virgin was sent to San Diego, where he was placed in prison but afterwards released to rejoin Smith. Warner states that Smith, himself, was conducted to San Diego but this is unsupported and seems improbable, Warner, "Reminiscences," in Southern California historical society *publications,* VII, 181 ff.

[458] Archivo del Arzobispado, MSS., V, part I, 27 and Departmental records, MSS., V, 45, cited by Bancroft, *California,* III, 156 footnote.

could not succeed in getting over. I returned to this place, it being the only point to kill meat, to wait a few weeks until the snow melts so that I can go on. The Indians here, also, being friendly, I consider it the most safe point for me to remain until such time as I can cross the mountains with my horses, having lost a great many in attempting to cross ten or fifteen days since. I am a long ways from home and am anxious to get there as soon as the nature of the case will admit. Our situation is quite unpleasant, being destitute of clothing and most necessaries of life, wild meat being our principal subsistence.

I am, reverend father, your strange but real friend and christian,

(signed) J. S. SMITH

May 19, 1827.[459]

Far from satisfying the authorities, this letter only roused them to greater exertions. By may 23 Echeandía, having learned of the situation, sent word to Smith, not knowing that he had already departed, ordering him to start homeward at once or else come to San Jose, or to sail on the first vessel that would convey him north on the forty-second parallel.[460] After it was discovered that the leader of the expedition had gone, however, less interest seems to have been taken in the Americans. From now on the little company on the Stanislaus continued unmolested either by the Mexicans or the Indians. Like countless thousands since, "they spoke in high terms of the climate,"[461] though they had become desperately short of food when Smith arrived empty-handed.

On the twentieth of september Smith and three of his men set out for San Jose, some seventy miles distant, hoping to procure supplies. He arrived on the

---

[459] In Guinn, "Captain Jedediah S. Smith," in Southern California historical society *publications*, III, part 4, 48 ff; also in Cronise, *Natural wealth of California*, 44-5. Padre Duran was in charge of the mission at San Jose and president of the Alta California missions 1825-1827.

[460] Echeandía to Martinez (acting commandant at San Francisco), Departmental records, MSS., V, 48, cited by Bancroft, *California*, III, 158 note.

[461] Sullivan, *op. cit.*, 35.

twenty-third, much to the consternation of Father
Duran, who deprived Smith of his horses and kept him
in partial confinement. Apparently not knowing just
how to proceed or what to do, Duran at last bethought
himself of the military authorities and sent for Lieutenant Martinez,[462] who came up from the presidio at
San Francisco. Smith was arraigned on the charge of
being an intruder and of laying claim to the country
on the Peticutsy (San Joaquin). Although Duran appeared particularly eager for Smith's conviction, a few
questions convinced Martinez of the preposterous character of the charges. The sole witness against Smith, a
renegade Indian, was ordered flogged, and at Smith's
request word was sent to Monterey for permission for
him to travel thither. Meantime Captain Cooper [463] and
Thomas B. Park, supercargo of the brig "Harbinger,"
both of Boston, had come up from Monterey to intervene on Smith's behalf.[464] After a fortnight of delay,
Smith

received a polite note from the governor to pay him a visit. Then he
was stript of his arms and accordingly complied and started well
guarded by four soldiers. The third day, at eleven o'clock at night,
he arrived in Montera, where the governor lived, and was immedi-

---

[462] Ex-governor Luis Antonio Arguello was captain of the company of San
Francisco. At this time he was absent and his place filled by Lieutenant
Ignacio Martinez. See Bancroft, *California*, II, 583.

[463] John Rogers Cooper, otherwise known as Juan Bautista Rogers Cooper,
and, from a deformity, Don Juan el Manco. Born on the island of Alderney
in 1792, he had come to Massachusetts as a mere boy with his mother. At
the age of twenty-one, master of the "Rover," port of Boston, he reached
California. Here he sold his ship but continued, for three years, to command
her on voyages to China. Abandoning the sea, he settled down to life in
Monterey where he was baptized, naturalized, and married. Until 1839 he
was in business in Monterey, but in that year resumed his sea-faring life,
making many voyages to the Mexican coast and to the islands. Later he resided in San Francisco, dying at the advanced age of ninety. Compare Bancroft, *California*, II, 765-766.

[464] Sullivan, *op. cit.*, 36, 37.

ately conveyed to the callibose without any refreshment whatever, where he remained until eleven o'clock next day, when a messenger arrived stating the governor was then ready to receive him. He was conveyed to his dwelling and met at the door by the governor, who invited him to partake of some refreshment, which he readily accepted. Mr. Smith soon found he could not have a perfect understanding with the governor for want of a proper interpreter. However, he obtained liberty of the limits of the town and harbor and of boarding with an American gentleman (Capt. Cooper) from Boston. Next day an interpreter was found by the name of Mr. Hartwell,[465] an English gentleman, to whom Smith is under many obligations for his kindness and liberality towards him. But yet he could not find out what his future fate was to be; the governor would sometimes say Mr. Smith must go to Mexico, at other times, Mr. S. and party must be sent off by water; again he would say, "Send fetch in the party here," and continued in the equivocating manner for several days.[466]

---

[465] William (Edward) Petty Hartnell, born 1798 in Lancashire, had lived in South America some time when he came to California on board the "John Begg" in 1822. He was member of the firm of McCulloch, Hartnell and company, agents for John Begg and company of Lima and for the Brothertons of Liverpool and Edinburgh. His firm contracted in 1823 to take the mission produce for two years and for a while did a large business. In 1824 he was baptized, the name, Edward, being added at this time, and in 1825 married María Teresa de la Guerra. His business prospered till 1826, but from that time till 1829 constantly declined. After a trip to South America, on which he dissolved his partnership, he returned heavily burdened with debt. He was naturalized in 1830, and in 1831 undertook the life of a *ranchero* at Alisal. In 1832 he was commander of the *Compañía Extranjera de Monterey* supporting Zamorano. From 1833 to 1836 he acted as agent for the Russian company. From 1839 to 1845 he was variously employed as interpreter, tithe collector, clerk, teacher, and customs officer. From 1845 to 1846 his attitude was unfriendly to the United States, until he lost all hope of an English protectorate, on which he had set his heart. The United States employed him from 1847 to 1850 as official interpreter and translator, in which capacity he rendered important services in connection with land titles and in the constitutional convention. He died in 1854. "Hartnell was a man who enjoyed and merited the respect and friendship of all who knew him, being perfectly honest, straightforward in all his transactions, of most genial temperament, and too liberal for his own interests. In some directions he was a man of rare ability, being master of the Spanish, French, and German languages, besides his own." Compare Bancroft, *California*, III, 777 ff; see also Ogden, "Hides and tallow," California historical society *quarterly*, VI, 254 ff.

[466] Brief sketch, etc., Kansas historical society MSS.

At length the interpreter, Mr. Hartnell, who consistently befriended Smith, bethought himself of an English law permitting the masters of vessels in a foreign port to act in case of emergency as consular agents until the government could be appraised of their proceedings. "Perhaps," said he, "the Americans have such a law." Echeandía, who was considerably embarrassed at having Smith on his hands again and who was hesitant about taking responsibility for any decision affecting him, jumped at this suggestion. Forthwith four masters in the port, two of whom were Captain Joseph Steele of the brig "Harbinger," and Captain Allan Tilton of the brig "Omega," [467] "took the responsibility on themselves and appointed Captain Cooper agent for the U. States in order to settle this matter in some shape or manner." [468] At first Echeandía insisted that Smith promise never to return to California under any pretense whatever and to withdraw from the territory south of the forty-second parallel. To both of these conditions Smith declined to agree, to the first as being an invasion of his rights as a citizen of the United States and to the latter because of the absence of any valid Spanish claim to the Salt lake and interior basin areas. An agreement satisfactory to all parties was finally arrived at whereby Captain Cooper agreed, under penalty of forfeiture of his own property, to guarantee the good conduct and behavior of Smith till he returned to his "deposit," that is, to the post at Great Salt lake, giving assurances that Smith would proceed from San Jose by way of Car-

---

[467] According to Smith's journal, Sullivan, *op. cit.*, 41. The instrument itself names Steele, Tomas B. Parc (Thomas B. Park) supercargo of the "Harbinger," Henry Pease, master of the "Hesper," Benjamin Clark, captain. Printed from one of the originals in the Bancroft library MSS. in Sullivan, *op. cit.*, 172.

[468] Brief sketch, etc., Kansas historical society MSS.

quinez strait and Bodega,[469] that he would delay no longer than was absolutely necessary to procure much needed mounts, arms, ammunition, and provisions and that he would make no expedition toward the coast or into the Salt lake region south of the forty-second parallel not authorized by his government and under legal passport.

By way of personal guarantee to Captain Cooper that this engagement would be fulfilled, Smith affixed his signature to the following instrument.[470]

I Jed S. Smith, of Green township in the state of Ohio, do hereby bind myself, my heirs, executors, and principals in the sum of thirty thousand dollars for the faithful performance of a certain bond, given to the Mexican government, dated at Monterey, 15 nov. 1827.

Witness, RUFUS PERKINS.

After receiving Echeandía's promise that his men would not be imprisoned but would be furnished with the necessary supplies, Smith wrote Harrison G. Rogers directing him to bring the company in to San Francisco. Accordingly on november 15, having furnished the bond quoted above, Smith set sail from Monterey on board the "Franklin," Captain Bradshaw. After a rough passage in which Smith suffered from sea sickness, they entered the Golden gate on the seventeenth, where Smith immediately called on the acting commander of the presidio, Don Luis Arguello, who found his papers satisfactory. The "Brief sketch" continues:

Mr. Smith, finding his party weak, knowing he had a great many more hostile tribes to pass, endeavored to strengthen his party by

[469] Smith had received a letter from the Russian agency at Bodega instructing the agent at Ross to provide him with whatever he might need, Sullivan, op. cit., 48.

[470] Smith's copy is in the Sublette MSS., carton 10, Missouri historical society.

engaging more ften [fifteen more men?]; found several willing to engage, both Americans and English, but would not be allowed permission to engage them. He then traded for some articles such as horses, mules, arms, ammunition, and other necessaries, merely to enable him to return back from whence he came. Then Mr. Smith went on to visit his party, found them in St. Francisco in a very deplorable state, and would have suffered immensely for want of victual and clothing, were it not for the timely assistance of Mr. Vermont, a German gentleman, who happened to be trading on the coast, to whom Mr. Smith is under many obligaitons.[471]

The men had brought up the stock of furs amounting in all to 1568 pounds of beaver and ten otter skins. Arrangements for their sale at two dollars and fifty cents per pound had been concluded at Monterey so that Smith realized nearly four thousand dollars for the lot. A week in San Francisco concluded with a dinner aboard the man-of-war, "Blossom," commanded by Captain Beechey, famed explorer who had aided Franklin and Perry in their polar expeditions. The company besides Smith consisted chiefly of Yankee skippers, including Captain Bradshaw of the ship "Franklin" from Boston, Captain Cressy of the "Sophia" of New Bedford, Captain Foster of the brig "Fulham," and no less than three masters of Nantucket ships, Moses Harris of the "Weymouth," Obadiah Swayne of the "Enterprise," and Benjamin Coleman of the "Eagle." Next day Smith made arrangements to move his men and horses from the barren hills of San Francisco, where

[471] Henry Virmond, a German merchant of Acapulco and Mexico City, was in Alta California as early as 1827 (therefore before 1828, the date given by Bancroft, *California,* v, 764). He did a large business in California, where he was well known by nearly everybody before he visited the country. He was a skillful intriguer, enjoyed extraordinary facilities for obtaining the ear of Mexican officials, and was always the man first sought for any favor by his California friends. He owned several vessels on the California coast. He was the tallest man ever seen in the country until the arrival of Doctor Semple in 1845.

the latter had nearly starved, down the peninsula to San Jose. Here Thomas Virgin, who had been left behind at the San Bernardino ranch, rejoined him. Virgin had been taken to San Diego, imprisoned, and half starved. Only Smith's persistence in dealing with Echeandía and the latter's explicit orders finally led to his release and permission to rejoin Smith's party at San Jose. Another month was consumed in procuring supplies and in bickering with the Spanish authorities as to his route. Arguello insisted that he cross at the Straits of Carquinez, called by Smith the mouth of the Buenaventura,[472] but refused to provide facilities for ferrying the men, horses, and supplies for the simple reason that they were not to be had.

Wearied of delay and burdened with mounting expense accounts, on december thirtieth, accordingly, Smith and his party set out on the long trek back to the United States, not, to be sure, by the direct eastern route across the Sierras and the Nevada deserts, which Smith had already proved by bitter experience to be impassable, but, as it was to turn out, by the unexplored upper valley of the Sacramento and along the wild northern California and Oregon coast, and the Willamette valley to the Columbia. This stage of the journey was destined to require seven months and the lives of all his men save two and to be carried through only in the face of such arduous effort that at one point, facing hardships almost unendurable for beast and man, the intrepid Rogers, in a moment of depression, poured out his hopes and fears in his diary, pleading, "Oh! God,

---

[472] This is about the last appearance of the Buenaventura, that mythical stream identified by Ashley with the Weber and now at length by Smith with the Sacramento. The reality of an interior basin whose rivers, contrary to all ordinary observation, failed to reach the sea, was at last becoming apparent.

may it please thee, in thy divine providence, to still guide and protect us through this wilderness of doubt and fear, as thou hast done heretofore, and be with us in the hour of danger and difficulty, as all praise is due to thee and not to man, oh! do not forsake us Lord, but be with us and direct us through."

Of three that were destined to survive, only two, Smith and the faithful Arthur Black, were destined to return to the United States and they not until the summer of 1830, two and a half years later. There were nineteen in the party all told. They had an experienced and resourceful commander, though he was only twenty-nine years of age. He was courageous, ingenious, humane, and indifferent to his own physical suffering. The faithful Rogers records on june first, while they were traveling through the rough country of the northern California coast counties, that "Capt. Smith got kicked by a mule and hurt pretty bad," [473] and the following day, "Capt. Smith goes about although he was much hurt by the kick he received yesterday." [474] Smith's entries in his own journal for these two days are very brief. No doubt he was suffering too painfully to spend much effort on his diary but there is no mention of this accident, nor even any indication of the discouragements that overtook Rogers now and then. To be kicked by a mule and barely able to get about was all in the day's work. Had Smith's orders been strictly followed, moreover, the cruel disaster that was to overtake them six months later would almost certainly have been avoided. Second in command was Harrison G. Rogers, known as the clerk of the expedition, and a faithful companion of Smith from the time they had left the rendezvous

[473] Entry of may 22.
[474] See page 255.

of 1826. Next in turn was Thomas Virgin, who but for Smith's insistence with the authorities would have been left behind to languish in the Mexican prison at San Diego. Then there was Arthur Black, the only member of the 1826 expedition except Smith himself who was destined to survive the massacre on the Umpqua the following summer.[475] Ten of the party belonged to the first expedition (1826), eight to the second expedition (1827), and one, Richard Leland, a young Englishman, had joined in California.

Although Smith recorded that he "could not say much of the enterprize of these people," he had gleaned some bits of geographical information from the Mexican authorities about northern California and about the possibility of returning to the United States by a more circuitous northern route. Arguello, he learned, some time before had sent an expedition up the Sacramento, accompanied by a man well acquainted with the Columbia who told them that "this river [the Sacramento] was a branch or rather bayou of the Columbia and that left it something like 600 miles from the bay of St. Francisco they were in a short distance of that river." [476] Although Smith appeared to take little stock in this statement, since he was interested in finding an eastern pass in the Sierras to the north of the one he had followed the year before, he was finally forced by the stubborn facts of northern California geography to head for the Columbia rather than eastward to Great Salt lake.

From the thirtieth of december to the twenty-first of january he struggled through the bogs, morasses,

[475] John Turner also escaped, but he had joined Smith's second California expedition that set out from the Bear lake rendezvous in the summer of 1827.
[476] Sullivan, *op. cit.*, 53.

and sloughs of the San Joaquin-Sacramento estuaries, finally on the latter date reaching the south bank of the Mokelumne, not far from the present town of Lodi. Another month was spent in trying to get his men and horses to the Sacramento, but this was the rainy season and the sloughs and swamps made the country impassable. He finally crossed the Mokelumne and on february twelfth managed to reach the east bank of the Sacramento, which he mistook at first for American river. Proceeding by gradual stages and stopping frequently to trap for beaver, Smith reached the American river on the twentieth, within a mile of the place where he had struck it the previous year on his first attempt to cross the Sierras and just east of the present city of Sacramento. Continuing northward and finding the ground firm and less mirey, he crossed Bear river, camping just to the north of Reed's creek.

Having wounded a brown bear one evening, Rogers set out the next morning with John Hannah to look for him. The bear had concealed himself in a thicket and at their approach suddenly attacked Rogers, clawing and biting him severely. Although shot a second time, the bear resumed the attack, inflicting several additional wounds on the unfortunate Rogers, who was brought into camp and treated by Smith "with plaster of soap and sugar." The next day Smith records Rogers's wounds as still being very painful. Four days later and after renewed applications of "cold water and salve of sugar and soap," [477] he was still suffering and two weeks later was still unable to travel more than a short distance, but thereafter seems to have recovered at least sufficiently to be no longer a matter of concern in Smith's journal.

[477] *Ibid.*, 68.

Crossing the Yuba on the fifteenth of march, not far from Marysville, the Honcut on the nineteenth, and Feather river on the twenty-sixth near Oroville, Smith proceeded in a northwesterly direction, camping on the east bank of the Sacramento again on march twenty-eighth just west of Chico. Finding the trapping satisfactory, they proceeded northward by easy stages until april tenth. Reconnoitering the country, Smith now observed that the Sacramento was coming in from the northeast through an extremely rough country and noting a gap in the low ranges to the west, he decided next day to cross the Sacramento [478] and to make for this low divide in the western hills.

Crossing the south fork and then the main fork of Cottonwood creek, Smith proceeded in a northwesterly direction, crossing the divide on april seventeenth and coming out on the headwaters of the Hay fork of Trinity river. Since the river flows slightly to the east of north at this point, Smith was apprehensive lest he might not actually have crossed the divide but might still be on a tributary of the Sacramento. The following day, however, he found the stream trending more and more to the northwest and on april twenty-first reached its confluence with the south fork of Trinity river. Crossing the Trinity and finding the canyon impassable, he followed up the north bank of Grouse creek. Continuing through this rough and broken country where he first noted the redwoods, he reached a point opposite the confluence of the Trinity with the Klamath river on may third. Still unable to proceed down the canyon, he struggled along the heavily timbered hills above the river, camping on the night of may ninth nearly opposite the mouth of Blue creek.

---

[478] Near Red Bluff.

From this point the second Harrison G. Rogers journal picks up the narrative with a wealth of detail generally omitted in the brief and laconic entries of Smith's
journal.

THE SECOND JOURNAL OF HARRISON G. ROGERS
Men's names with J. S. Smith [479]

J. S. Smith	Joseph Lapoint
H. G. Rogers	Abraham Laplant
Thos. Virgin	Thos. Daws
Arthur Black	Charles Swift
John Turner	Richard Layla [Leland]
John Gaiter	Martin McCoy
John Hanna	John Reubasco
Emannuel Lazarus	Toussaint Marishall
Joseph Palmer	John Peter Ranne
Peter Ranne	(a man of colour)

Many men of many minds, and many kinds of many,
Kinderate of God's creation.

When young in life and forced to guess my road,
  And not one friend to shield my bark from harm,
The world received me in its vast abode,
  And honest toil procured its plaudits warm.

SATURDAY, MAY 10TH, 1828. We made an early start
this morning, stearing N.W. about 5 miles, thence w. 7
miles and encamped, on a small creek, and built a pen

---

[479] Out of the eighteen men here listed (nineteen including Smith) the fol-
lowing were members of the first expedition: H. G. Rogers, Arthur Black,
John Gaiter, Emanuel Lazarus, Peter Ranne, Abraham Laplant, Martin Mc-
Coy, John Hanna, (John) Reubascan. The others, Charles Swift, Toussaint
Marishall, Thomas Virgin, John Turner, Joseph Palmer, Joseph Lapoint, and
Thomas Daws were new members taken by Smith when he started on his
second expedition. Richard Leland had joined the party in California. The
annual term of employment of Thomas Virgin, John Turner, and Joseph La-
point expired july 2, 1828, when they were reengaged. Peter Ranne, or John
Peter Ranne, seems to have been counted twice. An Indian boy, Marion, was
added to the party before they reached the Umpqua.

for our horses, as we could not get to grass for them. The travelling very bad, several very steep, rocky and brushy points of mountains to go up and down, with our band of horses, and a great many of them so lame and worn out that we can scarce force them along; 15 lossed on the way, in the brush, 2 of them with loads; the most of the men as much fatigued as the horses; one of the men, lossed his gun, and could not find it. We have had more trouble getting our horses on to-day, than we have had since we entered the mount. We crossed a creek close by the mouth 15 or 20 yards wide heading south, and emptying into the river east at an course, the current quite swift, and about belly deep to our horses. Some beavers sign discovered by the men. The day clear and warm. But one Ind. seen to-day; he was seen by Capt. Smith as he generally goes ahead, and I stay with the rear to see that things are kept in order.

SUNDAY, MAY 11, 1828. As our horses was without food last night, we was up early, and dispatched four men after those that was left back yesterday, and had the others packed and under way a little after sun rise, directing our course up a steep point of mountain, very rocky and brushy about ¾ of a mile. The course N.W. 2 miles and struck into an open point of mountain where there was good grass and encamped, as the most of our horses was nearly down. We had a great deal of trouble getting them up the mountain with there loads on; a number would fall with their packs, and roll 20 or 30 feet down among the sharp rocks, several badly cut to pieces with the rocks.

The four men that was sent back returned late in the evening. They had got 12 of the horses that were missing, and among them the 2 that had loads; the man that lost his gun could not find it. Three deer killed in the evening, the meat poor.

MONDAY, MAY 12TH. We concluded to remain here to-day and let the horses rest; 2 men sent back after the other horses that are still missing; one left yesterday that could not be got along, that had entirely given out. The two men returned late, found one of the lossed horses, but could not drive him to camp, consequently we shall loose them as Capt. Smith intends moving camp early to-morrow. The day clear and warm.

TUESDAY, MAY 13TH, 1828. All hands called early and ready for a start, directing our course N.W. over high ranges of rocky and brushy points of mountains, as usual, and travelled 6 m. and encamped on the side of a grassy mou., where there was an abundance of good grass for the horses, but little water for them. We had a great deal of difficulty to drive them on account of brush and the steepness of the points of mountain; two left that could not travel and a great many more very lame; the weather good.

WEDNESDAY, MAY 14TH. We made an early start, directing our course as yesterday N.W., and traveled 4 m. and enc. on the top of a high mountain, where there was but indifferent grass for our horses. The travelling amazing bad; we descended one point of brushy and rocky mountain, where it took us about 6 hours to get the horses down, some of them falling about 50 feet perpendicular down a steep place into a creek; one broke his neck; a number of packs left along the trail, as night was fast approaching, and we were oblige to leave them and get what horses we could collected at camp; a number more got badly hurt by the falls, but none killed but this one that broke his neck.

Saw some Inds. that crossed the river in a canoe and came to me; I give them some beads, as presents; they made signs that they wanted to trade for knives, but I told them that I had none; they give me a lamper eel dryed, but I could not eat it.

They appear afraid of horses; they are very light coloured Inds., quite small and talkative.[480] The weather still good.

THURSDAY, 15TH. MAY, 1828. The men was divided in parties this morning, some sent hunting, as we had no meat in camp, others sent back after horses and packs that was left back.

5 Inds. came to camp; I give them some beads; they appear quit friendly; shortly after fifteen or 20 came, and among them one squaw, a very good featured woman; she brought a dressed skin and 2 worked boles for sale; I bought them from her for beads. The hunters killed 5 deer. The balance of the horses and packs, was got to camp about 4 oc. in the evening; the men quit fatigued climbing up and down the hills. The weather still good. Some black bear seen by the hunters.

FRIDAY, MAY 16TH, 1828. We concluded that it was best to lie by today and send two men to look out a pass to travel, as the country looks awful a head, and let our poor horses rest, as there is pretty good grass about 1 mile off for them to feed on. 20 or 30 Inds. visited

480 The first account of the interesting Hupa Indians, of Athapascan stock, who were not encountered by the whites again till 1850. They occupied the Trinity river from its mouth to Burnt Ranch. They were a powerful and important tribe, whose language was the *lingua franca* among most of the tribes of northern California. All these tribes are described as "pudgy" except the Yuroks. For further comment on the Hupas see Powers, "Tribes of California," in U.S. Bureau of ethnology, *Contributions to North American ethnology*, 72-77. See also Goddard, "Life and culture of the Hupa," in University of California *publications in American archaeology and ethnology*, I. Goddard states that the coming of Smith made little, if any, impression on the tribe.

our camp in the course of the day, bringing eels for trade and roots; the men bought the most of them giving awls and beads in exchange. Capt. Smith made them some small presents, and bought one B. skin from them; the women does the principal trading. Those Inds. are quite civil and friendly; the weather still good.

SATURDAY, MAY 17TH, 1828. The 2 men that were sent on discovery yesterday returned this morning and say that we are 15 or 20 miles of[f] the North Paciffic ocean;[481] they report game plenty, such as elk and deer; they report the traveling favourable to what it has been for 30 or 40 m. back. On there return, we concluded to remain here again to-day on account of our horses being so very lame and soar from the bruises they got on the 14th inst. The morning cloudy and rainy. The 2 men, Marishall and Turner, that were sent off yesterday, killed 3 deer, and Capt. Smith has dispatched 2 men after the meat, as the camp is almost destitute.

Mr. Virgin and Ransa quite unwell this morning. The day continues cloudy and rainy, and quite cold towards evening.

SUNDAY, MAY 18TH, 1828. As we intended moving camp, the horses were sent for early, and got to camp about 10 oc. A.M., packed and started, directing our course W. 3 miles and struck into a small hill pararie, where there was grass and water, and encamped, as the distance were too great to go to any other place of grass to-day for the horses,[482] from what Turner and Marishall tell us about the route from here to the ocean. The morning being so thick with fogg, the men that was sent after the horses did not find them all; Capt. Smith took 2 men with him, and went back after those

---

481 The two men, Turner and Marishall, crossed the divide between the Klamath and the sea and sighted the Pacific north of Sharp point.

482 Still on the divide but presumably on the western slope.

that could not be found in the morning, and I went on with the company, and encamped before he joined me with those that he went back after; he found nine that was left and brought eight to camp, one being so lame that he could not travel, and he was oblige to leave him; the weather clear and windy.

MONDAY, MAY 19TH, 1828. We made an early start this morning, stearing our course as yesterday, 6 miles west, and encamped on the side of a mountain, where their was plenty of good grass and water for our horses. Just before we encamped, there was a small band of elk seen by Capt. Smith and those men that was in front with horses; they went after them and killed 6, two of which number were in good order. The travelling some better than it was back, although we have hills and brush to encounter yet; we encamped about 6 m. from the ocean, where we have a fair view of it.

4 Inds. came to camp in the evening and stay all night. Capt. Smith give them some small presents of beads and some elk meat; they eat a part and carried the balance off with them; they appear quit friendly as yet.[483]

TUESDAY, MAY 20TH. As our horses was lame and tired, we concluded to remain here and let them rest, and kill and dry meat, as elk appeared to be plenty from the sign.

After breakfast, myself and Mr. Virgin started on horse back for the sea shore, following an Ind. trail that led immediately there; after proceeding about 5 m. west, we found we could not get any further on horse back along the Ind. trail, so we struck out from the creek that we had followed down, about 3 miles

---

[483] Probably the Chillule, a tribe occupying the Redwoods for twenty miles from the coast. See Powers, *op. cit.*, 87.

from where we first struck it; this creek being about 40 yards wide, heading into a mou. south and emptying into the ocean at a N.W. direction.[484] After leaving the creek with considerable difficulty, we ascended a point of steep and brushy mountain, that runs along parallel with the sea shore, and followed that, until we could get no further for rocks and brush. We got within 80 or 100 yards of the beach, but, being pretty much fatigued and not able to ride down on account of rocks and brush, we did not proceed any further in that direction. Seeing that it was impossible to travel along where we had been with the company, we concluded to turn and travel across a point of mou. that run N.E., but we could not get along, the travelling so bad; we then concluded to stear for camp, as it was get[ting] on towards night. On our return we saw some elk; I went after them, and Mr. Virgin stay with the horses. I did not get to fire on them, and saw a black bare and made after him, and shot and wounded him very bad, and heard Mr. Virgin shoot and hollow in one minute after my gun were discharged, and tell me to come to him. I made all the haste I could in climbing the mou. to where Mr. Virgin was; he told me that some Inds. had attacked him in my absence, shoot a number of arrows at him and wounded the horses, and, he supposed, killed them by that time, that he had shot one, and was waiting for me. I rested a few minutes and proceed on cautiously to the place where we had left our horses, and found an Ind. lying dead and his dog by him, and Mr. Virgin's horse with 2 or 3 arrows in him, and he laying down. We got him up and made camp a little before night, and there was 7 or 8 Inds. at camp when we got there, and I made signs to them that we were attacked by some of there band, shoot at, one of our horses

---

484 Redwood creek.

wounded, and we had killed one; they packed up and put off very soon.[485] The day very foggy at times; some little rain in the evening. Mr. Smith told me that he had sent two men back after the horses that were missing with instructions to stay and hunt them until to-morrow, if they did not find them to-day.

WEDNESDAY, MAY 21ST. Still at the same camp; those two men that was sent after the lossed horses still absent. A considerable quantity of rain fell last night; the morning continues to be showery and foggy. The men that were sent back after horses yesterday returned, late in the evening, without finding but one; they say they suppose the Inds. to have killed the rest. The timber in this part of this country is principally hemlock, pine, and white ceadar, the most of the ceadar trees from 5 to 15 feet in diameter and tall in proportion to the thickness, the under brush, hazle, oak, briars, currents, goose berry, and Scotch cap bushes,[486] together with aldar, and sundry other shrubs too tedious to mention; the soil of the country rich and black, but very mountainous, which renders the travelling almost impassable with so many horses as we have got.

THURSDAY, MAY 22ND, 1828. All hands up early and preparing for a move, had the horses drove to camp and caught ready for packing up, and it commenced raining so fast that we concluded to remain here again to-day, as we could [not] see how to direct our course for fog along the mountains. We have not seen or heard any Inds. since the 20th that Mr. Virgin killed the one that shoot at his horse.

Oh! God, may it please thee, in thy divine provi-

---

[485] Rogers and Virgin, finding their way impeded, had turned northwest toward the sea, but here again finding their course impassable, they had struck back toward the slopes of the mountain range running parallel with the sea south of Sharp point. The attacking Indians were very likely Chiilule.

[486] The black raspberry, or thimbleberry, *rubus occidentalis*.

dence, to still guide and protect us through this wilderness of doubt and fear, as thou hast done heretofore, and be with us in the hour of danger and difficulty, as all praise is due to thee and not to man, oh! do not forsake us Lord, but be with us and direct us through.

FRIDAY, MAY 23RD, 1828. The morning being clear, we were ready for a start early, directing our course east, back on the trail we travelled on the 19th inst, and made the same camp and stopped, it being 6 miles, and concluded to remain the balance of the day and let our meat and other wet articles get dry.[487] We had but little difficulty getting along, as we had a good trail that were made by our horses passing along before; the day clear and pleasant.

SATURDAY, MAY 24TH. All hands up early and ready for a move about 8 oc. A.M., directing our course N.E., 4 miles, and encamped within 100 yards of Indian Scalp river,[488] on the side of the mountain where there was plenty of good grass for our horses.

Capt. Smith went down to the river, where there is a large Indian village on the opposite side, and called to the Inds., and there were 4 crossed over, 2 men, 1 woman and a boy about 12 or 14 years of age, and came to camp with him; he made them a present of a few beeds. The day cloudy and misty. There being some horses missing when we encamped, 2 men were sent immediately back in search of them and found them and got back a little after sun set. One mule killed this morning by haltering him and throwing him.

SUNDAY, MAY 25TH. As is usual when travelling, we

[487] Their course was a little to the south and east, taking them back to the camp of the nineteenth.

[488] Having started from their camp of the nineteenth, they crossed the ridge and encamped once more near the Klamath, called by Smith, Indian Scalp river.

was up and made an early start, directing our course
N.E. about 1 mile and struck Ind. Scalp river opposite
to an Ind. village, and got the Inds., with there canoes,
to cross our plunder and selves. We drove in our horses,
and they swam across, where they had to swim from
250 to 300 yards. We give those Inds. that assisted in
crossing our goods, beeds and razors for there trouble;
there was a number visited our camp in the course of
the day, men, women, and children; some brought
lamprey eels for sale; the men bought them, giving
beeds in exchange. Those Inds. live in lodges built
similar to our cabbins, with round holes about 18 inches
in diameter for doors; they appear friendly and say
nothing about the Ind. that Mr. Virgin killed on the
20th inst. About 10 oc. A.M., it commenced raining and
continued to rain on pretty fast during the day.

We cannot find out what those Inds. call themselves;
the most of them have wampum and pieces of knives.
Some have arrow points of iron; they also have some
few beaver and otter skins. Mr. Smith purchases all
the beaver fur he can from them. The foundation of
there lodges are built of stone with stone floors; the[y]
appear quit affraid when we first reached the river
and called to them, but, after coakesing, one came across
with his canoe, and, showing him by signs what we
wanted, he soon complied, and called to others who
came with canoes and comm. x our goods.[489] Deer
killed to-day; the meat all poor.

489 "Commenced crossing our goods." Smith and his party crossed the
Klamath and encamped on the eastern bank. The Indians encountered were
probably the Yurok, who had no name for themselves, but only names for
their individual villages. They are of Weitspeken linguistic stock, but their
language is distinct from the Hupa, being notable for its gutterals. They occupied the Klamath from the confluence of the Trinity to the sea and a short
distance along the coast. The house, which Rogers describes, is typical of
the Yurok and also of their neighbors, the Hupa, the construction of a stone

MONDAY, MAY 26TH, 1828. We made an early start this morning, directing our course N.E., and ascended a very long and steep point of grassy mountain, and reached the divide, and kept in about 6 miles, the travilling good, and encamped on the side of the mountain where there was pretty good grass for our horses. I killed one fat buck to-day, and Mr. Virgin killed a small doe, but poor fat. We counted our horses, and find that three got drowned yesterday in crossing the river, we saw one of them floating down the river this morning. The day clear and pleasant; 2 Inds. started with us this morning, as pilots, but soon got tired and left us.

TUESDAY, MAY 27TH. Capt. Smith and Mr. Virgin started early this morning ahead to look out a road to travel; I stay and had the horses caught and packed, and started following the blazes through the woods, a N.W. course, descending a very steep and brushy point of mountain, about 3 miles, and struck a creek [489a] 25 or 30 yards in width, heading east, and running west into Ind. Scalp river, and enc. (for the day), as there was some horses missing, and sent 3 men back on the trail to look after them. There was 8 or 10 Inds. came to camp, soon after we stoped; Capt. Smith give them a few beeds; they have a fishing establishment on the creek. The day pleasant and clear; one horse left to-day.

foundation being particularly characteristic of the latter. The Hupa excavated a round cellar three or four feet deep, which was walled with stone. Round the cellar and resting on the surface of the ground a circular wall was erected, on which poles, puncheons, and great strips of redwood bark were leaned in the form of a dome. Sometimes the stone wall was built outside the conical covering. Doors of the kind described by Rogers were made by boring a circular hole through one of the puncheons just large enough to admit an Indian crawling through on all fours. Some of these holes had sliding panels on the inside, rendering them "baby-tight" on occasion. Shell money, wampum, was the usual medium of exchange. See Powers, *op. cit.*, 45 ff, 74.

[489a] Blue creek (?)

WEDNESDAY, MAY 28TH. We made an early start this morning, stearing our course N.E. up a very steep and brushy point of the mountain, and got on the ridge, or divide, between the creek and river, and travelled about 7 miles on it, and enc. on the top of the mountain, where there was but little grass for horses.[490] The day so foggy that we could scarce see how to get along on the ridge, at times; late in the evening, it cleared off, and we had a fair view of the ocean. It appeared to be about 15 or 20 miles distant.

THURSDAY, MAY 29TH. All hands up early and making ready for a move; about 10 oc A.M., our horses were collected together, and we got under way, following the trail that we came yesterday, about 2 miles, S.W., and found some water in a ravine and encamped, the day being so foggy that we could not see how to direct our course to the river, and sent 2 men to hunt a pass to travel; they returned in the evening without finding any route that we could get along with our band of horses. The timber of the country as usual pine and white ceadar.

FRIDAY, MAY 30TH, 1828. All hands up early this morning and out after horses, as they were very much scattered, and got them collected about 10 oc., and star[ted] down a step and brushy ridge, a N.W. course, and travelled about 3 m., and struck a small creek, where there was a little bottom of good grass and clover, and encamped.[491] The horses got so that it was almost impossible to drive them down the mou. amongst the brush; 8 or 10 left back in the brush, and six men sent

---

[490] Again on the divide. From the ridge the ocean is easily visible, distant about seventeen miles. The mountains come so close to the river in the canyon of the Klamath that they found it impossible to proceed except along the ridge.

[491] Still traveling northwest, along the ridge, parallel to the Klamath. Several small streams enter the river on the east side.

back after them; they got them to camp just at dark;
one lost entirely that the men could not find; the rear
part of the compy, that stay with me, had a serious
time running up and down the mountain after horses
through the thickets of brush and briars. 2 elk killed
to day by Mr. Virgin; the morning clear, and the
evening foggy.

SATURDAY, MAY 31ST, 1828. Capt. Smith concluded
we would stay here a part of the day and send 2 men
to look out a pass to the river; they returned about 11
o.c' and say that we will be obliged to climb the mountain again at this place, and go along the ridge for 2
or 3 miles, and then descend to the main river, as it is
impossible to go along the creek with horses for cut
rocks. As it had commenced raining when those men
returned, we concluded to stay here to day, as there
was plenty of good grass for our horses. Two Inds [492]
came to camp in the rain, and brought a few rasberrys
that are larger than any species of rasberrys I ever saw;
the bush also differ from those I have been acquainted
with; the stock grow from 8 to 10 feet in heighth,
covered with briars, and branches off with a great many
boughs, the leaf is very similar to those vines I have
been acquainted with heretofore. Capt. Smith give
those Inds. some meat, and they say they will go with
us from here to the ocean.

It rained fast from the time it commenced in the
forenoon, untill night.

SUNDAY, JUNE 1ST, 1828. We got our horses about
10 o.c. A.M. and packed up and started in the rain, as it
had not quit from the time it commenced yesterday,
directing our course west, up a steep and brushy mountain, and travelled about 3 miles and enc. in a small

---

[492] Probably Yuroks.

bottom pararie, principally covered with ferns;[493] the travelling amazing bad; we left several packs of fur on the road and lost several pack horses and some loose horses, the day being so rainy that it was almost impossible to get up and down the mountains; the road became quite mirery and slippery. Capt. Smith got kicked by a mule and hurt pretty bad. When I reached camp with the rare [rear], it was night, and all hands very wet and tired.

MONDAY, JUNE 2ND, 1828. Capt. Smith concluded to remain here and send some men back after the fur that was left, and to hunt horses; they returned about noon, bringing all the horses and packs that was left. Some men went hunting but killed nothing. Two Inds.[494] came to camp and brought some rasberrys; Mr. Smith give them a few beeds. The morning wet; about 1 o.c. P.M., it cleared off, and the balance of the day fair. Capt. Smith goes about although he was much hurt by the kick he received yesterday.

TUESDAY, MAY [JUNE] 3RD, 1828. We made an early start this morning, directing our course N.W. up a steep point of brushy mou., and travelled about 2 m., and enc. in the river bottom, where there was but little for our horses to eat;[495] all hands working hard to get the horses on, as they have become so much worn out that it is almost impossible to drive through brush; we have two men every day that goes a head with axes to cut a road, and then it is with difficulty we can get along. The day clear and pleasant.

WEDNESDAY, MAY [JUNE] 4TH. As our horses were

---

493 After four miles of scrambling over the rough mountain side, they encamped not far from the river. They were now in Del Norte county.

494 Still the Yuroks.

495 At last they reached the river where, emerging from the mountains, it flows through a narrow valley before entering the sea.

very much fatigued, we made an early start again, this morning, to get to grass, but, the road proving both brushy and mirery, we only made 1½ miles, a N.W. course, during the day; the men almost as well as horses done out. We were obliged to enc. again in the river bottom and build a pen for our horses, as there was no grass for them.[496] 5 Inds. came to me and brought some rasberrys, and give me; I give them a few beeds and went on, and left a coloured man by the name of Ransa with them, and had not been absent but a few minutes before he called to me and said the Inds. wanted to rob him of his blanket, that they had rushed into the bushes and got there bows and arrows; he fired on them and they run off leaving 2 or 3 small fishes. The Inds. that have visited our camps some time back generally came without arms and appeared very friendly; those I left with Ransa had no arms at the time they came to me, which induced me to believe that he told me a lie, as I suppose he wanted to get some berrys and fish without pay, and the Inds. wanted his knife and he made a false alarm, for which I give him a severe reprimand. The day clear and warm.

THURSDAY, JUNE 5TH, 1828. Our horses being without food again last night, we packed up and made an early start, sending some men a head to cut a road to where there was a small bottom of grass on a creek that comes into Ind. Scalp river, about 10 yards wide; the distance being about 2 miles, a N.W. course.[497] We reached it about 11 o.c.' A.M., and enc., one mule and 2 horses left to-day, that could not travel. No Inds. seen to-day; one man sent hunting but killed nothing, and we are entirely out of provision with the exception of a

---

[496] Still along the river, which is heavily timbered on both banks.

[497] They were now near the mouth of the Klamath, not far from the present town of Requa.

few pounds of flour and rice. Capt. Smith give each man a half pint a flour last night for their supper; we can find no game to kill although there is plenty of elk and bear sign. The day clear and pleasant. The most of the men went hunting after they had enc., but found nothing to kill; we killed the last dog we had along, and give out some more flour.

FRIDAY, JUNE 6TH, 1828. Myself and six men started early hunting, but killed nothing; 5 others started after we returned, as we intend staying at this camp for several days for the purpose of recruiting our horses. 8 Inds ventured to camp and brought a few lamprey eels and some ransberrys; they were soon purchased by Mr. Smith and the men for beeds.[498] The morning foggy and cloudy, the after part of the day clear and pleasant.

The hunters all returned without getting meat, and we were obliged to kill a horse for to eat.

SATURDAY, JUNE 7TH, 1828. At the same camp; some men pressing beaver fur, and 2 sent hunting, and 3 others sent back to look for loossed horses. The horses hunters returned without finding but one horse; they report 2 dead that was left back. 18 or 20 Inds. visited camp again to-day with berrys, mussels, and lamprey eels for sale; those articles was soon purchased, with beeds, by Capt. Smith and the men, and when the Inds. left camp, they stole a small kittle belonging to one of the men; they come with out arms and appear friendly but inclined to steal. The day clear and pleasant.

SUNDAY, JUNE 8TH, 1828. As we intend moving camp, we was up and ready for a start, early, stearing

---

[498] The Indians of this vicinity lived chiefly on fish, catching eels in traps which they affixed to stakes driven in the river bottom, Powers, *op. cit.,* 103.

our course N.W., about 3½ miles over two small points
of mou. and enc. on the sea shore, where there was a
small bottom of grass for our horses.[499] The travelling
ruff, as we had several thickets to go through; it made
it bad on account of driving horses, as they can scarce
be forced through brush any more. There was several
Ind. lodges on the beach and some Inds.; we got a
few clams and some few dried fish from them. Some
horses being left, I took four men with me and went
back and stay all night in a small pararie.

MONDAY, JUNE 9TH. I was up early and started the
men that stay with me all night after horses and to
hunt at the same time for meat, as I had left the camp
entirely destitute; we hunted hard until 9 or 10 o.c.
A.M., but killed nothing. Gaiter wounded a black bear,
but did not get him. 6 horses was found that was left,
when all hands came in, we saddled up our horses and
started for camp, and reached it about the middle of
the day. All the men that was sent hunting in the morning from camp had come in without killing any thing.
Some Inds. in camp with a few small fishes and clams;
the men, being hungry, soon bought them and eat them.
They also brought cakes made of sea grass and weeds
and sold to the men for beeds. Where we encamped,
there was a small creek pulling into the ocean at a
south direction. Capt. Smith started out again to try
his luck and found a small band of elk and killed 3;
he returned to camp and got some men and horses and
brought all the meat in, which was a pleasing sight to
a set of hungry men. The day clear and pleasant.

TUESDAY, JUNE 10TH. We concluded to stay here to-
day, dry meat, make salt, and let our horses rest, as

---

[499] They had at last reached the sea, camping at the mouth of Wilson
creek. From this point to june twelfth the itinerary is difficult to follow for
the distances are underestimated.

there is good grass and clover for them. A number of Inds. in camp with berrys, but do not find so good a market for them as they did yesterday. The morning cloudy and foggy, some rain towards evening. The men appear better satisfied than they do when in a state of starvation.

WEDNESDAY, JUNE 11TH. As we intended moving camp, the men was called early, and, preparing for a start, we were under way about 9 o.c. in the morning, directing our course N.W. up a steep point of mou. along the sea coast, and travelled about 2 m., and entered the timber and brush, and kept along a small divide between the sea shore and creek [500] we left, and travelled 3 m. further and enc. in the woods, without grass for our horses, and built a pen and kept them in through the night. The travelling very bad on account of brush and fallen timber; several horses left with packs that got hid in the brush and was passed and not seen by the men. When we was ready for a start, our fellin axe and drawing knife was missing, and the Inds. had left the camp. Capt. Smith took 5 men with him and went to there lodges, and the Inds. fled to the mou. and rocks in the ocean; he caught one and tyed him, and we brought him on about 2 miles and released him. The axe was found where they had buryed it in the sand. The day cloudy and foggy.

THURSDAY, JUNE 12TH. All hands up early and ready for a start, directing our course W. about 2 miles and struck a small creek, where there was some grass on the mountain for our horses, and enc. for the day, the traveling very bad. The horses that was left yesterday, was found to-day, and brought to camp.[501] The day clear; some fog in the morning.

---

[500] Wilson creek.
[501] They camped about midway between Requa and Crescent City.

FRIDAY, JUNE 13TH, 1828. We made an early start again this morning, stearing N.W., about 6 m., and struck the ocean and enc. on the beach.[502] Plenty of grass on the mountain for our horses, but very steep for them to climb after it. The traveling very mountainous; some brush as yesterday. 2 mules left today that give out and could not travel; one young horse fell down a point of mou. and killed himself. The day clear and pleasant.

SATURDAY, JUNE 14TH, 1828. We made an early start again this morning, directing our course along the sea shore N., about 1 mile, and struck a low neck of land running into the sea, where there was plenty of clover and grass for our horse, and enc. for the day.[503] We travelled in the water of the ocean 3 or 4 hundred yards, when the swells some times would be as high as the horses backs. 2 men sent back after a load of fur that was lossed yesterday, and to look after horses. 2 hunters dispatched after elk as soon as we enc. One fat deer killed yesterday by J. Hanna. Seven or 8 Inds. came to camp; Capt. Smith give them some beads. The hunters returned without killing any game; saw plenty of elk sign. The day clear and windy.

SUNDAY, JUNE 15TH, 1828. Several men started hunting early, as we intended staying here to day and letting our horses rest. Joseph Lapoint killed a buck elk that weighed 695 lbs., neat weight; the balance of the hunters came in without killing. A number of Inds. visited our camp again to day, bringing fish, clams, strawberrys, and a root that is well known by the traders west of the Rocky mountains by the name of com-

---

[502] Finding their progress easier, they managed to reach a point just south of Crescent City, where they encamped. For a description of this stretch of coast, see Chase, *California coast trails*, 307 ff.

[503] A mile from the camp they struck the long neck of land called Point St. George, and encamped on the side facing the open sea.

meser,[504] for trade. All those articles was soon purchased. The day cloudy, windy, and foggy, some rain in the afternoon. Cap. Smith and Mr. Virgin went late in the evening to hunt a pass to travel and found a small band of elk and killed two.

MONDAY, JUNE 16TH. We made an early start this morning, directing our course N.N.W. across a neck of land projecting or running into the ocean, and travelled 4 m., and enc. in a pararie, where there was plenty of grass for our horses. We had considerable difficulty getting our horses a cross a small branch, that was a little mirery; we were obliged to make a pen on the bank to force them across, which detained us several hours.[505] The day clear and warm.

TUESDAY, JUNE 17TH, 1828. We started early again this morning, stearing our course, as yesterday, N.N.W., 2 miles, and found the travelling in the bottom so amazing brushy and mirery we concluded to go back a few hundred yards to the pararie and encamp, dry what meat we had on hand, and send some men to look out a pass to travel when we leave here.[506] We also sent some hunters out. Joseph Lapoint killed a fine buck elk, and Mr. McCoy killed a fawn elk. The day clear and warm, plenty of muskeatoes, large horse flies, and small knats to bite us and pesterous early of mornings and late in the evenings. The timber along the bottom, ceador, hemlock of the largest size, under brush, hazle, briars, aldar, and sundry other srubs; the soil very rich and black.

WEDNESDAY, JUNE 18TH, 1828. We concluded to

[504] The camas root.
[505] Proceeding along the point, they camped on its northern extremity near Lake Earl.
[506] They advanced a couple of miles but, finding the ground in the vicinity of Lake Earl swampy and impassable, they returned to the higher prairie and encamped.

stay here to day, and dry meat, and do some work that could not well be dispensed with, and send some men off to hunt a road to travel to-morrow, as those that were sent yesterday did not reach the ocean. They say the traveling was tolerable as far as they went. Some more hunters sent out this morning; and men sent after the meat that was killed last evening. The day clear and very warm. Those men that was sent to hunt a road, returned late in the evening and say that we cannot travel along the bottom for swamps and lakes.[507] The hunters returned without killing any game. A number of Inds. visited our camp with clams, fish, strawberrys, and some dressed skins for sale, also commerss roots, ready prepared for eating; they appear friendly but inclined to steal without watching; they differ from the Ind. Scalp river Inds. in speach a little.[508]

THURSDAY, JUNE 19TH. As those men that was sent to hunt a road yesterday, returned without assertaining what way we could travel from here, Capt. Smith concluded it was best for us to remain here again today, and that he would take two men with him and go to the N.E. across a ridge, and see what kind of travelling it would be in that direction. He started early in company with two of the men, and returned about 12 o.c., and says that he can pass on in a N.E. direction very well as far as he went; he discovered another small river heading in the mountain east of the ocean, and emptying into a bay west about 2½ or 3 miles wide.[509]

---

507 The same obstacles that had been encountered the day before.

508 The Indians were probably Tolowa, whose language resembles the Hupa more closely than the Yurok, Powers, *op. cit.*, 65.

509 Smith river, which enters the ocean a few miles south of the Oregon-California boundary. The main highway up the coast today follows the course pursued by Smith, Chase, *op. cit.*, 309 ff. I am indebted to Mr. David Rhys Jones of Yreka, California, for the following Indian version of Smith's progress through the country, who obtained it from the descendants

5 Inds. in camp today with strawberrys for sale; the day clear and warm.

FRIDAY, JUNE 20TH, 1828. Capt. Smith started early with one man to blaze the road and left me to bring on the compy. I was ready about 10 o.c. A.M., being detained collecting horses that was missing, and started and travelled along an Ind. trail, about 2 m. east, thence 1 mile N.E., on the blazed road, forded the river that Capt. Smith discovered yesterday, which was nearly swimming and from 60 to 70 yards wide, and enc. on the east side, in a bottom pararie that contained about 15 or 20 acres of good grass and clover.[510] About 20 Inds. came to camp in their canoes, and brought lamprey eels for sale; the men bought a number from them for beeds. Several of us went hunting, and I

of one of the chiefs. As told to Mr. Jones the story is as follows, "When my uncle was a young man—not yet married—he went *early one morning* in a canoe across Lake Earl, to make the rounds of his elk traps (pits for trapping elk). After crossing he was tired and lay down on the side of a little knoll to rest (perhaps to 'spot' a deer?), with his four dogs. He spread his arrows on the ground beside him. Presently one of the dogs indicated alarm. Swi-net-klas, my uncle looked up and he saw approaching a strange human, followed by an animal never before seen in this region; and two other such groups following this one. Swi-net-klas reasoned that it must be a human being, and believed that he would not be hurt by him; so he hastily gathered up his arrows, and remained. The approaching figure saw Swi-net-klas and motioned him to approach, which he did. They had 'friendly talk.' They talk, 'Which way you bound for?' White man pat his heart with his hand to show wish, then point up along coast. Swi-net-klas show wish to stay here —he pat his heart, then point to ground." In the Indian story Smith is described in the following words, "Him young man; other two, middleage. Him beard, long; from here (cheeks) down long (gesture to breast). Him not wear hat like white man wear when white man come to Crescent City. Him wear round hat of fur. Him have feet all up to here covered with skins (gesture to legs above the ankles). Indian think this kind of thing very good for keep feet not hurt. Him carry in one hand over shoulder something (rifle) and in other hand he have strings he lead strange animal. On back of animal something (saddle or pack saddle)."

[510] Travelling two miles east and one mile northeast, they struck Smith river some distance above its mouth, fording the stream six or eight miles from the sea, where its course is nearly due south and north.

killed a fine black tail buck, that was fat. Marichall killed a small deer.

SATURDAY, JUNE 21ST, 1828. All hands up early and preparing for start. We was under way about 8 o.c. A.M., directing our course up a steep brushy point of mountain, about 1½m. E, and struck an open grassy ridge, or rather a small divide, and kept it about 4½ miles N.E. and enc.[511] The travelling along the divide pretty good and most of the way clear of brush; some rock. I saw an elk, while moving on, and approached it, and killed it; it happened to be a very large and fat buck, that would weight, I should say, nearly 600, from appearance, as I judge from one that we weighed that was killed by Lapoint. Several deer killed by the compy. The day clear and cold.

SUNDAY, JUNE 22. We made an early start again this morning, directing our course N.W., in towards the ocean, as the travilling over the hills E. began to grow very rocky and brushy, and travelled 5 m. and enc. in a bottom prararie on a small branch. The road, to-day, brushy and some what stoney. Timber, hemlock and ceadar, of considerable size, and very thick on the ground; some trees from 10 to 15 feet in diamitar. The weather still remain good. We had some considerable trouble driving our horses through the brush.

MONDAY, JUNE 23RD. All hands up early and preparing for a start; we was under way about 9 o.c. A.M., directing our course as yesterday N.W., and traveled 8 m. and enc. 3 miles from camp we struck a creek [512] 20 or 30 yards wide and crossed it, thence 5 M. further, keeping under the mountain along the bottom and

---

[511] An east and northeast course of six miles brought them to the ridge, east of the town of Smith River.

[512] Probably Windchuck creek, almost exactly on the California-Oregon boundary.

sometimes along the beach of the ocean. When we enc., the hills come within ½ mile of the ocean pararie, covered with grass and brakes. A little before we enc., we discovered the mule that packed the amunition to be missing; four men was sent immediately back in search of it and found it, and brought to camp just at night. 1 mule that was lame give out and was left, and another run off from camp, and went back on the trail with a saddle and halter on. A number of Inds. visited our camp, bringing strawberrys and commass for sale; the men bought all they brought, giving beeds in exchange. We passed a number of wigwams during the day. One fine doe elk killed. The day good.

TUESDAY, JUNE 24TH. We made an early start again this morning, directing our course N.N.W., and travelled 5 miles, and struck a creek about 60 or 70 yards wide, and, the tide being in, we could not cross, and were obliged to encamp on the beach of the ocean for the day.[513] Sent two men back early after the mule that run off last night; they returned without finding it; and 2 more were immediately sent back in pursuit of it with orders to hunt all the afternoon and untill 10 or 11 o.c. tomorrow in case they could not find it this evening. The travelling pretty good yesterday and today; a great many little springs breaks out along under the mountain and makes it a little mirery in some of the branches. Enc. close by some Ind. lodges; they all had fled and left them; no visits from them as yet at this camp; 5 or six Inds. came to camp this morning, just before we started, and brought berries and fish for sale. Capt. Smith bought all they had and divided amongst the men. The day fair and pleasant.

[513] Starting from a point north of the boundary line, they proceeded five miles to Chetcoe river, Curry county, Oregon, where they camped.

WEDNESDAY, JUNE 25TH, 1828. On account of the tide being low, we were ready for a start a little after sun rise; started and crossed the creek with out difficulty, it being about belly deep to our horses, and directed our course again N.W., keeping along a cross the points of pararie near and on the beach of the ocean and travelled 12 m. and enc. on the N. side of a small branch at the mouth where it enters into the ocean, close by some Ind. lodges;[514] they had run off as yesterday and left their lodges. The 2 men that was sent back to hunt the mule, returned to camp a little after night and say the Inds sallied out from their village with bows and arrows and made after them, yelling and screaming, and tryed to surround them; they retreated on horseback and swam a small creek, and the Inds. gave up the chase. When our horses was drove in this morning, we found 3 of them badly wounded with arrows, but could see no Inds. untill we started; we then discovered a canoe loaded with them some distance up the creek close by a thicket and did not pursue them, knowing it was in vain. One deer killed, and several more wounded, and one elk wounded to-day while travilling. Deer and elk quite plenty. 2 horses left to-day that give out and could not travel. The travelling tolerable when compared to former days when in the mou. among the brush; some steep ravines to cross, but not very mirery. The day clear cold and windy for the season.

THURSDAY, JUNE 26TH, 1828. We made an early start again this morning, stearing, as yesterday, N.N.W. across several points of brushy and steep mou. and

---

[514] Crossing the Chetcoe at low tide, they traveled twelve miles, encamping at the mouth of Thoglas creek. The Indians encountered were Chetcos.

travelled 8 m. on a straight line, but to get to the place of enc., about 12 miles, and struck a creek about 30 yards wide at the entrance into the ocean, and, it being high water, we enc. for the day.[515] 2 deer killed to-day. When we come to count our horses, we found one very valuable one missing that was killed, I suppose, by the Inds. on the 24 inst., when they wounded the other 3. We followed an Ind. trail from the time we started in the morning untill we enc.

FRIDAY, JUNE 27TH. All hands up early and under way a little after sun rise, and started along the beach of the ocean, crossed the creek at the mouth, where it was nearly belly deep to our horses, and purs[u]ed our route along the beach, it bearing N.N.W., and travelled about 7 miles and struck a river about 100 yards wide at the mouth and very deep, that makes a considerable bay and enc., and commenced getting timber for rafts.[516] A number of Ind. lodges on both sides of the river; they had run off, as usual, and left their lodges and large baskets; we tore down one lodge to get the puncheons to make rafts, as timber was scarce along the beach. The weather clear and windy. The Inds. that run off raised smokes on the north side of the bay, I suppose, for signals to those that were absent, or some other villages, to let them know that we were close at hand. All the Inds. for several days past runs off and do not come to us any more.[517]

[515] They probably camped on the southern bank of Pistol river.

[516] Presumably crossing Pistol river, they proceeded along the beach until they struck Rogue river, where they encamped. The distance is underestimated.

[517] The prevailing Indian stock along the coast is Athapascan. The Taltushtuntude lived about the mouth of Rogue river, the Mishikhwutmetunne farther north, near the mouth of the Coquille.

SATURDAY, JUNE 28TH, 1828. All hands up early, some fixing the rafts for crossing the river and others sent after the horses. We had all our goods crossed by 9 o.c. A.M., and then proceeded to drive in the horses; there was 12 drowned in crossing, and I know not the reason without it was driving them in too much crowded one upon another. We have lossed 23 horses and mules within 3 days past. After crossing the river, we packed up and started along the sea shore, a N.N.W. course, and travelled about 6 miles and enc.,[518] sometimes on the beach and sometimes along the points of pararie hills that keeps in close to the ocean; the country back looks broken, and thickety, timbered with low scrubby pines and ceadars, the pararie hills covered with good grass and blue clover; the country has been similar as respects timber and soil for several days past, also grass and herbage. One deer killed to-day.

SUNDAY, JUNE 29TH, 1828. We made an early start again this morning, stearing as yesterday N.N.W. along the beach and hills, and travelled 5M. and enc.[519] on account of the water being high, which prevented us from getting along the shore, or we should have travelled a great deal further, as the point of the mou. was too ruff that come into the beach to get along. The travelling yesterday and to-day much alike. I killed one deer after we enc. The day clear and warm.

MONDAY, JUNE 30TH, 1828. We was up and under way in good season, directing our course N.N.W. along the beach 1 mile, then took a steep point of mountain, keeping the same course, and travelled over it and

---

[518] Crossing Rogue river, they travelled six miles, camping near Ophir. Compare U.S. Geological survey, *Port Orford quadrangle* (topographic sheet).

[519] Near the mouth of Mussel creek.

along the beach 6 miles more, and encamped.[520] Lossed one mule last night, that fell in a pitt that was made by Inds. for the purpose of catching elk, and smothered to death; one other fell down a point of mou. today and got killed by the fall. The day clear and pleasant.

TUESDAY, JULY 1ST, 1828. All hands up early and under way, stearing as yesterday N. along the beach of the ocean and across the points of small hills and travelled 12 miles and enc.[521] The day clear and warm; one Ind. in camp early this morning. The country for several days past well calculated for raising stock, both cattle and hogs, as it abounds in good grass and small lakes a little off from the beach where there is good roots grows for hogs. One horse killed again to-day by falling.

WEDNESDAY, JULY 2ND, 1828. We made a pretty early start again this morning, stearing N., and travelled 12 miles, and enc.[522] No accident has happened in regard to horses to-day. We travelled pretty much along the beach and over small sand hills; the timber, small pine; the grass not so plenty nor so good as it has been some days past. The country, for 3 days past, appears to leave the effects of earth quakes at some period past, as it is quite cut to pieces in places and very broken, although it affords such an abundance of good grass and clover. The weather still good. As the most of the mens times expired this evening, Capt. Smith called all hands and give them up there articles, and engaged

---

[520] A little over a mile brought them to Humbug mountain, which they crossed. Six miles brought them to the vicinity of Port Orford.

[521] They camped at the mouth of Sixes river.

[522] Twelve miles took them to the mouth of Johnson creek, Coos county, Oregon. Compare U.S. Geological survey, *Coos bay quadrangle* (topographic sheet). Smith noted the passing of one of the little lakes en route, Sullivan, *op. cit.,* 104.

the following men to go on with him, at one dollar per day, untill he reaches the place of deposit, viz;

John Gaiter	Abraham Laplant
Arthur Black	Charles Swift
John Hanna	Thos. Daws
Emanuel Lazarus	Tousaint Marishall

Daws time to commence when he gets well enough for duty.

Also Peter Ranne and Joseph Palmer, at the above named price, one dollar per day, and Martin McCoy, 200 dollars, from the time he left the Spanish country, untill he reaches the deposit.

THURSDAY, JULY 3RD, 1828. We made a pretty early start, stearing N. along the pine flatts close by the beach of the ocean, and travelled 2 m., and struck a river about 2 hundred yards wide, and crossed it in an Ind. canoe. Capt. Smith, being a head, saw the Inds. in the canoe, and they tryed to get off but he pursued them so closely that they run and left it. They tryed to split the canoe to pieces with thir poles, but he screamed at them, and they fled, and left it, which saved us of a great deal of hard labour making rafts. After crossing our goods, we drove in our horses, and they all swam over, but one; he drowned pretty near the shore. We packed up and started again, after crossing along the beach N., and travelled 5 miles more, and encamped.[523] Saw some Inds. on a point close by the ocean; Marishall caught a boy about 10 years old and brought him to camp. I give him some beads and dryed meat; he appears well and satisfied, and makes signs that the Inds. have all fled in their canoes and left him.[524] I killed one deer

---

[523] After traveling two miles, they reached and crossed the Coquille. Continuing north along the beach, they camped not far south of Whiskey Run.

[524] The Indian boy was given the name, Marion, and was among those

to-day. The country similar to yesterday; the day warm and pleasant.

FRIDAY, JULY 4TH. We made a start early, stearing N.N.W. 9 m., and enc. The travelling pretty bad, as we were obliged to cross the low hills, as they came in close to the beach, and the beach being so bad that we could not get along, thicketty and timbered, and some very bad ravenes to cross. We enc. on a long point, where there was but little grass for the horses.[525] Good deal of elk signs, and several hunters out but killed nothing, the weather still good.

SATURDAY, JULY 5TH, 1828. We travelled 1½ miles to-day N. and, finding good grass, enc. as our horses was pretty tired.[526] Two Inds., who speak Chinook,[527] came to our camp; they tell us we are ten days travell from Catapos on the wel Hamett, which is pleasing news to us.[528] Plenty of elk signs, and several hunters out, but killed nothing.

SUNDAY, JULY 6TH. N. 2 miles to-day and enc., the travelling very bad, mirery and brushy; several horses snagged very bad passing over fallen hemlock; after encamping, two elk killed.[529]

---

who perished at the Umpqua. "Casualty list," Superintendent of Indian affairs, Letter book, 299-300, Kansas historical society MSS.

[525] Nine miles north-northwest carried them across the steep and broken ravines known as the Seven Devils. They camped south of Cape Arago.

[526] A mile and a half north brought them to the vicinity of Big creek.

[527] The Chinook jargon. This is the first instance of the use, so far south, of what later became the *lingua franca* of the entire Pacific coast from California to Alaska. It was first noticed about 1810, and at that time consisted only of Indian words, but later it incorporated English, French, and, perhaps, Russian roots. In 1841 the number of words in the jargon was estimated at two hundred fifty.

[528] The Kalapooian tribes of the Willamette and upper Umpqua comprise a distinct linguistic group. They seem to have suffered severely from an epidemic about four years before Smith's visit. They were usually at war with the Umpqua Indians, who dwelt farther down the river of that name.

[529] They crossed Big creek, finding their way brushy and miry.

MONDAY, JULY 7TH, 1828. We concluded to stay here to-day for the purpose of resting our horses and getting meat and clearing a road to the mouth of a large river that is in sight, about 2 miles distant that we cannot get too without.[530] About 100 Inds. in camp, with fish and mussels for sale; Capt. Smith bought a sea otter skin from the chief; one of them have a fuzill, all have knives and tommahawks. One a blanket cappon, and a number have pieces of cloth. The weather for several days past good.

TUESDAY, JULY 8TH, 1828. We made an early start, directing our course N. along the beach and low hills; the travelling very bad on account of ravenes, fallen timber, and brush. We made 2 miles and struck the river and enc. The river at the mouth is about 1 m. wide, the Inds. very numerous, they call themselves the Ka Koosh.[531] They commenced trading shell and scale fish, rasberrys, strawberrys, and 2 other kinds of bury that I am unacquainted with, also some fur skins. In the evening, we found they had been shooting arrows into 8 of our horses and mules; 3 mules and one horse died shortly after they were shot. The Inds. all left camp, but the 2 that acts as interpreters; they tell us that one Ind. got mad on account of a trade he made and killed the mules and horses. The weather still good. One horse left today that was ma[i]m[ed].

WEDNESDAY, JULY 9TH. We made an early start again this morning, and crossed the 1st fork of the river, which is 400 or 500 yards wide, and got all our things safe

---

[530] They cleared a road east to the South slough, which, not unnaturally, was mistaken for a river of some size.

[531] They reached the mouth of South slough. The Indians are probably the Coos or Kusan tribe, as the name suggests, a very small group now practically extinct. It is possible, however, that Rogers refers to the Kuitsch, a Yakonan tribe, inhabiting the lower Umpqua and the coast. Much confusion has arisen through the similarity of names.

across about 9 o.c. A.M., then packed up and started along the beach along the river N., and travelled about 2 miles, and struck another river and enc.[532] We crossed in Ind. canoes; a great many Inds. live along the river bank; there houses built after the fashion of a shed.[533] A great many Inds. in camp with fish and berris for sale; the men bought them as fast as they brought them. We talked with the chiefs about those Inds. shooting our horses, but could get but little satisfaction as they say that they were not accessary to it, and we, finding them so numerous and the travelling being so bad, we thought it advisable to let it pass at present without notice. We bought a number of beaver, land, and sea otter skins from them in the course of the day.

THURSDAY, JULY 10TH, 1828. We commenced crossing the river early, as we had engaged canoes last night; we drove in our horses and they swam across; they had to swim about 600 yards. Our goods was all crossed about 9 o.c. A.M. and 2 horses that was wounded, and one was much, remained, that Capt. Smith and 5 men stay to cross; the 2 horses dyed of there wounds, and Capt. Smith swam the mule along side of the canoe. He was some what of opinion the Inds. had a mind to attact him from there behaviour, and he crossed over where the swells was running pretty high, and, there being good grass, we enc. for the day; the Inds. pretty shy.

The river we crossed to-day unites with the one we crossed yesterday and makes an extensive bay that runs

---

[532] The words "1st fork of the" are crossed out in the MS. Having crossed South slough, they turned north along the east side of Coos bay but, after proceeding more than two miles, they struck Coos river itself at the point where it flows west.

[533] I.e., of boards, as distinct from the bark hives of the tribes farther south.

back into the hills; it runs N. and S., or rather heads N.E. and enters the ocean S.W., at the entrance into the ocean its about 1½ miles wide.[534]

FRIDAY, JULY 11, 1828. All hands up early and under way, had an Ind. who speaks Chinook along as a guide. Our course was N. along the beach of the ocean, 15 miles, and struck [another] river that is about 300 yards wide at the mouth and enc., as it was not fordable. We crossed a small creek, 3 yards wide, 10 miles from camp.[535] To-day we enc. where there was some Inds. living; a number of them speak Chinook; 70 or 80 in camp; they bring us fish and berris and appear friendly; we buy those articles from them at a pretty dear rate. Those Inds call themselves the Omp quch.[536]

The day windy and cold. Several of the men worn out.

Peter Ranne has been sick for 6 weeks, with a swelling in his legs. The country about ½ mile back from the ocean sand hills covered with small pine and brush, the sand beach, quit.[537]

SATURDAY, JULY 12TH. We commenced crossing the river early and had our goods and horses over by 8 o.c., then packed up and started a N.E. course up the river and travelled 3 M. and enc.[538] Had several Inds. along; one of the Ind. stole an ax and we were obliged to seize

---

[534] They crossed Coos river, perhaps above Empire, striking the long sand spit on the west side of the bay. The description of the bay as running north and south makes it clear that they did not explore the country to the east of South slough, where the bay takes a quite different form, like an inverted Y.

[535] Following the beach, they crossed Eel creek, reaching the Umpqua river in Douglas county, Oregon.

[536] The Umpquas, an Athapascan tribe, living along the lower stretches of the Umpqua river. They number at the present time less than one hundred.

[537] The manuscript breaks off abruptly at this point.

[538] They probably crossed from Winchester Head at the mouth of the river which they could easily have done at low tide. Travelling three miles up the river they probably encamped near the site of old Fort Umpqua, a favored Indian camp site in early days.

him for the purpose of tying him before we could scare him to make him give it up. Capt. Smith and one of them caught him and put a cord round his neck, and the rest of us stood with our guns ready in case they made any resistance, there was about 50 Inds. present but did not pretend to resist tying the other.[539] The river at this place is about 300 yards wide and make a large bay that extends 4 or 5 miles up in the pine hills. The country similar to yesterday. We traded some land and sea otter and beaver fur in the course of the day. Those Inds. bring Pacific rasberrys and other berries.

SUNDAY, JULY 13, 1828. We made a pretty good start this morning, directing our course along the bay, east and travelled 4 miles and enc.[540] 50 or 60 Inds in camp again to-day (we traded 15 or 20 beaver skins from them, some elk meat and tallow, also some lamprey eels). The traveling quit mirery in places; we got a number of our pack horses mired, and had to bridge several places. A considerable thunder shower this morning, and rain at intervals through the day. Those Inds. tell us after we get up the river 15 or 20 miles we will have good travelling to the Wel Hammett or Multinomah, where the Callipoo Inds. live.[541]

[539] The stealing of the axe and the binding of the Indian according to several accounts became one of the most important factors in the Indian attack of july 13. The chiefs of the Umpquas so reported three months later to Alexander McLeod, the leader of the Hudson's Bay company force sent to recover Smith's property, McLeod, "Journal," in Sullivan, *op. cit.,* 123. See also Simpson's "Report," *ibid,* 148 and the McLaughlin narrative in Clarke, *Pioneer days of Oregon history,* I, 216. McLaughlin had the story from Arthur Black, one of the survivors.

[540] Probably below or near the mouth of Smith's river. For topographical details of the Umpqua region I am indebted to Dr. William Kuykendall of Eugene, Oregon.

[541] The Indians directed them up the Umpqua to Elk creek and thence over a low divide to the Coast fork of the Willamette, near Drain, Oregon. They understate the distance however.

Harrison G. Rogers' book continued from the 10th of
may, 1828. Jedediah S. Smith capt. of
the compy.

MAY 23RD. One thousand eight hundred and twenty
eight.

I promise and oblige myself to pay unto John D.
Daggett, one hundred pounds, good and lawful money
of the United States, for value recd' of him, as witness
my hand this 23rd day of may, one thousand eight hundred and twenty eight.

This book commences 10th may, 1828.

Up to this point the general attitude of the Indians
toward the little party had been friendly. They had
furnished them food in exchange for beads and baubles.
To be sure, many of the savages encountered had been
overcome with fear at first sight of the whites and had
fled precipitately, only to be coaxed back with difficulty. Smith had made every effort to keep on peaceful
terms with them. The severe reprimand administered
to the negro, Ransa, june fourth, for having given a
false alarm, and Thomas Virgin's manifest regret at
being under the necessity of shooting an Indian a fortnight before, together with the efforts made on that occasion to explain to the savages that the whites had not
been the aggressors, point clearly to Smith's earnest
desire for peace with them all.[542] By the thirteenth of
july the worst of their journey seemed over. Fifteen or
twenty miles of easy traveling would bring them to the
Willamette valley, whence lay an open road to the
Columbia. The Umpqua Indians, moreover, seemed
singularly friendly. They brought fish and beaver

[542] Despite the claims of the Hudson's Bay officials to the contrary. See
Simpson, "Report," Sullivan, *op. cit.,* 148.

skins to trade. Two days earlier, it is true, one of them was accused of having stolen an axe. Smith had ordered him tied up and a rope put round his neck, releasing him only after the axe had been found buried in the sand. The following day the incident seemed to be forgotten, for fifty or sixty Indians came into camp to trade.

That night, the thirteenth, their attitude apparently changed, or else, from the first, Smith, despite his experience with the Indian character, had been deceived by their seeming friendliness.[543] With their usual precautions the men had pitched camp sunday evening near the river. Monday morning, leaving the rest of the party still in camp, Smith after breakfast set out with two men in a canoe to find the route for the day, just as he had done many times before.[544] The party had already crossed the Umpqua but had found the traveling on the north side of the stream unusually difficult, chiefly on account of the heavy rains, that had

[543] Gustavus Hines states that Smith and his party were thrown off their guard by the apparent good-will of the Indians, Hines, *Oregon,* 110. Hines had his information directly or indirectly from McLaughlin, who, in turn, had it from Smith himself. Fremont comments on the treacherous disposition of the Indians south of the Columbia. He writes, "I was not unmindful of the disasters which Smith and other travellers had met in this country."— Fremont, *op. cit.,* 205.

[544] One of these may have been the young Englishman, Richard Leland, who had joined the party in California (Victor, *River of the west,* 34) and the other John Turner (Hines, *Oregon,* 110, 111). "On the 14th july, Mr. Smith had left the encampment in order to search out a road, the country being very swampy in the lowlands and woody in the mountains."—Brief sketch, Kansas historical society MSS. The McLaughlin narrative states that Smith started with two men and an Indian in a canoe. Clarke (*Pioneer days of Oregon history,* I, 216) states that with one man he was searching for a ford. Hines (*Oregon,* 110) says that he proceeded up the river on foot with one man. Warner (*op. cit.,* VII, 182) says that with one man he was searching for a ford. Victor (*River of the west,* 34) states that he was on a raft at the time and had with him "a little Englishman and one Indian." Smith's account alone can be accepted as accurate.

begun with a thunder storm sunday morning and had kept up off and on all that day, but partly, too, because of the naturally soggy marshy ground along the river bottoms. Perhaps also it was because they had covered only four miles the day before that Smith resolved to find a better road before all the company broke camp.

Returning from his reconnaissance and before beaching his canoe, he suddenly discovered something of what had taken place. Evidently in grave danger and without any chance to investigate or to attempt a recovery of his property, Smith and his companion set out at once up the Umpqua in the direction they would have naturally pursued. After severe hardships they finally, on august tenth, reached the shelter of Fort Vancouver.[545] What was their surprise to discover Arthur Black, the only other survivor, who had arrived two days before. His experiences had been equally distressing. Black, as it appeared, had just finished cleaning and loading his rifle at the moment of the Indian attack. Three Indians had leaped upon him. He shook them off and seeing all his comrades struggling on the ground and the Indians assailing them, had fired into the crowd and rushed to the woods with several of them in hot pursuit. Fortunately he had succeeded in eluding them. Aware that safety lay in reaching the Hudson's Bay company's establishment, he had turned north, just as Smith and Turner had done, except that he had kept closer to the coast. Lack of shelter and food, save a few berries, rendered him so helpless in the course of a week or so, that he voluntarily gave himself up to the Tillamook Indians. They had treated him with humanity, fed and sheltered him, and conducted him to Fort Vancouver.

---

545 Simpson, "Report," in Sullivan, *op. cit.*, 147.

There are several versions as to the actual details of the massacre, all of them stemming either from the report given by the Umpqua chief to Alexander McLeod three months after the massacre or from the story told by Arthur Black. According to McLeod the Indian who had been tied up for the alleged theft of the axe had been so incensed that he demanded instant revenge but had been overruled by a chieftain of higher rank. While Smith was out searching the route, Rogers, who had been left in charge, allowed the Indians to come into the camp. When this second chief, so McLeod was told, just for the amusement of riding, mounted one of the horses he was threatened with a gun. This affront, it was said, led to the general attack.[546] The wily old Umpqua chief, in telling the story to McLeod, added a further reason to the effect that the Indians had been much influenced by the Americans' claim that they were a "different people from the British and would soon monopolize the trade and turn the latter out of the country."[547] An additional factor appears in the account given years later by Doctor McLaughlin, who not only had McLeod's report but also the eye-witness statement of Arthur Black. The trouble started, so the latter said, following the admission of squaws to the camp. The Umpqua chief did not mention this in telling the story to McLeod. However, Governor George Simpson in his report to the Hudson's Bay

---

[546] Sullivan, *op. cit.*, 123, 124. Arthur Black confirmed this but denied that the Indians had been threatened.

[547] The Indians were said to have "communicated something about territorial claims, and that they (the Americans) would soon possess themselves of the country, make the natives about us very inquisitive not having ever heard such a thing before, and we avoid giving them any information, and treat the subject with derision." Smith on hearing of this said he did not doubt it but asserted that any such boast was made without his knowledge and probably through the medium of the Indians who had joined the party.

company, dated march 1, 1829, elaborates this point, asserting that Harrison G. Rogers, while attempting to force a woman into his tent, knocked down the woman's brother, who had rushed gallantly to the defense of her virtue, whereupon "seeing the opportunity favorable, as some of the people were asleep, others eating and none on their guard, they rose in a body and despatched the whole party except the man who fled." [548] Whatever the truth of the last details, there is no question but what the relaxation of discipline with the admission of Indians to their camp was the occasion, if not the primary cause, of the disaster.

Dr. John McLaughlin, the chief factor, foreseeing the significance of the step he was taking, gave liberal rewards to the savages who had brought Arthur Black to Fort Vancouver and expressed the hope that in the future they would continue to render assistance to the whites whenever occasion might arise. At the same time he dispatched Thomas McKay, a half-breed, and Michel La Framboise, a former Astor employee, to proceed as rapidly as possible to the old Hudson's Bay fort on the Umpqua to recover the property if possible.

With characteristic humanity McLaughlin resolved to take still further steps to avenge the disaster.[549] Smith, not unnaturally, was urging punishment of the

548 Arthur Black. Smith, whose veracity was above reproach, denied the probability of this. For a contrary slant on Rogers's lustful impulses under other but somewhat similar conditions see page 217.

549 "It is an act of justice to say also that the treatment received by Mr. Smith at Fort Vancouver was kind and hospitable, that personally, he owes thanks to Governor Simpson and to the gentlemen of the H. B. company for the hospitable entertainment which he received from them, and for the efficient and successful aid which they gave him in recovering from the Umpqua Indians a quantity of furs," Smith, Jackson, and Sublette to John Eaton, secretary of war, St. Louis, october 29, 1830 in U.S. Senate, *Executive documents*, 21 cong., 2 sess., I, no. 39, 23.

Indians and expressed the hope that he might be allowed to participate in any move that might be made against them. Although McLaughlin was inclined to agree, fearing that if they let this incident pass British security and prestige might be endangered, his chief trader, Alexander McLeod, with whom he discussed the matter and who was about to start on the fall hunt, was inclined to question whether in undertaking to recover and restore Smith's property and to capture and punish the murderers, they might not be attempting more than they could effectively accomplish. Probably he was also inclined to think there might be two sides to the story Smith and Arthur Black had told. He further raised the larger question of the propriety of making war on the natives on whom the company was in part dependent for its trade in furs. Smith and his men, however, were allowed to join McLeod's party which left Fort Vancouver september sixth. Two days later they met McKay and La Framboise returning from the Umpqua country, who reported that the Umpqua chief had expressed great friendliness for the British and much exasperation with the Keliwatset Indians, who were alleged to have been the perpetrators of the massacre. They further reported that the Umpquas had several of Smith's horses in their possession. It was evident, however, that Smith's property, including all his equipment and his furs, a few of which La Framboise had found even among the distant Willamette Indians, were scattered over the country in the hands of various tribes.[550]

McKay and La Framboise hastened on to Fort Vancouver, where they made a similar report to Doctor McLaughlin. The latter, now fully convinced of the

[550] McLeod "Journal," Sullivan, *op. cit.,* 113.

soundness of McLeod's position, wrote Smith a letter expressing his sympathy but leaving such steps as might be taken in avenging the massacre to McLeod's judgment and experience in handling the Indian tribes. This he also confirmed in a letter to McLeod, although he did not fail to point out the desirability from the strictly British point of view of taking a firm stand in dealing with the situation.[551]

McLeod's party, accompanied by Smith and his men, continued up the Willamette. Various Hudson's Bay employees encountered on their way gave disturbing reports of the attitude of the Umpqua Indians, who, they claimed, had supported the Keliwatsets, the actual murderers, and were preparing to ambush McLeod's party. As they proceeded the Indians fled before them, so that they encountered none till the eleventh of october, when the Umpqua chief and a dozen of his tribe came to their camp near the old fort on the Umpqua. They related the story of the massacre as told above. At this point the expedition succeeded in recovering a considerable number of horses, and it was decided to leave the main body encamped near the mouth of Mill creek, at the site of the present city of Scottsburg, with McKay in charge, while Smith and one of his men accompanied the main detachment down the Umpqua to the Indian villages and the coast. On october twenty-first, just above the site of the massacre, they encountered what McLeod calls a populous Indian village. A message was sent demanding the restoration of any of Smith's property they had in their possession. The Indians complied and Smith recovered rifles, pistols,

---

[551] Letters of McLaughlin to Smith and McLaughlin to McLeod, both dated september 12, 1828 in Sullivan, *op. cit.*, 109, 110, 111. These letters were dispatched by McKay, who delivered them the following day.

beaver and other skins, shirts, medicines, some books and other papers,[552] charts, even "½ doz. led pencils." The property was sent back to base camp and the party proceeded farther down stream to a second village, where the same performance was repeated save that the quantity of goods recovered was somewhat less. On the twenty-eighth of october, on their way to the ocean, they stopped at the confluence of the north branch (Smith's fork), where the massacre took place, to provide decent interment and pay their last respects to eleven of Smith's men whose skeletons were found lying about the camp site. Near the mouth of the Umpqua they recovered more of Smith's property and proceeding along the seashore to the Siuslaw, recovered, bit by bit, a considerable quantity of his effects amounting in all to 216 beaver skins, 47 otter skins, 24 horses and mules, 4 kettles, quantities of traps and miscellaneous articles. The final amount came to 700 beaver skins and 39 horses.[553] Returning to their camp at the mouth of the Umpqua, they proceeded up stream, renaming the north fork, Defeat river as a reminder of Smith's disaster. Here Smith, with three Indians and two Hudson's Bay men, took a short cut, rejoining the main expedition near the site of Scottsburg. On november twenty-second they were at base camp, where McKay, who had been left in charge, had also recovered several articles belonging to Smith. The main body of McLeod's party, to which Smith entrusted his horses, was

---

[552] Including the journal of Harrison G. Rogers and probably Smith's also.

[553] Letter of Governor Simpson to Smith, Sullivan, *op. cit.*, 137. See also Smith, Jackson, and Sublette letter to John Eaton, in U.S. Senate, *op. cit.* Not all the property was recovered. The following may Ogden discovered among a tribe of Indians east of Pitt river arms and ammunition which he suspected had been the property of Smith's men. See Ogden "Journal," entry of may 28, 1829, Oregon historical society *quarterly*, XI, 395.

left here, while McLeod and Smith with a few others hastened down to Fort Vancouver, where they arrived shortly before Christmas.

Although Governor Simpson estimated that the recovery of Smith's property cost the company one thousand pounds without considering the loss in their own business occasioned thereby, he declined to accept any remuneration for the services rendered, saying "that the satisfaction we have derived from these good offices will repay the honble Hudsons Bay compy amply for any loss or inconvenience in rendering them." [554]

Smith was now faced with the serious problem of his future course. Winter was at hand and he had but two men left of his original company. Despite the lateness of the season, he at first determined to proceed at once up the Columbia to the Hudson's Bay station at Fort Walla Walla, procuring horses there in exchange for the mounts he had left in the company's charge in the Umpqua country, and thence to hasten on to Salt lake. Governor Simpson of the Hudson's Bay company, who had arrived at Fort Vancouver two months before on a tour of the company's posts, not only declined to furnish him horses at Walla Walla because of the shortage there, but emphatically called his attention to the great hazards to be encountered in undertaking a journey to Salt lake in the midst of winter by way of the Blue mountains and the Snake river. As an alternative he offered to buy Smith's furs at three dollars per skin and his horses at forty shillings per head and to provide him free passage either the following spring to the Red River post of the Hud-

---

[554] Letter of Governor Simpson, cited above. Cf. Chittenden, *American fur trade*, I, 286; Bancroft, *History of the northwest coast*, II, 452, citing Robert Newell in the *Democratic herald*, october 3, 1866.

son's Bay company, whence he could proceed to St.
Louis by way of Prairie du Chien, or with the Snake
country expedition the following fall by which he could
find safe conduct to Salt lake. Smith decided to abandon his plans for reaching Salt lake, accepted the company's offer for his furs, receiving thirty-two hundred
dollars in payment,[555] and accordingly spent the winter
at Fort Vancouver, where he was a welcome guest.
The valorous John Turner, however, abandoned
Smith's service here, but only to start back again into
the very country from which he had so narrowly escaped. He joined the expedition conducted by Alexander McLeod, which had set out for the country
south to the forty-second parallel, in which, by the
treaty of joint occupancy, the British had equal hunting
rights with the Americans.[556]

On the twelfth of march 1829 Smith and Arthur
Black left Fort Vancouver, traveling up the Columbia
to the Kettle falls, thence to Fort Colville and Flathead
House, and on to the rendezvous of his company, thence
southward into the upper Snake river country, where
he encountered a detachment of his company's men in
Pierre's Hole (Teton basin).[557]

[555] According to McLaughlin, Clarke, *op. cit.,* I, 217. Sullivan (*op. cit.,* 152)
says $2600; Merk (*Fur trade and empire,* 307 note) says £550.2.6.

[556] Warner, "Reminiscences," in Southern California historical society
publications, VII, 183 ff; Bancroft, *California,* III, 161-162. Turner was in
California in 1835, returning to Oregon that year, after meeting with a narrow escape on Rogue river. He was a member of the Willamette Cattle
company, organized by Ewing Young in 1837, and with that company came
overland again from California to Oregon. He was with the so-called
second relief party sent out from Sutter's fort in march 1847 to assist the
Donner party, Bancroft, *op. cit.,* v, 540; Lang, H. O., *History of the Willamette valley,* 226, 230; Houghton, E. P. D., *Donner party and its tragic fate,*
104.

[557] Smith, Jackson, and Sublette to John Eaton, in U.S. Senate, *op. cit.;*
Brief sketch, Kansas historical society MSS.

During Smith's prolonged absence the other partners had maintained a hundred men in the field but divided into groups, which had operated on the usual streams of the interior basin and in adjoining territory. In the fall of 1826 and spring of 1827 they had pushed north to the southern tributaries of the Columbia, but, by keeping well to the east, had avoided the Hudson's Bay company's Snake expedition of that year, commanded by Peter Skene Ogden.[558] During the spring hunt it is highly probable that one detachment penetrated as far as the Yellowstone national park, and that one of the party wrote the graphic description of that region which appeared in *Niles register* of october 6, 1827. This description, having apparently escaped the notice of the historian of the park, deserves to be quoted in full.[559]

SWEET LAKE, july 8, 1827

Shortly after writing to you last, I took my departure for the Black Feet country much against my will, but I could not make a party for any other route. We took a northerly direction about fifty miles, where we crossed Snake river, or the south fork of Columbia, at the forks of Henry's and Lewis's; at this place we were daily harassed by the Black Feet; from thence we went up Henry's or north fork, which bears north of east thirty miles, and crossed a large rugged mountain which separated the two forks; from thence, east up the other branch to its source, which heads on the top of the great chain of Rocky mountains which separates the waters of the Atlantic from those of the Pacific; at or near this place heads the Suchkadee or California,

---

[558] There is no mention of Americans in the Ogden "Journal, 1826-1827," *Oregon historical society quarterly,* XI, 204 ff.

[559] Chittenden says that the description of the park written by W. A. Ferris (*Life in the Rocky mountains*) published first in the *Western literary messenger* (Buffalo), 1841-1842 and reprinted in the *Wasp* (Nauvoo, Illinois), august 13, 1842, "forms the most interesting and authentic reference to the geyser regions published prior to 1870," Chittenden, *Yellowstone national park,* 40. This description from *Niles register,* however, antedates Ferris's account by fifteen years.

sticking [Stinking?] fork, Yellow Stone, south fork of Masiori [*sic*], and Henry's fork; all those head at one angular point; that of the Yellow Stone has a large freshwater lake near its head at the very top of the mountains, which is about 100 by 40 miles in diameter, and as clear as crystal. On the south border of this lake is a number of hot and boiling springs, some of water and others of most beautiful fine clay, resembling a mush pot, and throwing particles to the immense height of from 20 to 30 feet. The clay is of a white, and of a pink color, and the water appears fathomless, as it appears to be entirely hollow underneath. There is also a number of places where pure sulphur is sent forth in abundance. One of our men visited one of these whilst taking his recreation, there, at an instant, the earth began a tremendous trembling, and he with difficulty made his escape, when an explosion took place, resembling that of thunder. During our stay in that quarter I heard it every day. From this place by a circuitous route to the north west was returned.

Two others and myself pushed on in advance for the purpose of accumulating a few more beaver, and in the act of passing through a narrow confine in the mountain, we were met plump in the face by a large party of Black Feet Indians, who, not knowing our number, fled into the mountains in confusion; we retired to a small grove of willows; here we made every preparation for battle, after which, finding our enemy as much alarmed as ourselves, we mounted our horses, which we hastily loaded, and took the back retreat. We here put whips to our horses and they pursued us in close quarters until we reached the plains, where we left them behind. On this trip, one man was closely fired on by a party of Black Feet; several others were closely pursued.

On this trip I lost one horse by accident, and the last spring two by the Utaws, who killed three for the purpose of eating them, one of which was a favorite buffaloe horse. This loss cannot be computed at less than four hundred and fifty dollars. A few days previous to my arrival at this place, a party of about 120 Black Feet approached the camp and killed a Snake Indian and his squaw. The alarm was immediately given and the Snakes, Utaws, and whites sallied forth for battle, the enemy fled to the mountain to a small concavity thickly grown with small timber surrounded by open ground. In this engagement, the squaws were busily engaged in throwing up batteries and dragging off the dead. There were only six whites engaged in this battle, who immediately advanced within pistol shot, and you may be assured that almost every shot counted one. The loss of the Snakes was three killed, one wounded, and two narrowly made their escape; that of the Utaws was none, though they gained great applause for their bravery. The loss of the enemy is not known; six were found dead on the ground; a great number besides were carried off on horses. To-morrow I depart for the west.[560]

By july the scattered detachments reunited for rendezvous at Bear lake, where Smith joined them on his return from his first California expedition.

With the conclusion of rendezvous and the departure of Smith the second time to California, the fall hunt began, lasting this year well into the winter. In general the men confined their operations to Weiser river, Reed's river, Payette river, Riviere aux Malades, and the Portneuf, tributaries of the Snake, but without great success, so thoroughly had all this area been trapped by English and Americans since first the Astorians toiled through it.[561] One detachment fell in with Ogden's men early in the season, remained with them two months, and then set out november 30 for Great Salt lake.[562] On Christmas eve a second detachment, commanded by the veteran Samuel Tullock, which was also trapping the Snake country, joined the Britishers in camp. They stayed four months simply because they could not push through to their headquarters. They were prevented partly because the winter of 1827-1828 was unusually severe but largely because of Ogden's influence with

---

[560] Smith, Jackson, and Sublette were probably the only Americans engaged in the country fifty miles south of Snake river as early as the year 1827. They also traded with the Blackfeet this season, and one of their parties, commanded by Robert Campbell, penetrated this region the following year. Letter of W. H. Ashley to T. H. Benton, St. Louis, january 20, 1829, in U.S. Senate, *Executive documents,* 20 cong., 2 sess., I, no. 67.

[561] Ogden, "Journal, 1827-1828," Oregon historical society *quarterly,* XI, 362 ff.

[562] *Idem,* XI, 365.

the Indians. The latter refused to sell Tullock snow-shoes, though he offered as high as twenty-five dollars for a single pair. Tullock at length determined to make the attempt without snow-shoes but failed. Then he tried to engage an Indian to carry letters through to the post at Great Salt lake. Ogden writes

Jan. 20, 1828, Tullock, the American, who failed to get thro' the snow to Salt lake, tried to engage an Indian to carry letters to the American depot at Salt lake. This I cannot prevent. It is impossible for me to bribe so many Indians with my party. I have succeeded in preventing them from providing snow shoes.

And three days later

The American is now very low spirited. He cannot hire a man to go to his cache nor snow shoes, nor does he suspect that I prevented. This day he offered 8 beaver and 50 dollars for a pair and a prime horse to any one who would carry a letter to the American camp. In this he also failed.

Ogden, however, overestimated his own subtlety. Tullock did, as a matter of fact, suspect his influence with the Indians, though he was probably shrewd enough not to let his suspicions become known to him. When he met William Sublette, next spring, he told him of the difficulties he had encountered and stated clearly his suspicions of Ogden. These suspicions Sublette, in turn, passed on to Ashley on his return to the states in the winter of 1828-1829, who incorporated them in a letter to Thomas Hart Benton. In this way they found permanent record in a public document.[563]

Finally, however, Tullock and his companions, having given up all hope of purchasing snow-shoes, set out to make some for themselves, "which," says Ogden, "they ought to have done 2 weeks ago." Their achieve-

---

[563] U.S. Senate, *op. cit.*

ments were pathetic and certain to give them trouble.[564] Tullock, however, with one companion set out on the twenty-eighth of january for Great Salt lake. Neither of them had had any experience with snow-shoes. Trouble began at the start. In crossing Snake river the ice gave way; Tullock's companion was swept into the current and only saved himself by a heroic struggle. Undaunted, they struggled on through deep snows and ice-locked valleys, making but slow progress, until they finally reached the headwaters of the Portneuf, where, despairing of continuing further, they turned about and made their way back to Ogden's camp, arriving on the fourth of february. After resting a week they set out again and had not gone far when they met Robert Campbell, coming up from Great Salt lake. Campbell was nearly destitute, and, accordingly, they turned about again, reaching Ogden's quarters on the sixteenth. Meantime another detachment had been feeling the severity of this winter on Bear river, perhaps at the old wintering grounds in Cache valley.[565]

After a week with the English, Tullock and Campbell, with most of their men, set out northward. Their departure was taken so quietly and their destination left so vague that Ogden suspected, probably with some foundation, that they were bound for the forks of the Missouri and the land of the Blackfeet, who, as it happened, had been singularly docile this year.[566] His suspicions were confirmed when he learned that they

---

[564] Oregon historical society *quarterly*, XI, 372.

[565] *Idem,* XI, 371, 373, 374.

[566] *Idem,* XI, 375. "These people [the Blackfeet] had always been considered enemies to our traders; but about that time [1827-1828] some of them manifested a friendly disposition, invited a friendly intercourse and trade, and did actually dispose of a portion of their furs to Messers Smith, Jackson, and Sublette."—Letter of W. H. Ashley to T. H. Benton, january 20, 1829, in U.S. Senate, *op. cit.*

had arranged their summer rendezvous for the Flat-head country, not far distant from the Three Forks. Tullock was equally suspicious of the designs of Ogden, placing a sinister interpretation on a misfortune which befell him shortly after his departure. Within three or four days of Ogden's camp a detachment of his men were suddenly attacked by thirty or forty Blackfeet, who killed three and made off with about forty thousand dollars' worth of furs, forty-four horses, and a considerable quantity of merchandise.[567]

Disaster followed disaster for Smith, Jackson, and Sublette in the year 1828. Besides the loss of Tullock's men and the massacre on the Umpqua, misfortune befell another division of fifteen or twenty men, who were crossing from the Columbia to Great Salt lake through the dangerous and little-known deserts of southern Oregon. Four of the party had strayed from the main detachment to explore several small streams along the way. They planned to rejoin their companions in three or four days but were never heard of again.[568]

After the return of the various detachments to Great Salt lake in the fall of 1828, William Sublette set out for St. Louis with the accumulated furs. Arriving before Christmas he procured a fresh supply of horses, mules, and merchandise, enlisted sixty men, and started for the mountains in march 1829. He followed the now well-trodden route of the North Platte but, instead of proceeding through the South pass to Green river

---

[567] *Idem*. Ogden afterwards saw the clothing, horses, etc., of some men, Oregon historical society *quarterly*, XI, 378. He was, however, in no way responsible for the attack, as hinted by Sublette to Ashley. Among those killed was Pinckney Sublette, a relative (brother?) of William Sublette. Five other men were lost in the course of the year, U.S. Senate, *op. cit.*

[568] *Idem*. Their names were Ephraim Logan, Jacob O'Harra, William Bell, and James Scott.

and the interior basin, he turned north from the Sweetwater to the valley of the Popo Agie, where he arrived
for a rendezvous about the first of july.[569] David E.
Jackson was absent, having remained for the spring
and summer in the Snake river and Great Salt lake
country.[570]

After rendezvous the company as usual divided,
Milton Sublette, William's brother, with two free
trappers, Henry Fraeb and Baptiste Gervais, going
into the familiar region of the Big Horn, abandoned
five years before, while William Sublette, with the
main body, pushed westward into the Snake river country, hoping to meet here his long-absent partner, Jedediah Smith, as had been agreed between them before
the latter returned to California. Pursuing the old
route of the overland Astorians he ascended Wind river,
crossed the Union pass to the Hoback, which he descended to its confluence with the left fork of Snake
river, and then, turning north to Jackson's Hole, met
there his partner for whom this charming valley was
named. Together they camped on the shores of Jackson's
lake under the shadow of the Tetons to await Smith's
arrival. But he did not come. Finally, detachments were
sent out in various directions to search for him. One
of these, of which Joseph L. Meek was a member, ran
across him and the faithful Arthur Black, beyond the
Tetons, in Pierre's Hole. Thither the entire camp removed.

In return for the favors extended him by the Hud-

---

[569] Victor, *River of the west*, 43, 48. The reason for abandoning Bear lake
or Great Salt lake as the place of rendezvous is not entirely clear, but it may
have been due to the fact that Smith, Jackson, and Sublette were operating
more and more to the north, in the vicinity of their old fields about the upper
Missouri and its tributaries, which were more easily accessible from the states
via the Big Horn basin than via Great Salt lake.

[570] Victor, *op. cit.*, 57.

son's Bay company at Fort Vancouver, Smith, it is said, promised Doctor McLaughlin that he and his partners would abandon their operations in the Snake river country, thereby giving the English a free rein in this much worked field. Mindful of his promise, Smith now, apparently, induced Sublette and Jackson to agree, rather reluctantly, to this arrangement.[571] In october, accordingly, after a brief hunt along Henry's fork, the whole outfit moved north and east through the North pass to Missouri lake, the source of the Madison fork, a region rich in furs but dangerous through the presence of the Blackfeet.[572] Smith assumed general command. For a time the men were unmolested and in november pushed still farther north and east, across the Gallatin fork into the lofty divide between that stream and the Yellowstone. On their way a band of Blackfeet pounced upon them, killing two of their number. The rest fled confusedly in scattered groups, reuniting, without further loss of life, on the Stinking fork of the Big Horn.[573] Continuing eastward they finally joined Milton Sublette's party. After caching their furs the entire company turned south across the Big Horn mountains to the Wind River valley, which

[571] *Idem*, 58 ff.

[572] *Idem*, 64. With this expedition went, besides Smith and Sublette, Thomas Fitzpatrick, Joseph L. Meek, James Bridger, Craig, Nelson, and Reese.

[573] In the course of the engagement with the Blackfeet, Meek, like the rest, fled to the mountains about the Yellowstone river. He was alone. "At his feet rolled the Yellowstone river, coursing away through the great plain to the eastward. To the north, his eye followed the windings of the Missouri, as upon a map, but playing hide-and-seek in amongst the mountains. Looking back, he saw the River Snake stretching its serpentine length through lava plains, far away, to its junction with the Columbia."—Victor, *op cit.,* 73 ff. Suffice it to say that there is no mountain from which such a view may be obtained. Seeking to escape from his predicament and rejoin his companions or find refuge among the Crows, Meek turned southeast, passing through Yellowstone park, where he met two of his companions.

they reached about Christmas. During the ensuing winter, William Sublette returned to St. Louis.[574]

On the first of january 1830 the two remaining partners, leaving their winter quarters on Wind river, moved the entire camp north to the buffalo country on Powder river. The winter was proving severe and the supply of grass in Wind river valley insufficient for the horses. The journey was accomplished in a fortnight. The camp then settled down for the remainder of the winter.

Through the day, hunting parties were coming and going, men were cooking, drying meat, making moccasins, cleaning their arms, wrestling, playing games, and, in short, everything that an isolated community of hardy men could resort to for occupation, was resorted to by these mountaineers. Nor was there wanting, in the appearance of the camp, the variety, and that picturesque air imparted by a mingling of the native element; for what with their Indian allies, their native wives, and numerous children, the mountaineers' camp was a motley assemblage; and the trappers themselves, with their affection of Indian coxcombry, not the least picturesque individuals.

The change wrought in a wilderness landscape by the arrival of the grand camp was wonderful indeed. Instead of Nature's superb silence and majestic loneliness, there was the sound of men's voices in boisterous laughter, or the busy hum of conversation; the loud-resounding stroke of the axe; the sharp report of the rifle; the neighing of horses, and braying of mules; the Indian whoop and yell; and all that now unpleasing confusion of sound which accompanies the movements of the creature man. Over the plain, only dotted until now with the shadow of the clouds, or the transitory passage of the deer, the antelope, or the bear, were scattered hundreds of lodges and immense herds of grazing animals. Even the atmosphere itself seemed changed from its original purity, and became clouded with the smoke of many camp-fires. And all this change might go as quickly as it came. The tent struck and the march resumed, solitude reigned once more, and only the cloud dotted the silent landscape.

574 Victor, op. cit., 79 ff. Jedediah Smith sent a letter out by Sublette to his brother, Ralph, dated december 24, 1829, Smith MSS., Kansas historical society.

If the day was busy and gleesome, the night had its charms as well. Gathered about the shining fires, groups of men in fantastic costumes told tales of marvelous adventures, or sung some old-remembered song, or were absorbed in games of chance. Some of the better educated men, who had once known and loved books, but whom some mishap in life had banished to the wilderness, recalled their favorite authors, and recited passages once treasured, now growing unfamiliar; or whispered to some chosen confrere the saddened history of his earlier years, and charged him thus and thus, should ever-ready death surprise himself in the next spring's hunt.[575]

The spring hunt opened in april, and the company was again divided. Jackson, with about half the men, went across the mountains to his old haunts on Snake river, despite Smith's alleged promise to the British. With James Bridger as pilot and Jedediah Smith as commander, the remaining men crossed the series of parallel ridges dividing the southern tributaries of the Yellowstone. Crossing Tongue river and the Big Horn, they reached Bovey's fork, a tributary of the latter. Here a serious accident occurred. A light fall of snow had suddenly melted in the warm spring sun, swelling the mountain streams far above their normal flood. Bovey's fork was a torrent, and, in attempting to cross it, thirty head of horses with three hundred traps were swept away.

It was Smith's intention, despite the disaster of 1828 and the attack of the previous year, to press once more into the rich country of the Blackfeet. Accordingly, undismayed by this latest disaster, he continued westward to Pryor's fork, then over the low divide, Pryor's gap, to Clark's fork of the Yellowstone, then to the Rosebud, and so to the Yellowstone itself, "where it makes a great bend to the east." The river was so high that Smith was obliged to construct bull-boats to cross.

[575] Victor, op. cit., 83-84.

They were soon in the heart of the Blackfoot country. With renewed precautions and doubled guard Smith cautiously moved his company to the Musselshell and the Judith. Beaver were plentiful but danger imminent. The men were soon made aware of the presence, not far distant, of a large village of Blackfeet. Every day they stole traps but made no overt attack on the men themselves. After several weeks of high tension, to the great relief of the men, Smith gave the command to turn south again. On the whole they had had a successful hunt, and, returning by the same route they had come, they hastened back to Wind river. On the way a detachment commanded by Samuel Tullock raised the cache of furs on the Big Horn.

Early in july preparations were made for rendezvous on Wind river, and on the tenth of the month William Sublette arrived with ten wagons, two Dearborn buggies, four head of cattle, and a milch cow, having left St. Louis just three months before.[576] Rendezvous lasted three weeks. It was the last conducted by Smith, Jackson, and Sublette. On the fourth of august the three partners sold their business to Thomas Fitzpatrick, Milton Sublette, James Bridger, Henry Fraeb, and Baptiste Gervais,[577] who continued operations until 1834 as the Rocky Mountain Fur company. The same day, with one hundred ninety packs of beaver, the

[576] Smith, Jackson, and Sublette to John Eaton, St. Louis, october 29, 1830, in U.S. Senate, *Executive documents,* 21 cong., 2 sess., no. 39. Victor (*op. cit.,* 89) gives the statistics of the expedition as fourteen wagons and two hundred men.

[577] The documents of this transaction and the business accounts of the Rocky Mountain Fur company are in the Sublette MSS., carton 10, Missouri historical society. The retiring firm accepted, in part payment, a note for sixteen thousand dollars payable june 15, 1831. At Taos in New Mexico, august 23, 1831, Jackson and Sublette executed a power of attorney to David Waldo, afterward Jackson's partner, to collect this note in cash or in beaver at $4.25 a pound. The note was then in the hands of W. H. Ashley.

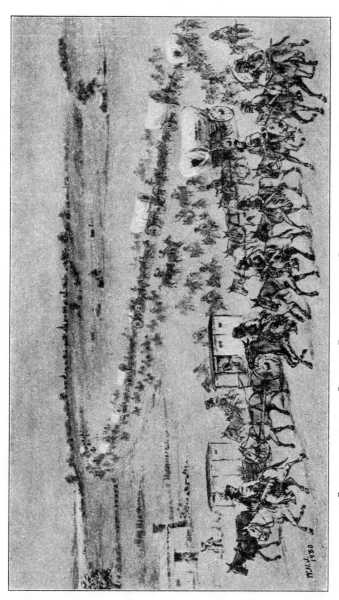

SUPPLY TRAIN OF SMITH, JACKSON, AND SUBLETTE, JULY 10, 1830
Painting by William H. Jackson

retiring partners started back for St. Louis, arriving in that city the tenth of october. The cattle and wagons they also brought back with them, leaving the Dearborn buggies in the mountains.[578] So large a wagon-train and so great a quantity of valuable furs had never been brought out of the mountains before, and their arrival in St. Louis created something of a sensation.[579]

The future plans of the three partners were probably undetermined when they reached St. Louis. Smith, perhaps, had decided definitely not to return again to the mountains. So he told J. J. Warner, a young man who had arrived in St. Louis from his home in New London, Connecticut, just as Smith, Jackson, and Sublette were getting in. Warner, having come west for his health, sought an interview with Smith, hearing that he had lived for years in the mountains and could tell him something of the climate and general conditions of health prevailing in the far west. Warner described his interview thus:

Instead of finding a leather stocking, I met a well-bred, intelligent, and christian gentleman, who repressed my youthful ardor and fancied pleasure for the life of a trapper and mountaineer by informing me that if I went into the Rocky mountains, the chances were much greater in favor of meeting death than of finding restoration to health, and that if I escaped the former and secured the latter, the probabilities were that I would be ruined for anything else in life than such things as would be agreeable to the passions of the semi-savage. He said that he had spent above eight years in the mountains and should not return to them.[580]

---

[578] Smith, Jackson, and Sublette to John Eaton, St. Louis, october 29, 1830, in U.S. Senate, *op. cit.*

[579] Warner, "Reminiscences," Southern California historical society *publications*, VII, 176.

[580] *Idem.* This is confirmed by Smith's letter to his brother, Ralph, dated Blue fork of Kansas river, september 10, 1830, Smith MSS., Kansas historical society.

Smith found in the city two of his younger brothers awaiting his arrival. He had already written to his brother, Ralph, urging him to come to St. Louis. The latter seems to have been unable to comply, and so two other brothers, Peter and Austin, came instead. Smith found them both in desperate straits financially but, with characteristic generosity, agreed to furnish them an outfit with which to go to Santa Fe the following spring. It may have been Milton Sublette, a member of the recently formed Rocky Mountain Fur company, who turned Smith's attention in this direction. Milton Sublette had been in New Mexico two years before trapping with Ewing Young and had learned much about the Santa Fe trade.[581] It was Smith's first intention to furnish the capital and outfit, while his brothers made the actual journey to and from Santa Fe. Later he determined to enlarge the venture and accompany it himself. In organizing the party he offered young Warner a position as clerk, which the latter gladly accepted.[582]

By 1830 the Santa Fe trade offered much greater opportunities for wealth than the fur-trade. In the latter competition was constantly increasing, furs were becoming scarcer and harder to procure, and withal, the market price was positively declining. The Rocky Mountain Fur company was obliged to dissolve partnership within four years simply because the business was no longer profitable, and that despite the fact that the members of this company were among the ablest,

---

[581] Gregg, Josiah, *Commerce of the prairies,* in Thwaites, *Early western travels,* XX, 23-24.

[582] Warner, "Reminiscences," *op. cit.,* VII, 177; Smith, E. F., "Jedediah Smith and the settlement of Kansas," in Kansas historical society *collections,* XII, 258. Warner and also Samuel Parkman witnessed Smith's will, drawn april 30, 1831 and printed in Sullivan, *op. cit.,* 157, 158.

shrewdest, and most experienced mountain men in the country. In the Santa Fe trade, on the other hand, returns had constantly increased in volume ever since William Becknell in the fall of 1821 sold for seven hundred dollars in Santa Fe the wagon load of goods which he had brought from Franklin, Missouri. During the ensuing ten years many others had followed Becknell. James McNight, Thomas James, and Colonel Hugh Glenn had all made the trip that first year, 1821, though not with wagons.[583] In 1822 William Becknell returned a second time, and, the same year, Braxton Cooper,[584] a Mr. Heath,[585] and, in the fall, James Baird and Samuel Chambers [586] went. Gregg says, "It is from this period – the year 1822 – that the virtual commencement of the Santa Fe trade may be dated."

A single expedition in 1823 was followed in 1824 by the largest company that had hitherto made the journey, comprising eighty-one men, one hundred fifty-six horses and mules, twenty-five wagons, and about thirty thousand dollars' worth of merchandise.[587] The same year Braxton Cooper returned again, and also William Becknell; Joseph Robidoux went out for the first but not the last time,[588] and James O. Pattie.

This year, too, thanks to the efforts of Senator Thomas Hart Benton, congress appropriated ten thou-

---

[583] Compare Coues, *Journal of Jacob Fowler*, 74, 79, 142 and *passim;* James, *Three years among the Indians and Mexicans*, 47 ff; Chittenden, *American fur trade*, II, 500 ff.

[584] Gregg, *Commerce of the prairies*, in Thwaites, *op. cit.*, XIX, 178; *Missouri intelligencer*, september 23, 1822.

[585] Compare Chittenden, *American fur trade*, II, 503.

[586] *Missouri intelligencer*, september 2 and 17, 1822.

[587] Gregg, *op. cit.*, XX, 180.

[588] "Sept. 20, 1824. Robidoux party started for St. Afee to-day. . . August 30, 1825. Robidoux party arrived from Tous [Taos]."—Kennerly, "Journal," Kennerly MSS., Missouri historical society.

sand dollars for the construction of a road to Santa Fe
and twenty thousand dollars to purchase a right of way
through the Indian country. Work was begun the following spring, and the highway completed in about
three years. The road extended from Fort Osage to
Taos, following the old trail.[589] Its completion revolu-
tionized the Santa Fe trade.[590]

As this trade increased in volume, however, the ever-
attendant danger from Indian attack likewise increased
until in 1829 the United States government tried the
expedient of accompanying the annual caravan with a
detachment of infantry. This, apparently, was just the
provocation needed to bring on a concerted Indian attack. Beyond Chouteau's island in the Arkansas river,
the road, in approaching the Cimarron, lay in Mexican
territory, which, of course, prevented the American
troops from proceeding further. The great caravan,
now deprived of its escort, continued its way. It was
scarcely out of sight when a band of Kiowa Indians
pounced upon it. Fortunately Major Riley, commanding the United States forces, had camped near the
Arkansas and, on learning of the danger, hastened to
the relief of the traders. The Indians fled, and Riley

[589] There is valuable data on the construction of the road in the letters
of George C. Sibley, 1825, Sibley MSS., III, Missouri historical society.

[590] The following figures compiled from Chittenden (*American fur trade,*
II, 519) show the magnitude of the commerce of the prairies:

YEAR	AM'T MDSE.	WAGONS	MEN
1822	$15,000		70
1823	12,000		50
1824	35,000	26	100
1825	65,000	37	130
1826	90,000	60	100
1827	85,000	55	90
1828	150,000	100	200
1829	60,000	30	50
1830	120,000	70	140

Not all the mechandise was taken as far as Santa Fe.

continued with the expedition as far as Sand creek, where, perceiving no indication of further danger, he returned to the Arkansas to await the return of the caravan in the fall. On their way back from Santa Fe the traders secured the protection of a detachment of Mexican troops under Colonel Viscara as far as the Arkansas, where Riley and his men met them again and accompanied them the remainder of the distance. The government did not look approvingly on this arrangement, and, the next year, the escort was withdrawn with disastrous results.

There was little in common between the fur-trade and the Santa Fe trade. In the former it was customary to employ a considerable number of men over a wide extent of territory. The furs which were collected in the spring and fall hunts were conveyed annually from rendezvous to St. Louis. Smith, Jackson, and Sublette had conducted their business on this basis. Jackson and Sublette remained continually in the mountains in command of the hundred or more men in their employ. Jackson, as resident partner, maintained his headquarters, first, in the vicinity of Great Salt lake, and later east of the mountains, near the head of the Sweetwater, while Smith, the explorer, sought out new fields for exploitation. Sublette, on the other hand, each year made the trip back and forth from St. Louis, bringing in the stores of Indian goods, blankets, powder, shot, traps, liquor, etc., for the trappers, and returned with the year's accumulations of fur.

In the Santa Fe trade fewer men were employed and they were all attached to a single expedition. There were clerks, drivers, horse wranglers, guards and so on. The goods that were taken out, being destined for a civilized people, consisted largely of textiles, cottons, silks, calicos, velvets, and finer weaves, hardware, and Yankee notions. The goods were conveyed to the markets of Taos and Santa Fe and there disposed of for horses, mules, and sometimes also, furs (from the Colorado mountains), but especially for gold and silver bullion. From these points the American goods made their way into the interior of Mexico and even to California.

This was the business to which Smith and his two partners turned in the spring of 1831, at what seemed a most favorable moment. The *Missouri intelligencer* of february 12, 1830, affirmed

The inland trade between the United States and Mexico is increasing rapidly. This is perhaps the most curious species of foreign intercourse which the ingenuity and enterprise of American traders ever originated. The extent of country which the caravans travel, the long journeys they have to make, the rivers and morasses to cross, the prairies, the forests, and all but African deserts to penetrate require the most steel-formed constitution and the most energetic minds.

Smith, Jackson, and Sublette possessed the last qualifications, if ever men did.

In the spring of 1831 a number of parties set out for Santa Fe. One of these, including among its members Josiah Gregg, the historian of the Santa Fe trade, started soon after Smith, and another party a week after Gregg.[591] Smith's party comprised eighty-five men, including David E. Jackson, William Sublette, J. J. Warner, Smith's two brothers, and a considerable force of employees.[592] Setting out from St. Louis on the tenth of april, they traveled leisurely up the Missouri valley by the Boone's Lick road, stopping a week or two in Lexington and a few days in Independence. While the

---

[591] Gregg, *Commerce of the prairies,* in Thwaites, *op. cit.,* XIX, 193.
[592] "Eulogy," in Sabin, *Kit Carson days,* 515.

party was in Lexington, Thomas Fitzpatrick, Smith's friend and former employee and now his business successor, came in from winter quarters on the Yellowstone. On learning the nature of Smith's venture, he gladly joined the expedition, accompanying it the entire distance.[593] From Independence the caravan at last, on the fourth of may, began the actual journey to Santa Fe. Ten wagons belonged to Jedediah Smith, a like number to Jackson and Sublette, one to Messrs. Wells and Chadwick of St. Louis, another to a Mr. Flournoy of Independence, and another jointly to Smith, Jackson, and Sublette.[594] This last supported a small field piece on the rear axle, "the wagon [being] so constructed that it could be readily uncoupled, and the hind wheels with the piece of artillery mounted thereon drawn out ready for action." [595]

Little difficulty or danger was encountered on the first stage of the journey. One of the employees, Merton by name, while they were still north of the Arkansas, ventured some distance from the main company in pursuit of antelope and was unfortunately overtaken and slain by the Pawnees.[596] They crossed the Arkansas without further mishap, finding that stream very low because of an unusually dry season. Once across, there stretched ahead of them sixty-five miles of burning

[593] Warner, "Reminiscences," *op. cit.*, VII, 177; Victor, *op. cit.*, 101.

[594] I have followed E. D. Smith *(op. cit.)* in this, though he, apparently, based his account on Warner. Warner, however, declares that Jackson and Sublette owned ten wagons, Wells and Chadwick, ten, Flournoy, one, and Smith, Jackson, and Sublette, one. This would make Smith's share in the whole outfit only a part interest in one wagon, which is certainly incorrect.

[595] Warner, "Reminiscences," *op. cit.*, VII, 177. Smith calls it a six-pounder, the traditional piece of artillery taken to the mountains, Smith, *op. cit., loc. cit.* It was a six-pounder that Ashley was incorrectly supposed to have conveyed to the mountains in 1826 (1827).

[596] Warner, "Reminiscences," *op. cit.*, VII, 177. Compare Gregg, *op. cit.*, XIX, 238. Gregg calls him Minter.

plains to the forks of the Cimarron. These mountain men must, indeed, have longed for the snow-chilled winds of the Rockies and the ever recurring springs that freshen the hottest days of mid-summer. Instead, they faced a searing south wind. As the entire party was unfamiliar with the road, no one knew where to seek the water-holes, those miniature oases, which an experienced traveler of the plains could have discovered and which, even in so dry a season as that of 1831, would have offered at least a temporary relief.[597] At some points, moreover, the road lay a considerable distance from any water whatever, which, of course, doomed many a feverish search of the inexperienced to futility.[598]

For two days they struggled valiantly forward, bewildered by the network of buffalo traces criss-crossing the trail in every direction, tempting paths for thirsty men. They followed some of them, no doubt, but only in vain, for at this season of the year the drinking pools were as destitute of moisture as the cruel mirages which likewise tempted them from the well-beaten track. On the second day their situation became desperate. The horses were dying, and the men were approaching that unstable equilibrium of mind which a prolonged thirst has been known so often to produce. It is a frenzy which drives a man so suffering to expend the very final ounce of his energy in one supreme effort to reach water, instead of conserving his strength to cover a greater distance and perhaps attain thereby his goal. Instinct was supplanting reason.

---

[597] Compare *idem*, XIX, 236.

[598] Gregg mentions a point where a spring, the so-called "Upper spring," was a quarter of a mile from the road, which ran along an adjacent ridge. The spring was reached by a path winding through dense thickets of underbrush. See *idem*, XIX, 233.

On the third day, may 27, the party divided. Some struck off to the east, others to the west, while Smith and Fitzpatrick bravely plunged to the south along the choking road that lay ahead.[599] After great effort they reached a deep hollow where water was usually to be found, but it was now dry. Smith, leaving Fitzpatrick here to await the arrival of the main party, turned south in the direction of some broken ground a few miles distant.[600] Following him with his spy-glass, Fitzpatrick watched him urge along his tottering animal until, some

[599] J. J. Warner ("Reminiscences," *op. cit.,* VII, 177) says that Smith set out to find water in the morning of the second day. The "Eulogy" (Sabin, *op. cit.,* 515) says after they had been out nearly three days. Mrs. Peter Smith's narrative (Southern California historical society *publications,* III, part 4, 53) says three days. The sources for the events of these last days of Smith's life are, in the order of their value: (1) A letter of Austin Smith in Smith MSS., Kansas historical society. Smith accompanied the expedition. He wrote this letter to his father from "Walnut creek on the Arkansas, three hundred miles from the settlements of Missouri, september 24, 1831," on his return from Santa Fe. He probably learned the details after reaching that city. (2) The reminiscences of J. J. Warner, who was a member of the party and had the story of Smith's death from a group of Mexican traders, who, in turn, had it from the Indians who murdered him. He wrote his reminiscences a number of years later. They are printed in Southern California historical society *publications,* VII. (3) Josiah Gregg's *Commerce of the prairies.* Gregg followed the trail a short time after Smith and learned the incidents of his death from a Mexican cibolero, or buffalo hunter, and from New Mexicans in Santa Fe, who had purchased Smith's rifle and pistols from the assassins. The most available edition of Gregg is in R. G. Thwaites's *Early western travels,* XIX, XX. (4) Mrs. Peter Smith's narrative in Southern California historical society *publications,* III, part 4. Mrs. Smith had the story from her husband who accompanied the expedition. (5) The "Eulogy," written less than a year after the event by an unknown author, who endeavored to ascertain the facts and whose account is based in large measure on information derived from Mexicans, who, in turn were informed by Smith's assassins. (6) William Waldo's "Reminiscences" in Waldo MSS., Missouri historical society. William Waldo had the story from his uncle, David Waldo, who was in Santa Fe at the time of Smith's death and who soon after engaged in business with David E. Jackson, a member of the expedition.

[600] Gregg and Mrs. Peter Smith state that he set out alone; the "Eulogy" that he was accompanied part way by Thomas Fitzpatrick; Warner that he "rode on in advance of the party."

three miles away, he dropped behind a low eminence and disappeared from sight.[601]

Smith and his languid horse stumbled on mile after mile through the dancing heat until, following perhaps the unerring instinct of the beast, he espied what seemed to be a river course. He was now fifteen miles from his company. Fearing, perhaps, that it was only a mirage that mocked him, he urged forward his jaded horse to test his own eyes and soon, to his delight, dropped over the grassy bank and down into the gravelly bed of the Cimarron. He found no constant stream but only here and there a small pool of precious water.[602] From the largest and the freshest, Smith and his horse drank. So eager had he been to reach the stream, that he had neglected the usual precautions. Refreshed at last and on the point of mounting and riding back with the good news to Fitzpatrick and the rest, he suddenly perceived his fatal rashness. Alone, with no available ambuscade and retreat cut off, he saw himself surrounded by a hostile band of Comanches.

They succeeded in alarming his animal, not daring to fire on him so long as they kept face to face. As soon as his animal turned, they fired and wounded him in the shoulder. He then fired his gun and killed the head chief.[603]

Two more of the savages he is said to have shot, badly crippled though he was, before he was finally done to death.[604]

---

[601] The "Eulogy."

[602] Warner; Mrs. Peter Smith; the "Eulogy." Gregg says that he was obliged to scoop out a hole in the sand into which the water slowly oozed.

[603] Austin Smith and Mrs. Peter Smith. Warner says that he was struck by a spear which pierced his body; Gregg, that he was pierced with arrows.

[604] E. D. Smith, with admirable devotion, has him rush in with an axe and slay thirteen out of the twenty Comanches. The "Eulogy" differs from the other narratives in stating that Smith "discovered them approaching when

The company, having apparently given him up for dead either from exhaustion or at the hands of Indians, pushed on along the main highway to the nearest point on the Cimarron. Having refreshed their horses and themselves, at this stream, they seemingly made no effort to assure themselves of Smith's fate but, instead, proceeded on their way to Santa Fe.[605] After an encounter with a huge band of Blackfeet and Gros Ventres, roaming far to the south of their usual haunts, which would very likely have terminated in a disaster had it not been for the cool head and native courage of William Sublette, they entered the New Mexican capital july fourth, 1831.[606] Here they definitely learned Smith's fate. As it happened, a company of Mexican traders came in at just the same time, having in their possession a rifle and a brace of large silver-mounted pistols, which Peter Smith at once recognized as the property of his brother.[607] The traders had purchased them of a war party of Comanches, who had related how they had seen a solitary horseman approach the Cimarron, how he had first watered his horse and then slaked his own thirst, how they had watched closely for a time and then rushed upon him and killed him. The

they were within a half a mile's distance; and, knowing that it was too late for flight, he rode directly towards them. At a short distance, they halted at his order, and made efforts to frighten his horse, wishing to fire on him when he was turned from them. After conversing among themselves about fifteen minutes, in Spanish, which Mr. Smith did not understand, they succeeded in scaring and turning his horse, when they immediately fired. A ball entered his body, near the left shoulder. Smith turned, levelled his rifle, and with the same ball shot the chief and another Indian, who was immediately behind him, and before he could get command of his pistols, they rushed upon him, and despatched him with their spears. His body was probably thrown into a ravine, as nothing could be found of it, when search was made for it two days afterwards."

[605] This is the implication in Gregg.

[606] Gregg and Warner.

[607] Guinn, *op. cit.*, III, part 4, 53.

pistols they were anxious to dispose of, either because they were percussion locks, with which they were not familiar, or else because, having killed their chief, they might be regarded as evil medicine.

In accordance with Smith's request,[608] William H. Ashley was appointed the administrator of his estate, and to him was transferred, regularly, Smith's share of the payments of the note given by Fitzpatrick, Sublette, and Bridger and the other members of the Rocky Mountain Fur company to Smith, Jackson, and Sublette. The sums paid at sundry times were sufficient to give a fair portion to Smith's many brothers and sisters, who, as he died unmarried, were his only lawful heirs.[609]

"A very mild man and a christian; and there were very few of them in the mountains," is the estimate of Smith's character from one of his mountaineer contemporaries.[610] Certainly no one of his western associates gave so much earnest thought to religious matters as did Smith.[611] His letters express his spiritual longings and the crushing sense of his own sin and unworthiness. He lived in a period of religious flux and unrest. New sects were springing up all through the West; religion had become to the backwoodsman the one great vital issue of life. Western New York, where Smith had been brought up, was the most notable scene of this religious intoxication. A namesake of his and, like him, of New

---

[608] Letter of Jedediah S. Smith to Ralph Smith, dated Blue fork of Kansas river, september 10, 1830, Smith MSS., Kansas historical society.

[609] The documents covering the administration of Smith's estate are among the Sublette MSS., cartons 6 and 10, Missouri historical society. The exact extent of his estate cannot be determined.

[610] Victor, *River of the west*, 79.

[611] That this trait was early recognized is evident in the letter written by Hugh Glass to the uncle of John S. Gardner killed in the Arikara campaign, "Mr. Smith," says Glass, "a young man of our company made a powerful prayer which moved us all greatly." The letter is printed in South Dakota historical society *collections*, I, 247.

England extraction, established only a few miles from Smith's early home one of these new and typically western sects. The same sense of unregeneration and of unsatisfied groping after spiritual justification which drew Smith's neighbors to the Church of Jesus Christ of Latter-day Saints, led him to express himself thus,

As it respects my spiritual welfare, I hardly durst speak. I find myself one of the most ungrateful, unthankful creatures imaginable. Oh, when shall I be under the care of a christian church? I have need of your prayers. I wish our society to bear me up before a Throne of Grace. I must tell you for my part, that I am much behind hand. Oh, the perverseness of my wicked heart! I entangle myself too much in the things of time. I must depend entirely upon the mercy of that Being, who is abundant in goodness and will not cast off any, who call sincerely upon Him. Again, I say, pray for me, my brother, and may He before whom not a sparrow falls without notice, bring us in His own good time together again.[612]

Nor was Smith's religion essentially demonstrative alone. "He made religion an active principle from the duties of which nothing could seduce him." [613]

He was a man of great courage and devotion to the task in hand, in the performance of which he never spared nor sheltered himself at the risk of his men. His entire effort was not for himself at all but for his family and his friends. No thought of personal gain actuated him; he strove rather to procure the wherewithal to repay those to whom he was indebted and to help those for whom he felt personally responsible. It is with no insincerity that he wrote,

It is that I may be able to help those who stand in need, that I face every danger. It is for this, that I traverse the mountains covered with eternal snow. It is for this, that I pass over the sandy plains, in heat

---

[612] Letter of Jedediah S. Smith to Ralph Smith, dated Wind river, december 24, 1829, Smith MSS., Kansas historical society.

[613] The "Eulogy," in Sabin, *op. cit.*, 517.

of summer, thirsting for water where I may cool my overheated body. It is for this, that I go for days without eating, and am pretty well satisfied if I can gather a few roots, a few snails, or, better satisfied if we can afford ourselves a piece of horse flesh, or a fine roasted dog, and, most of all, it is for this, that I deprive myself of the privilege of society and the satisfaction of the converse of my friends! But I shall count all this pleasure, if I am at last allowed, by the alwise Ruler, the privelege of joining my friends. Oh, my brother, let us render to Him, to whom all things belong, a proper proportion of what is His due.[614]

Smith was a very brave christian gentleman.

Had he lived, Smith would very likely have made a contribution of great value to geographic science. In the brief space of six years he had crossed and recrossed (in many cases, the first white man to do so) the American west from the upper Missouri southward to the Platte and from the Columbia to the Colorado and westward to the Pacific. His geographic knowledge excelled that of all his contemporaries. He traveled, too, with wide-open eyes. Everywhere observant and greedy for information, he returned from each expedition with something more than a superficial acquaintance with the business resources of the regions he had traversed.[616] He intended to publish his journals entire, and he also had in mind the preparation of an atlas that should, by embodying his discoveries, correct the prevailing mis-

---

[614] Letter of Jedediah S. Smith to Ralph Smith, dated Wind river, december 24, 1829, Smith MSS., Kansas historical society.

[615] It has been suggested (Sabin, *Kit Carson days*, 140), that it was Smith who sowed the first seeds of christianity among the Flatheads, which, in fruition, led that tribe to send a deputation to St. Louis in 1832, seeking religious instruction for their people. Even if this Flathead deputation was actually sent, Smith's contribution is problematical as his sojourn among them at Flathead House, in the winter of 1824-1825 and in 1829, was very brief.

[616] Compare Smith's report to Ashley, page 153 f; his report to General Atkinson, U.S. House, *Executive documents*, 19 cong., 1 sess., VI, no. 117; and his report with Jackson and Sublette to John H. Eaton, secretary of war, U.S. Senate, *Executive documents*, 21 cong., 2 sess., I, no. 39.

conceptions concerning the geography of the West.[617]

After his death his notes and journals were collated and arranged for the press. Unfortunately, however, like the originals of the Bonneville journals, they were destroyed by fire in St. Louis.[618] Some of his expert knowledge, however, did find embodiment in maps of the period. Three, in particular, were in a large measure, directly or indirectly, his work. The first is the careful map accompanying Albert Gallatin's *Synopsis of the Indian tribes within the United States.*[619] This was probably the best map of the west at the date of its publication, 1836, and it far excelled many that followed. The extent of Smith's contribution may be gauged from the following in Gallatin's text.

Some unforeseen circumstances have prevented General Ashley of Missouri from communicating to me in time, as he intended, some further information respecting the country which he explored in the Rocky mountains and thence in a southwardly direction beyond Lake Timpanogo. But he has transmitted to me a manuscript map with numerous explanatory notes, the materials for which consist of various journeys and explorations by some of our own enterprising traders and hunters [among others, Jedediah S. Smith].[620] It is on that authority and subject to such correction as more complete exploration and scientific observation will hereafter render necessary, that several geological innovations have been introduced in the small map annexed to this essay.[621]

Smith's services are then directly acknowledged.

The Lake Timpanogo has been found and is laid down in the same latitude and longitude nearly as has been assigned to it by Baron

---

617 The "Eulogy" in Sabin, *op. cit.,* 514; Waldo, William, "Reminiscences," Waldo MSS., Missouri historical society.

618 Guinn, *op. cit.,* III, part 4, 53.

619 American antiquarian society *transactions,* II.

620 Ashley communicated this information to Gallatin long before the publication of his memoir.

621 American antiquarian society *transactions,* II, 140 ff.

Humboldt. It received two rivers from the east, which issue from mountains west of the Colorado, is known to Americans as Great Salt lake, and has no outlet whatever towards the sea. General Ashley's own explorations extend as far south as another small lake, to which his name has been given, and which is situated about eighty miles south of the southeastern extremity of Lake Timpanogo. It is also fed by a river coming from the mountains in the south-east and has no outlet. The discoveries south and west of that place appear to belong to others, and principally to J. S. Smith. Another river known by the name of Last [sic for Lost] river, coming also from the coast, falls into another lake, also without outlet, situated in thirty-eight degrees north latitude and in the same longitude as Lake Timpanogo.

J. S. Smith descended the Rio Colorado of California, in the year 1826, as far south as the thirty-fifth degree of north latitude. Proceeding thence westwardly, he reached the Spanish missions of San Pedro and San Diego, near the Pacific. The ensuing year, he visited Monterey and St. Francisco; ascended the river Buenaventura some distance, and recrossed the Californian chain of mountains, called there Mount Joseph, in about the thirty-ninth degree of latitude. He thence proceeded north of west, and reached the southwestern extremity of Lake Timpanogo. The eastern foot of the Californian chain, where he recrossed it, is about one hundred and eighty miles from the Pacific. There he crossed some streams, coming from the south, which may either be lost in the sands, or, breaking through the mountains, north of Mount Joseph, unite with the river Buenaventura. The course of this last river, so far as is known, is from north to south between and parallel to the Californian chain and the Pacific.

Smith also contributed to the map accompanying Reverend Samuel Parker's *Journal of an exploring tour beyond the Rocky mountains* (Ithaca, 1838).[622]

[622] According to the "Eulogy" this map is almost entirely the work of Smith, aided by Jackson and Sublette. It was intended to be published just as he left it. It has generally been supposed, however, that the Parker map was based partly on Parker's own observations and partly on Vancouver's chart and the explorations of Samuel Black, a Hudson's Bay company factor, as stated by Parker (*Journal of an exploring tour beyond the Rocky mountains,* v). The "Eulogy" mentions Smith's contributions, and an editorial in

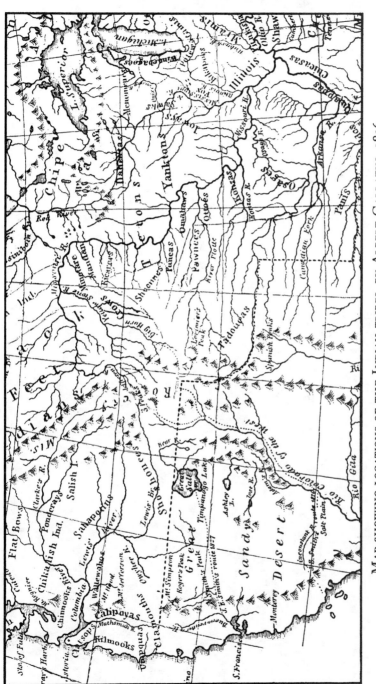

MAP SHOWING LOCATIONS OF THE INDIAN TRIBES, BY ALBERT GALLATIN, 1836
Reproduced from his "Synopsis of the Indian tribes of North America," in the *Transactions*
of the American Antiquarian society (Cambridge, 1836) II.
Both Ashley and Smith contributed to this map.

The southern portion of the map, perhaps below the forty-fifth parallel, is the work of Smith. Its accuracy is striking, and, so far as it goes (it does not extend below the thirty-ninth parallel), it excels the Gallatin map, which, however, has the merit of covering the area as far south as thirty degrees.

The map, also of 1839, prepared by David H. Burr, geographer to the house of representatives, must have been drawn largely from data obtainable in Smith's journals and sketches.[623]

Smith's contribution to cartography, together with his own journals and diaries and sketches, although the last have unfortunately perished, entitle him to rank with Lewis and Clark in the group of foremost American explorers. They discovered the first overland route to the Pacific; he discovered the second. Lewis and Clark followed the northern and, at their time, the easiest route, owing to the existence of water courses the entire way. Jedediah Smith, following, in general, the footsteps of William H. Ashley to the Great Salt lake, continued southwest to the Pacific, returning by a different route. Going and returning, he crossed untracked deserts. Lewis and Clark crossed merely from the upper Missouri area to the Columbia basin; Smith crossed from the central Missouri area to the interior basin,

---

the *Oregonian and Indians' advocate,* february 1839 (I, no. 5, 158-159) distributes the indebtedness as follows, "The . . . coast is copied from the chart drawn by Vancouver, after a minute survey which he made. The one from which Mr. P. copied is preserved at Fort Vancouver. The middle country is put down according to Mr. P.'s own directions. The north is from the surveys of a Mr. Black, and the south from the sketches of Mr. Smith. . . To Mr. Black the world is indebted for the greater part of the geographical knowledge which has been published of the country west of the Rocky mountains." —Wilkes, Charles, *Narrative of the United States exploring expedition 1838-1842,* IV, 369.

[623] Printed as a frontispiece in Sullivan, *op. cit.*

thence to the Colorado basin, and thence to the Pacific drainage.

If there is any merit in untiring perseverance and terrible suffering in the prosecution of trade, in searching out new channels of commerce, in tracing out the courses of unknown rivers, in discovering the resources of unknown regions, in delineating the characters, situation, numbers, and habits of unknown nations, Smith's name must be enrolled with those of Franklin and Parry, of Clapperton and Park.[624]

---

[624] The "Eulogy" in Sabin, *op. cit.*, 514.

Bibliography

The bibliography is not intended to be exhaustive. Only those manuscripts and books are listed that have been utilized in the preparation of this volume.

Manuscript Sources

KANSAS HISTORICAL SOCIETY. A brief sketch of accidents, misfortunes, and depredations, committed by Indians on the firm of Smith, Jackson, and Sublette, Indian traders on the east and west side of the Rocky mountains, since july 1, 1826 to the present, 1829.

Contains a list of the men lost.

———— McCoy, Reverend Isaac. A diary covering the years 1817 to 1823 and 1828 to 1841.

Mentions William Henry Ashley.

———— St. Louis Missouri Fur company, Records.

Covers the financial operations of the company.

———— Jedediah S. Smith.

Comprises most of the correspondence of Jedediah S. Smith that has survived, as well as letters of Austin Smith and Peter Smith, his brothers.

———— Superintendent of Indian affairs. Letter book, 1830-1832.

Contains tables of Indian depredations from 1823 to 1832 and an important report on the fur-trade made by William Gordon to Lewis Cass, secretary of war, dated october 3, 1831.

MISSOURI HISTORICAL SOCIETY. William Henry Ashley.

Comprises drafts of Ashley's letters and his business accounts. The collection includes the letter of december 1825, and the Harrison G. Rogers journals, printed in the text.

———— Chouteau, Pierre and Auguste.

These contain the correspondence and business accounts of Pierre and Auguste Chouteau, covering the period 1778-1850.

———— Crooks, Ramsay.

Consists of copies of the correspondence of Crooks from the collection of Mr. C. M. Burton of Detroit.

———— Drips, Andrew.

Andrew Drips was an employee of the American Fur company. The manuscripts include his correspondence and business accounts.

MISSOURI HISTORICAL SOCIETY. Hood, Washington.

Consists of an itinerary of a route for wheeled vehicles across the Rocky mountains by way of the South pass and Jackson's Hole.

―――― Kearny, Stephen Watts.

Contains the journals of Stephen Watts Kearny, 1820 and 1824, 1825.

―――― Kennerly, James. 2 cartons.

Contains the diary of James Kennerly at Fort Atkinson, 1824, 1825.

―――― Sibley, George C. 3 vols.

Includes material on the early history of the Santa Fe trade and on the construction of the Santa Fe road.

―――― Sublette, William, Milton, and Andrew. 13 cartons.

Comprises most of the business correspondence of the firm of Smith, Jackson, and Sublette and papers covering the administration of Jedediah S. Smith's estate. Of first importance.

―――― Vasquez, Louis and Benito. 5 cartons.

Louis Vasquez was an employee of Ashley and Henry and subsequently of Smith, Jackson, and Sublette. He became a member of the Rocky Mountain Fur company. The collection contains also material on James Bridger, who was Vasquez's companion and partner.

―――― Waldo, William.

Comprises the reminiscences of William Waldo, whose uncle, David Waldo, was a friend and companion of Smith.

Printed Sources

BANCROFT, H. H. History of Arizona and New Mexico (San Francisco, 1888).

―――― History of California (San Francisco, 1884-1890) 7 vols.

―――― History of the northwest coast (San Francisco, 1884) 2 vols.

―――― History of Oregon (San Francisco, 1886-1888) 2 vols.

―――― History of Utah (San Francisco, 1889).

The Bancroft histories, though quite unreliable in many respects, contain a wealth of source material for the study of the history of the west. Especially useful for the identification of early settlers.

BEEKLY, A. L. Geology and coal resources of North Park, Colorado. U.S. Geological survey bulletin 596 (Washington, 1915).

Contains descriptions and maps of a portion of the area traversed by Ashley in 1824, 1825.

BENTON, THOMAS HART. Speech in the senate, reprinted in "Proceedings of the senate of the United States on the bill for the protection of the fur trade" (St. Louis, 1824). Pamphlet.

Presents a summary of the situation of the trade in 1824 by a well-informed statesman.

BIDWELL, JOHN. "The first emigrant train to California," in Century magazine, XIX (New York, 1890).

Bidwell entered California by the valley of the Stanislaus, the route which Smith followed in the opposite direction on his first return from California, 1827.

BILLON, F. L. Annals of St. Louis (St. Louis, 1880).

A collection of source material relating to the early history of St. Louis.

———— Annals of St. Louis in its territorial days (St. Louis, 1888).

A continuation of the former, containing a number of important documents bearing on the early operations of the St. Louis fur companies.

BONNER, T. D. The life and adventures of James P. Beckwourth (New York, 1856).

An important narrative greatly undervalued. Especially useful for Ashley's expedition of 1824, 1825. The work comprises Beckwourth's personal reminiscences as he related them orally to Bonner. For the incidents in which Beckwourth himself participated he is, aside from his ever patent egotism, singularly reliable.

BRACKENRIDGE, H. M. Views of Louisiana (Pittsburgh, 1814).

BRADBURY, JOHN. Travels in the interior of America (London, 1819).

Reprinted in Thwaites, R. G., *Early western travels, 1748-1846,* v (Cleveland, Arthur H. Clark company, 1904).

BRYANT, WILLIAM. What I saw in California (New York, 1849).

BURPEE, L. J., editor. "Journal de Larocque," in Publications des archives canadiennes, no. 3 (Ottawa, 1911).

Larocque, an employee of the Northwest company, examined the upper Missouri and Yellowstone country contemporaneously with Lewis and Clark.

CAMP, C. L., editor. James Clyman (San Francisco, 1928).

Contains Clyman's narrative (dictated in 1871) of the Ashley expedition of 1823-1824.

CAREY, M. General atlas (Philadelphia, 1814).

Contains maps showing contemporary conceptions of western geography.

CHASE, J. S. California coast trails (Boston, 1913).

A description of the country which Smith traversed in 1828 on his way to the Umpqua.

CHITTENDEN, HIRAM M. The American fur trade of the far west (New York, 1902) 3 vols.

The standard history of the fur-trade.

———— History of early steamboat navigation on the Missouri river (New York, 1903) 2 vols.

Useful for the operations of the Missouri Fur company and the American Fur company.

CHITTENDEN, HIRAM M. The Yellowstone national park (Cincinnati, 1915).

Useful for the wanderings of John Colter.

CLARKE, S. A. Pioneer days of Oregon history (Portland, 1905) 2 vols.

Contains Dr. John McLaughlin's account of Smith's disaster on the Umpqua.

CONRAD, H. L. Uncle Dick Wootton (Chicago, 1890).

COOKE, P. ST. GEORGE. Scenes and adventures in the army (Philadelphia, 1857).

COUES, ELLIOTT. The expeditions of Zebulon Montgomery Pike (New York, 1895) 4 vols.

The best edition of Pike.

———— Forty years a fur-trader (New York, 1898) 2 vols.

The personal narrative of Charles Larpenteur, an employee of the American Fur company, on the upper Missouri, 1833-1872.

———— History of the expedition under the command of Captains Lewis and Clark (New York, 1893) 4 vols.

A well-edited history of the Lewis and Clark expeditions.

———— Journal of Jacob Fowler (New York, 1898).

Contains material on the earliest expeditions to Santa Fe.

———— New light on the great northwest: the Henry-Thompson journals (New York, 1897) 3 vols.

Important for the early examination of the Columbia.

COUTANT, C. G. History of Wyoming (Laramie, Wyoming, 1899).

Of slight value.

COYNER, D. H. The lost trappers (Cincinnati, 1859).

Covers the wanderings of Ezekiel Williams, 1807 (?) to 1814 (?). Fictitious but with a basis of fact.

CRONISE, T. F. The natural wealth of California (San Francisco, 1868).

Contains Smith's letter to Padre Duran.

DALE, H. C. "Did the returning Astorians use the South pass?" in Oregon historical society quarterly, XVII (Portland, 1916).

Contains a letter of Ramsay Crooks, a leader of the returning Astorians, reprinted from the *Deseret news* of november 5, 1856 (Salt Lake City, 1856).

DARBY, WILLIAM. The map of the United States (New York, ca 1818).

Useful for early geographic conceptions.

DAVIS, W. R. and D. S. DURRIE. Illustrated history of Missouri (St. Louis, 1876).

DE Bow, J. B. Industrial resources of the south and west (New York, 1854).

DELLENBAUGH, F. S. A canyon voyage (New York, 1908).

—— The romance of the Colorado river (New York, 1906).

Dellenbaugh was the official artist of the Powell expedition in 1871.

DODGE, GRENVILLE M. A brief biographical sketch of James Bridger (New York, 1905). Pamphlet.

DODGE, HENRY. "Report of the expedition with dragoons to the Rocky mountains during the summer of 1835, etc." in U.S. Senate, Executive documents, 24 cong., 1 sess., no. 209 (Washington, 1836).

DOUGLAS, W. B. "Manuel Lisa," in Missouri historical society collections, III (St. Louis, 1911).

A scholarly monograph.

EDWARDS, R. and M. HOPEWELL. Edwards's great west (St. Louis, s.d.).

ELLIOTT, T. C., editor. "Alexander Ross, journal, 1824," in Oregon historical society quarterly, XIV (Portland, 1913).

—— "Alexander Ross, journal, Flathead post, 1825," in Oregon historical society quarterly, XIV (Portland, 1913).

The Ross journals throw light on the operations of the Hudson's Bay company in the Snake country.

—— "Peter Skene Ogden," in Oregon historical society quarterly, XI (Portland, 1910).

A sketch of Ogden's career.

——, editor. "Peter Skene Ogden, journals, 1825-1826, 1826-1827, 1827-1828, 1828-1829," in Oregon historical society quarterly, X and XI (Portland, 1909, 1910).

Of prime value for the exploration of the Columbia drainage area and the northern portion of the interior basin.

EYRIÉS, J. B., P. F. de Larénaudière, et J. H. Klaproth. Nouvelles annales des voyages, series II (Paris, 1833-1836).

Contains Smith's letter describing his first journey to California.

FARNHAM, T. J. Travels in the great western prairies, etc. (London, 1843).

Reprinted in Thwaites, Early western travels, 1748-1846, XVIII-XIX (Cleveland, Arthur H. Clark company, 1906).

A description of much of the area traversed by Ashley.

FENNEMAN, N. M. "Physiographic boundaries within the United States," in Association of American geographers annals, IV (New York, 1914).

An illuminating article.

FINLEY, ANTHONY. New and general atlas (Philadelphia, 1826).

Useful for early geographic conceptions of the west.

FLETCHER, F. N. "Eastbound route of Jedediah S. Smith, 1827," in California historical society quarterly, VII (January 1924).

Supports the view that Smith crossed by way of the Stanislaus and the Sonora pass.

FLINT, T., editor. The personal narrative of James O. Pattie of Kentucky (Cincinnati, 1831).

Reprinted as "Pattie's personal narrative" in Thwaites, *Early western travels, 1748-1846*, XVIII (Cleveland, Arthur H. Clark company, 1905).
Pattie reached California overland just after Smith.

FREMONT, J. C. Report of the exploring expedition to the Rocky mountains in 1842, and to Oregon and North California in 1843-1844 (Washington, 1845).

Contains the official narratives of Fremont's expeditions of 1842, 1843, and 1844.

GALES, J. and W. W. SEATON. Register of debates 1833-1837 (Washington, 1833-1837).

Contains material on Ashley's career in congress.

GALLATIN, ALBERT. "Synopsis of the Indian tribes within the United States east of the Rocky mountains and in the British and Russian possessions of North America," in American antiquarian society transactions, II (Cambridge, 1836).

Mentions Ashley's and Smith's contributions to cartography.

GARRISON, G. P. Texas (American commonwealths), (Boston, 1903).

For early lead-mining in Missouri.

GASS, PATRICK. Journal (Philadelphia, 1810).

For the Lewis and Clark expedition.

GILBERT, E. W. The exploration of western America (Cambridge, 1933).

GODDARD, P. E. "The life and culture of the Hupa," in University of California publications in American archaeology and ethnology, I (Berkeley, 1903).

GREGG, JOSIAH. The commerce of the prairies (New York, 1845) 2 vols.

Reprinted in Thwaites, *Early western travels, 1748-1846*, XIX-XX (Cleveland, Arthur H. Clark company, 1905).
A classic.

GUINN, J. M. "Captain Jedediah S. Smith," in Southern California historical society publications, III, part 4 (Los Angeles, 1897).

A not very accurate account of Smith's activities in California.

HAFEN, LeRoy R. and W. J. GHENT. Broken hand (Denver, 1929).

> For Thomas Fitzpatrick.

HARRIS, W. R. The Catholic church in Utah (Salt Lake City, 1909).

> Contains an English translation of the *Diaria* of Escalante. Useful also for Etienne Provot.

HINES, GUSTAVUS. Oregon (Buffalo, 1851).

> Based on interviews with Oregon pioneers, including Doctor Mc-Laughlin. Contains material on Smith's disaster on the Umpqua.

HISTORY of Franklin, Jefferson, Washington, Crawford, and Gasconade counties, Missouri (Chicago, 1888).

> Contains material on Ashley's and Henry's mining and manufacturing ventures.

HODGE, F. W. Handbook of American Indians, U.S. Bureau of American ethnology bulletin 30 (Washington, 1907, 1910) 2 vols.

HOLMAN, FREDERICK V. Dr. John McLoughlin, the father of Oregon (Cleveland, Arthur H. Clark company, 1907).

HOUGHTON, E. P. D. The Donner party and its tragic fate (Glendale, Arthur H. Clark company, 1924).

> Mentions John Turner, one of Smith's employees.

HUMBOLDT, ALEXANDER VON. Political essay on the kingdom of New Spain, translated by John Black (London, 1811) 3 vols.

> Contains a summary of early exploration including the journeys of Dominguez and Escalante. The map, portions of which are reproduced in the translation, is particularly valuable.

HUNTER, JOHN. Memoir of a captivity among the Indians of North America (London, 1824).

ILLUSTRATED HISTORY of southern California (Chicago, 1890).

IRVING, WASHINGTON. Astoria (Philadelphia, 1841) 2 vols.

> The most important secondary account of the Astor enterprise. Especially valuable for the group which returned overland from Astoria.

—— Rocky mountain sketches (Philadelphia, 1832) 2 vols.

JAMES, EDWIN. Account of the expedition from Pittsburgh to the Rocky mountains, etc. (London, 1823) 3 vols.

> Reprinted in Thwaites, *Early western travels, 1748-1846,* XIV-XVII (Cleveland, Arthur H. Clark company, 1905).
>
> An account of Stephen H. Long's expedition. Ashley in 1824 covered a portion of Long's route of 1820.

JAMES, THOMAS. Three years among the Indians and Mexicans (Waterloo, Illinois, 1846).

> A very rare pamphlet containing the reminiscences of one of Manuel Lisa's employees on the upper Missouri who was later one of the first

Americans to make the journey overland to Santa Fe. Especially valuable for the years 1809 to 1811. A new edition edited by W. B. Douglas for the Missouri historical society was published in St. Louis, 1916.

KOLB, E. L. Through the Grand canyon from Wyoming to Mexico (New York, 1914).

A record of a recent expedition down Green river and the Colorado.

LANG, H. O. History of the Willamette valley (Portland, 1885).

LATHAM, R. G. "On the language of the northern, western, and central Americas," in London philological society transactions (London, 1856).

Useful for the Indian tribes encountered by Smith in northern California and Oregon.

LAVOISNE, C. V. Atlas (Philadelphia, 1821).

——, editor. A complete historical, chronological, and geographical atlas accompanying Le Sage's atlas (Philadelphia, 1822).

Useful for early geographic conceptions of the West.

LYMAN, H. S. History of Oregon (New York, 1903) 4 vols.

MANLY, W. L. Death valley in 1849 (San Jose, 1894).

Manly descended Green river for some distance in 1849 en route to California.

MAP of Spanish North America, published as the act directs, aug't 20, 1818 by Longmans, Hurst, Rees, Orme, and Brown, Paternoster row, London, engraved by Sidy Hall.

A map of unusual value, possibly based on a copy of Dominguez, Francisco Atanasio, and Silvestre Velez Escalante, "Plano geografico de la tiera descubierta y demarcada por Dn Bernardo de Miera," etc. (s. d., ca. 1777) in United States Library of congress, Woodbury Lowery collection, no. 593.

MAXIMILIAN (Prince of Wied). Travels in the interior of North America (London, 1843).

Reprinted in Thwaites, Early western travels, 1748-1846, XXII-XXIV (Cleveland, Arthur H. Clark company, 1906).

MEADE, WILLIAM. Old churches, ministers, and families of Virginia (Philadelphia, 1861).

Throws some light on Ashley's ancestry.

MELISH, JOHN. Map of the United States with the contiguous British and Spanish possessions (Philadelphia, ca. 1816).

Contains good early maps.

MERIAM, C. H. "The route of Jedediah S. Smith in 1826," in California historical society quarterly, II (October 1923).

Interprets Smith's route across Utah and Nevada.

—— "Jedediah Smith's route across the Sierra in 1827. A reply to F. N. Fletcher," in California historical society quarterly, III (April 1927).

> An unconvincing reply to Fletcher's contention (C.H.S.Q., II) that Smith crossed the Sierras by the Sonora pass in may 1827.

MERK, FREDERICK. Fur trade and empire (Cambridge, 1931).

> Contains Governor George Simpson's journal and excerpts and summaries of the Hudson's Bay company correspondence, with an admirable introduction.

———— "Snake country expeditions, 1824-1825," in Mississippi valley historical review, XXI, 49-75.

> Correspondence in the files of the Hudson's Bay company covering the Snake country expeditions of 1824-1825.

MISSOURI HISTORICAL SOCIETY collections, III and IV (St. Louis, 1908-1911).

> Contains a number of valuable articles. Volume IV includes a summary of the material on Ezekiel Williams.

———— Collections of newspaper excerpts.

> Clippings from early Missouri newspapers, chiefly from 1808 to 1830.

MISSOURI INTELLIGENCER (St. Louis) 1822 to 1826.

> Useful for the early history of the fur-trade.

MISSOURI REPUBLICAN (St. Louis) 1818 to 1822 and 1827 to 1831.

> Contains material on the operations of Ashley and Smith.

MOFRAS, E. D. DE. Exploration du territoire de l'Oregon (Paris, 1844).

> Covers the entire Pacific coast.

MONTAGNES, FRANÇOIS DES (pseudonym). "The plains," in the Western journal, IX (St. Louis, 1852).

> Contains material on Thomas Fitzpatrick.

NEIHARDT, J. G. The song of Hugh Glass (New York, 1915).

> A metrical account of Glass's adventures.

NILES REGISTER (Baltimore) 1818 to 1856.

> These volumes contain many valuable items covering the west in general and the activities of the fur companies in particular.

OGDEN, W. F. "Hides and tallow," in California historical society quarterly, VI.

OREGONIAN and Indians' advocate (Lynn, Massachusetts) 1838, 1839.

> Refers to Smith's contributions to cartography.

PARKER, SAMUEL. Journal of an exploring tour beyond the Rocky mountains (Auburn, 1846).

> Includes a map to which Smith contributed.

PERRIN DU LAC, F. M. Voyages dans les deux Louisianes et chez les nations sauvages du Missouri, par les États-Unis, l'Ohio et les provinces qui le bord, en 1801, 1802, et 1803 (Paris, 1805).

Shows the geographic conception of the west at the beginning of the nineteenth century.

POWELL, J. W. Exploration of the Colorado river of the west (Washington, 1878).

The first carefully recorded descent of the upper Colorado (Green river) after Ashley.

POWERS, STEPHEN. "Indian tribes of California," in U.S. Bureau of ethnology contributions to North American ethnology (Washington, 1877).

Useful for the Indian tribes encountered by Smith.

PRYOR, NATHANIEL. "Letter to William Clark, october 16, 1807," in Annals of Iowa (Des Moines, 1896), third ser., I.

For Manuel Lisa.

QUAIFE, M. M. "The journals of Captain Meriwether Lewis and Sergeant John Ordway," in Wisconsin state historical society collections, XXII (Madison, 1916).

QUIGLEY, HUGH. The Irish race in California (San Francisco, 1878).

RAYNOLDS, W. F. "Report of the exploration of the Yellowstone river, 1867," in U.S. Senate, Executive documents, 40 cong., 2 sess., no. 77.

REEVES, L. U. The life and military services of General William S. Harney (St. Louis, 1878).

Mentions Ashley's return to St. Louis by way of the Big Horn and the Yellowstone to the Missouri.

REPORT of exploration and survey to ascertain the most practicable and economic route for a railroad from the Mississippi river to the Pacific ocean, made under direction of the secretary of war in 1853-1856, being U.S. Senate, Executive documents, 33 cong., 2 sess., no. 78 (12 vols.); also U.S. House, Executive documents, 33 cong., 2 sess., no. 91.

Volume XI contains Lieutenant G. K. Warren's "Memoir to accompany the map of the territory of the United States from the Mississippi river to the Pacific ocean, giving a brief account of each of the exploring expeditions since A.D. 1800, with a detailed description of the methods adopted in compiling the general map."

RICHMAN, I. B. California under Spain and Mexico (Boston, 1911).

Contains a useful map.

[ROBB, JOHN S.] SOLITAIRE (pseudonym). "Major Fitzpatrick, the discoverer of the South pass," in the St. Louis reveille, march 1, 1847.

ROBINSON, DOANE. "Official correspondence of the Leavenworth expedition into South Dakota in 1823," in South Dakota historical society collections, I (Aberdeen, 1902).

ROLLINS, P. A. The discovery of the Oregon trail (New York, 1935).

> Contains Robert Stuart's so-called journal and traveling memoranda of his overland trip eastward from Astoria in 1812-13 and a translation of Wilson Price Hunt's diary of his overland trip westward to Astoria in 1811-12, from *Nouvelles annales des voyages*.

ROSS, ALEXANDER. Adventures of the first settlers of the Oregon or Columbia river (London, 1849).

> Reprinted in Thwaites, *Early western travels, 1748-1846*, VII (Cleveland, Arthur H. Clark company, 1904).
> Contains material on the Pacific coast venture of John Jacob Astor. Particularly valuable for events at Astoria.

—— Fur hunters of the far west (London, 1855) 2 vols.

> Based in part on Ross's journal of 1824.

SAGE, R. B. Rocky mountain life (Boston, 1860).

> Useful in determining Ashley's route in 1824.

ST. LOUIS REVEILLE, 1847.

> Contains material on Thomas Fitzpatrick.

SCHOOLCRAFT, H. R. Journal of a tour into the interior of Missouri and Arkansas (London, 1821).

—— Scenes and adventures in the semi-alpine regions of the Ozark mountains (Philadelphia, 1853).

—— View of the lead mines of Missouri (New York, 1819).

SIMPSON, J. H. Report of explorations across the great basin of Utah for a direct wagon-route from Camp Floyd to Genoa in Carson valley in 1859 (Washington, 1876).

SMITH, JEDEDIAH STRONG. "Eulogy of that most romantic and pious of mountain men, first American by land into California," originally in the Illinois magazine (June 1832) and reprinted in Sabin, Kit Carson days (Chicago, 1914).

> Throws light on Smith's contributions to geographic discovery and cartography.

SMITH, E. D. "Jedediah Smith and the settlement of Kansas," in Kansas historical society collections, XII (Topeka, 1912).

> Utilizes the manuscript material in the Kansas historical society but is inflated and inaccurate.

STANSBURY, HOWARD. Exploration and survey of the valley of the Great Salt lake of Utah (Philadelphia, 1855).

SULLIVAN, M. S. The travels of Jedediah Smith (Santa Ana, 1934).

Contains fragments of Smith's narrative of his experiences of 1822, his actual journal for the period june 22 to july 3, 1827, Smith's summary account for the period july 13 to november 7, 1827, evidently based on Smith's journal, his journal from november 7, 1827 to july 3, 1828. Included also are several documents from the files of the Hudson's Bay company, including correspondence between Dr. John McLaughlin, Governor George Simpson, Alexander McLeod, and Jedediah Smith, McLeod's journal for the fall of 1828, and Smith's will.

SWITZLER, W. F. "General William Henry Ashley," in the American monthly magazine, XXXII (Washington, 1908).

A biographical sketch of slight value.

——— "Historical sketch of Missouri," in Barnes, The commonwealth of Missouri, part 2 (St. Louis, 1878).

TEGGART, F. J. "Notes supplementary to any edition of Lewis and Clark," in American historical association annual report, 1908 (Washington, 1909).

A commentary on the explorations of Trudeau and his contemporaries.

THOMPSON and WEST. History of Los Angeles county, California (Oakland, 1880).

THWAITES, R. G. Early western travels, 1748-1846 (Cleveland, Arthur H. Clark company, 1904-1906) 32 vols.

Volumes V to XXX contain a vast amount of descriptive material for the far west in general.

——— Original journals of the Lewis and Clark expeditions (New York, 1904, 1905) 8 vols.

The best edition of Lewis and Clark.

TRAITS of American Indian life (Santa Fe, 1933).

TRUDEAU, JEAN BAPTISTE. "Journal, part I," in American historical review, XIX (New York, 1914); "part III (II)," (translation), in Missouri historical society collections, V (St. Louis, 1912).

Throws light on a number of interesting points connected with the early exploration of the Missouri.

TWITCHELL, R. E. Leading facts of New Mexican history (Cedar Rapids, 1911) 2 vols.

UNITED STATES: American state papers, Indian affairs (Washington, 1832 and 1834) 2 vols.

Contains scattered data on the fur-trade.

——— Bureau of American ethnology, second annual report, 1885, 1886 (Washington, 1891).

UNITED STATES: Department of the interior, report of the geological exploration of the fortieth parallel (Washington, 1876).

The King survey. The accompanying geological and topographical atlas is useful.

———— Geological survey, Big Trees, Bridgeport, Carson, Coos bay, Cucamonga, Dardanelles, Fort Steele, Jackson, Marsh peak, Pasadena, Peal, Port Orford, Pyramid, St. Thomas, Sonora, Wabuska, Wellington, Yosemite quadrangles (topographic sheets), (Washington, 1893-1914).

———— House, Executive documents, 19th congress, 1st session, I, no. 117.

Contains "Licenses to trade with the Indians, 1823."

———— House, Executive documents, 19th congress, 1st session, I.

Contains letters of Brigadier-general Henry Atkinson to Major-general Brown, november 23, 1825.

———— Senate, Executive documents, 18th congress, 1st session, I.

Contains a letter of Benjamin O'Fallon to Brigadier-general Henry Atkinson, july 3, 1823; "Licenses to trade with the Indians, 1822;" letter of W. H. Ashley to Colonel Leavenworth, june 4, 1823, describing the Arikara fight; letter of Brigadier-general Atkinson to Major-general Gaines, St. Louis, august 17, 1823; letter of W. H. Ashley to Colonel O'Fallon, Fort Brasseaux, july 19, 1823, describing the Arikara fight; and a letter of Major-general Gaines, august 15, 1823, alluding to the same.

———— Senate, Executive documents, 20th congress, 2d session, I, no. 67.

Contains a letter of W. H. Ashley to Thomas Hart Benton.

———— Senate, Executive documents, 21st congress, 2d session, I, no. 39.

Contains a letter of W. H. Ashley to General A. Macomb, march 1829; also a report of Smith, Jackson, and Sublette to John Eaton, secretary of war, october 29, 1830.

———— Senate, Executive documents, 22d congress, 1st session, II, no. 90.

Contains a report of Joshua Pilcher on the fur-trade, 1831 and a letter of Thomas Forsyth to Lewis Cass, secretary of war, october 24, 1831.

———— War department, Map of the military department of the Platte, Wyoming (Washington, 1874).

———— War department, Missouri river commission, map of the Missouri river (Washington, 1892-1895).

VELEZ ESCALANTE, SILVESTRE. "Diaria," in W. R. Harris's The Catholic church in Utah (Salt Lake City, 1909).

Contains an English translation.

VICTOR, F. F. The river of the west (Hartford, 1870).

> Based on the personal reminiscences of Joseph L. Meek as related by him to Mrs. Victor. Useful for the operations of Smith, Jackson, and Sublette, 1827 to 1830.

VINTON, STALLO. John Colter, discoverer of Yellowstone park (New York, 1926).

WALLACE, DILLON. Saddle and camp in the Rockies (New York, 1911).

WARNER, J. J. "Reminiscences of early California from 1831 to 1846," in Southern California historical society publications, VII (Los Angeles, 1906).

> For Smith's last journey and death.

WETMORE, A. Gazetteer of Missouri (St. Louis, 1837).

WILKES, CHARLES. The narrative of the United States exploring expedition during the years 1838, 1839, 1840, 1841, and 1842 (Philadelphia, 1845) 5 vols.

WILLIAM AND MARY COLLEGE quarterly, XXI (Richmond, 1913).

> Contains material on Ashley's ancestry and early life.

WISLIZENUS, F. A. Ein Ausflug nach den Felsen Gebirgen im jahre 1839 (St. Louis, 1840) ; reprinted, with a translation, as A journey to the Rocky mountains in the year 1839 (St. Louis, 1912).

> Covers much of the area traversed by Ashley.

WORK, JOHN, Journals, edited by William S. Lewis and Paul C. Phillips (Cleveland, Arthur H. Clark company, 1923).

WYETH, N. J. "Letters and journals," in Young, Sources of the history of Oregon (Eugene, 1899).

YOUNT, GEORGE C. "Chronicles," in California historical society quarterly, II (April 1923).

> Excerpts from the Clark manuscript containing Yount's story of his life and adventures.

Index

Clark, William: 29, 182, 226; map, 25, 28

Clarke (Neb.): 117

Clark's Fork (of Columbia): 19, 42, 48, 50, 153, 179; explored by David Thompson, 40; trapped by Smith, 92, 295

Clay County (Mo.): 169 footnote

Clearwater River: 34

Clover: 253, 259, 260, 263, 268

Clyman, James: 83, 88 footnote, 91, 136 footnote; employee of Ashley, 66; encounter with Arikara Indians, 70; cares for Smith after attack by bear, 86; sketch, 66 footnote

Coast Range: 20, 25

Coleman, Benjamin: 236

Collins, John: killed by Arikara Indians, 71 footnote

Colorado (state): 19, 50, 114, 125 footnote, 181

Colorado Drainage Area: 19, 20, 21, 25, 50, 51; defined, 19, 20

Colorado River [Rio Colorado, Seedskedee, Siskadee, Suchadee] [Spanish]: 15, 20, 21, 33, 88 footnote, 98, 132, 147 footnote, 148, 151 footnote, 152 footnote, 153, 186, 229, 286, 312, 314; Ashley-Henry men on 147; descended by Smith (1826), 16, 185, 193 footnote, 314; described by Smith, 185; Smith on (1827) 227; massacre of Smith's men, 228

Colter, John: explorations, 17, 27-28, 33, 49; route, 28, 35; guide, 28 footnote

Colter's River: 35, 99 footnote

Columbia Drainage Area: 20, 21, 32, 48, 97, 317; defined, 20; exploration, 48, 49-50, 96

Columbia Fur Company: 56, 107

Columbia River [River of West]: 16, 18, 20, 25, 28, 36, 37, 41, 48, 98, 101 footnote, 105, 114, 132, 150, 151, 153, 179, 181, 226, 230, 237, 239, 276, 286, 291, 312; overland Astorians on, 34; explored by David Thompson, 40; Cascades, 42

Comanche Indians: 51, 146 footnote, 152 footnote, 309; slay Smith, 308

Compañia Extranjera de Monterey: 200 footnote, 216 footnote, 233 footnote

Compagnie de Comerce pour decouverte des nations du Haut du Missouri: 22, 26; explorations, 23-24

Connecticut: 60

Cooke Creek: 129 footnote

Cooper, Braxton (Santa Fé trader): 301

Cooper, John Rogers: 232; sketch, 232 footnote; becomes accountable for Smith, 234-235

Cooper (Colo.): 124 footnote

Coos Bay: Smith on, 273 footnote

Coos Indians: 272 footnote

Coos River: Smith crosses, 273 footnote, 274 footnote

Coquille River: 267 footnote; Smith crosses, 270 footnote

Cordillera Mountains: 25, 31, 48, 53, 97

Corn: 185

Cotton: cultivated by Mohave Indians, 185

Cottonwood [populus angulata and p. angustifolia]: 117, 123, 124, 125, 128, 134, 135, 136, 144

Cottonwood Creek: 241

Council Bluffs: 55, 73, 116 footnote, 158, 160

Coureurs de bois: 21

Craig, —: 293 footnote

Crater Lake: 46

Crescent City: 260 footnote; Smith's camp near, 259 footnote

Cressy, Captain—(of ship *Sophia*): 236

Crook County (Oregon): 45

Crooked River: Ogden on, 45

Crooks, Ramsay: 17; heads division

explores shore of the Pacific, 248;
gifts to Indians, 256; reprimands
Ranna, 256; as hunter, 264; journals of, 14; recovered from Indians, 283 footnote; precipitated
Umpqua massacre, 280; *First Journal,* 183 footnote, 190, 192, 193, 224
footnote; *Second Journal,* 192, 242,
276; quoted, 192, 237-238
Rogue River: 285 footnote; Ogden
on, 47, 48; Smith's camp on, 267
footnote; Smith crosses, 268 footnote
Rose (half-breed interpreter): 86
Rose, Edward: 35 footnote, 36 footnote, 68 footnote, 83, 85, 87; overland Astorian, 33; in Arikara campaign, 76
Rosebud River: Smith on (1830), 295
Ross, Alexander: 17, 43, 45, 94, 101,
179; quoted, 43 footnote, 44; heads
Snake country expedition, 42, 43, 44,
93; explorations, 44, 48; at Flathead House, 44, 95, 179, 181; *Fur
hunters of Far West* cited in footnotes on following pages, 30, 41,
42, 43, 44, 92, 93, 94, 96, 107, 134;
Journals, 15; *Journal, Flathead
House,* cited, 96 footnote; *Journal
of Snake River Expedition, 1824*
cited in footnotes on following
pages, 44, 90, 92, 93, 94, 95, 96, 101,
104
Ross's Hole: 96
Ruiz, Maria del Carmen: 216 footnote
Russian agency at Bodega: letter
from, 235 footnote

SACRAMENTO River: 20, 21, 48, 237,
239, 240, 241
Sacramento *Standard:* cited, 100 footnote
Sage Creek: Ashley's men on, 163
Sage-brush (*artemisia tridentata*):
131

St. Abbiso, Francis: 218
St. Anne (farm near San Gabriel):
221
St. Anthony (Idaho): 31
St. Charles (Mo.): 66 footnote, 160
Saint Fernando: *see* San Fernando
Saint Gabriel: *see* San Gabriel
St. Louis: 24, 26, 27, 29, 57, 58, 59,
62, 64, 65, 66, 73, 74 footnote, 82,
90 footnote, 113 footnote, 115, 147
footnote, 161, 164, 165, 167, 168
footnote, 171, 172, 177, 179, 181,
214 footnote, 228 footnote, 285, 291,
299, 303, 304, 313; center of fur-
trade, 21, 55; petition of citizens of,
54; arrival of Ashley, 1825, 159;
of Smith, Jackson, and Sublette,
1830, 299; Wm. Sublette returns
to, 294
St. Louis Missouri Fur Company: *see*
Missouri Fur Company
St. Louis *Reveille:* cited in footnotes
on following pages, 83, 88, 92, 113,
167
St. Paul (apostle): 211
St. Thomas (Nev.): 227
Salish House: 153 footnote
Salmon River: 94, 102; Snake country expedition on, 43 footnote, 44
Salt: 43, 150 footnote, 154, 184, 186,
258
Salt Lake: *see* Great Salt Lake
Salt Lake City: 141 footnote, 142
footnote, 143 footnote
Salt River: 97; overland Astorians
on, 37 footnote; trapped by Ash-
ley's men, 161
Saltpetre: 61
Sampatch Indians: *see* Sanpete Indi-
ans
San Bernardino Mission: sketch, 223
footnote; Smith encamped near,
188 footnote, 222, 224; Smith's
party at and near, 222
Sanchez, Jose Bernardo (head of
Mission of San Gabriel): 213 foot-